The Rising Gorge

S. J. PERELMAN

PENGUIN BOOKS

PENGUIN BOOKS
Viking Penguin Inc., 40 West 23rd Street,
New York, New York 10010, U.S.A.
Penguin Books Ltd, Harmondsworth,
Middlesex, England
Penguin Books Australia Ltd, Ringwood,
Victoria, Australia
Penguin Books Canada Limited, 2801 John Street,
Markham, Ontario, Canada L3R 1B4
Penguin Books (N.Z.) Ltd, 182–190 Wairau Road,
Auckland 10, New Zealand

First published in the United States of America by
Simon and Schuster 1961
Published in Penguin Books 1987

All the pieces in this book appeared originally in *The New Yorker*, except for
"Impresario on the Lam," based in part on "Say a Few Words, Georgie," which
appeared in *Holiday* magazine; "In Pixie Land I'll Take My Stand" and "Birth of a
Conquistador," which appeared in *Redbook*; "Love Sends a Little Gift of Noses,"
originally entitled "Love My Toucan," which appeared in *This Week* magazine; and
"The Importance of Healing Ernest," which appeared in *What's New*.

LIBRARY OF CONGRESS CATALOGING IN PUBLICATION DATA
Perelman, S. J. (Sidney Joseph), 1904–1979.
  The rising gorge.
  Includes index.
  I. Title.
PS3531.E6544R5   1987   818'.5209   86-30226
ISBN 0 14 00.8041 4

Printed in the United States of America by
R. R. Donnelley & Sons Company, Harrisonburg, Virginia
Set in Linotype DeVinne

For Al Hirschfeld

Contents

Call and I Follow, I Follow!

FOR THE CASUAL VISITOR in London averse to ostentation and uncushioned by expense account, few hotels offer the advantages of Peacock's, in Clarges Street. Its rates are modest and its service amiable, its cuisine, by and large, free of the viscous sauces that agglutinate the English menu. The clientele, picturesque without being intrusive, consists in the main of dehydrated colonials with saffron faces, bishops in gaiters, and elderly spinsters who still cling to ruching and avian headgear. For me the chief attraction of Peacock's is its proximity to the shops around Piccadilly and St. James's. After a tonic interval of caressing cardigans and chess sets in the Burlington Arcade, pricing wafer-thin diaries at Mudie's, and rubbering at the Golconda of neckwear and sponges, boots and guns, along Jermyn Street, I love to saunter home leisurely through the twilit Green Park, preening myself on my asceticism. By the time I reach the hotel, my frustration is such that I compensate with a Gargantuan tea of watercress sandwiches, rock buns, and pastry that utterly ruins my digestion. It makes for a stimulating afternoon.

One early evening during my last stay there, I approached the porter's desk brimful of euphoria and bile to discover a whole sheaf of messages awaiting me. The majority, while flattering, were hardly of paramount importance. Hooper's, the renowned coachbuilders, had rung up to advise that they could supply a Rolls-Royce sedan-de-ville as per my specifications, with built-in writing desk and poudoir—the exact duplicate of one furnished to His Arabic Highness the Sheik of Kuwait—for £9,250 nett. A firm of hairdressers in Bury Street wished to inform me that its celebrated pomade, by appointment to the Duke of Rotherhithe, King Philip of Greece, and the Coldstream Guards, was available at three guineas the tin. Kittredge & Bolsover, Ltd., of Pall Mall, would be gratified to have me inspect their summer collection of canes, shooting sticks, riding crops, and whips. Should I require anything exotic in the last, they added, their special-order department was at my disposal.

The final message, though, had a distinct note of urgency. A woman I'll cheerfully call Mrs. Elaine Strangeways had phoned twice during the hour, identifying herself as an old friend and entreating me to ring her at Viburnum 3774 upon my return. The name awoke no immediate response, but the supplication, patently, was too crucial to ignore. Some poor soul—willowy, as I envisioned her, with ash-blond hair and violet eyes—was desperately awaiting succor in, as I further visualized it, a negligee of crêpe de Chine. Vacillation, misanthropy in the circumstances was unthinkable. I instantly bolted upstairs to phone or, rather, as it turned out, to get lost in the Kafkalike network of passages surrounding my room. When I ultimately found the door and forced it, I got an unexpected surprise. A strong whiff of curry assailed my nostrils, and I was confronted by a copper-colored brigadier with tufted white eyebrows, straight out of the pages of *Chatterbox*, lacing himself into a corset. A second later, the scent of brimstone replaced that of curry, and I slunk off peppered by some of the most lurid cavalry oaths in my experience.

Slightly unnerved by the contretemps, I was not at concert

pitch when I managed to get through to Viburnum 3774, and my voice may have sounded a trifle brusque. Mrs. Strangeways, in contrast, was excessively kittenish, determined, so it seemed, to tax me for my failure to recognize her. "You faithless man," she simpered. "Have you forgotten me so soon? You used to call me your Lily Maid of Astolat."

"I did?" I stammered, vainly racking my brain for a clue. It was a good thirty years since I had used language like that, and even then I had used it with diffidence. "When was that?"

"Why, in 1926," she said in plummiest tones. "Down at that divine little studio of yours on West Tenth Street. Don't you remember Elaine Abercorn, the tawny-haired goddess you were always writing poems to?" I did not recall myself in any bardic role, but her self-description was promising. "There was one you wrote about my eyes I still quote whenever I'm a bit squiffy. It went: 'Let me drown in the deeps of those luminous orbs/Where many a shipwrecked mariner lies—' "

Crimson at the scope of my youthful ardor, I halted her in mid-dactyl. "Well, well—Elaine Abercorn, as I live and breathe!" I exclaimed. "How in the world did you know I was here?" Some movie quidnunc, it appeared, was her informant, and nothing must stand in the way of our instant reunion. "But, of course, my dear," I said, probing warily. "I'd be charmed to meet your—ah—husband sometime—"

"You probably have already," she said frothily. "I've had four since I knew you." The present incumbent, a zoologist at Manchester University, was in Ostend that week, meeting a consignment of Belgian hares or some such jazz, and Elaine was patently avid for companionship. "Do let's have dinner tonight and chat over old times, shall we, lamb?" she begged. "Oh, I've thought about you *so* often over the years!"

I gallantly assured her that she, too, had never ceased to haunt me, and we arranged a rendezvous two hours thence, at a smart sea-food restaurant in Curzon Street. The problem of what to wear gave me pause; ordinarily, I prefer black tie for these sentimental occasions, as a cummerbund flattens the belly, but lacking one at the moment—the cummerbund, not the belly—I compromised on a vest, and flicked a bath towel over my shoes. The bar at Florio's was jammed when I arrived, and I spent a tempestuous half hour buffeted by theatregoers noisily downing triple whiskeys and shellfish. Just as I was dispatching Elaine to the special purgatory reserved for old sweethearts, a giantess in an emerald-green frock trimmed with salmon beads, a veritable grenadier of a woman, wove through the crush and pinioned me. Askew on her head she wore a fawn-colored duvetyn turban whose aigrette was secured by the Hope diamond or its rhinestone equivalent, and from the odor of malt pervading her embrace, I judged that she had fortified herself for our soirée.

"Dear boy, you haven't altered a whit!" she trilled. "Oh, yes, you've lost most of your hair and gained a few stone, but I'd know you anywhere!" She cocked her head archly. "I'm changed, though, aren't I? Go ahead—say it."

"Elaine," I began fervently. "I give you my word of honor—" Luckily, I was saved from perjury by the barman's request for her pleasure—a champagne cocktail, it proved, followed in lightning succession by two more. Elaine apologized; her constitution rebelled at anything but bubbly, and, moreover, she was completely spent from a Homeric day's shopping. Could she recount her purchases? I would be fascinated, I asserted, striking a pose like the physician in Sir Luke Fildes' Victorian masterpiece.

"Well," she said, signaling the barman for a refill, "every time Nevil's abroad, I steal into Fortnum's and buy up all the tidbits he won't permit me. You know, potted shrimps, and Malaga grapes, and honey from Mount Hymettus—that sort of thing. Anyway, today I just went absolutely berserker. I bought three pounds of caviar, and a jar of those luscious Smyrna figs, and some greengage preserve, and a brandied plum pudding—" She leveled a demure glance at me from under her lashes. "You think I'm hopelessly extravagant, don't you?"

"Not at all," I disclaimed. "I'm sure zoologists do very well."

"Nevil?" she said with contempt. "Poor sod, he hasn't a bean —ours was a love match. . . . Thank you, I will have another, but a touch more brandy. My dear," she breathed, enveloping my hand in her dinosaur paw, "it's angelic seeing you again. I can't wait for you to meet Nevil; he's the handsomest thing. People always mistake him for Rex Harrison." I timidly observed that the same folk were wont to confuse me with Warren William, but Elaine was off on a nostalgic tack of her own. "I'll tell you something weird," she confided. "I met Nevil in this very restaurant, while I was still married to Hilary, my third husband. But what makes it so uncanny, Nevil was corespondent when Hilary divorced me, just as Hilary was named by the man who preceded *him*."

"I—I say, oughtn't we be considering food?" I blurted, overcome by dark premonitions. "We don't have to stay here necessarily—"

"But I want to," she pouted. "I adore this place, though, *entre nous,* darling, Nevil and I never come here any more— they're absolute robbers."

"Then why don't we—ahem—skip dinner, as it were?" I suggested brightly. "You probably aren't hungry anyhow, after noshing on all those sweets at Fortnum's."

My supposition, unhappily, was incorrect; with the emphatic avowal that she was famished, Elaine bore me in to the expectant brigands. Their eyes sparkled and their pencils flew as she proceeded to eviscerate my wallet—pâté, Whitstable oysters, a sole, filet mignon, and a favorite salad of the Nizam of Hyderabad made of shredded five-pound notes. Only cobwebs remained in the wine cellar when she had finished rifling it, and even the sommelier stood awe-stricken. Meanwhile, her effervescence soaring with the intake of champagne, my Lily Maid continued her marital saga.

"You never knew my first husband, did you?" she asked. "Benno Vontz, the sculptor—he used to hang around the Jumble Shop and all those bohemian spots you adored. He did that horn-

bill in welded steel on top of Neiman-Marcus. A brilliant boy, but
terribly erratic, and so jealous—he nearly drove me insane. For
six years he kept spying on me and reading my mail everywhere
we went—Woodstock, Santa Fe, Redondo Beach, even in Cuernavaca. I didn't have a moment's peace. He'd wake me up in the
middle of the day and accuse me of affairs with all kinds of people,
like osteopaths, carhops, bakers. I was practically on the verge
of a breakdown when I met Ricky.''

''What line was he in?'' I murmured, making an irrevocable
vow to join some Trappist order in the morning.

''He was an auctioneer,'' said Elaine. ''One of those criminally
good-looking, virile types—you know, like Dean Martin or Robert
Alda. I happened into his place on the boardwalk in Atlantic
City, to appraise this ring some woman had given Benno. Well,
it proved to be a fake, just carbon, and when I broke down and
cried, Ricky bought me a drink to console me. He was so attentive
and sweet I just couldn't resist confiding in him, and, of course,
one thing led to another. One night, as we were driving home in
a downpour, the brakes on his Cord overheated near Arverne and
we had to take refuge in a motel. The next thing anybody knew,
Benno and this awful private eye were all over us with cameras
and flash bulbs. The little skunk had been following me for days;
my dear, it was too sorbid. Naturally, he named Ricky, along
with all those chiropractors and bakers, though he didn't have
a smidgen of proof.''

The realization that I was in the toils of a python far more
lethal than any I had ever encountered in Malaya so constricted
my throat that speech deserted me. ''Wha—what happened
then?'' I croaked.

''Just what you'd expect,'' she said, scornfully draining her
goblet. ''Once the decree was final and we married, I got Ricky's
measure *subito*. He was forever mousing around with some popsy,
kiting checks and flogging my jewelry until I was frantic. His
mother finally crashed through with a few bob so we could come
over here. That was when I met Hilary—''

"In this very restaurant, no doubt," I conjectured. Subtly avoiding the pressure of her knee, I moved to extricate myself from our banquette. "Forgive me a second, Elai—" I froze at the sudden expression of terror on her face. "What's the matter?"

"Over there—by the entrance," she said in a low, agitated voice. "Don't look now. It's Nevil. He—he must have got back from Ostend sooner than I thought. . . . Oh, Lord, I can't imagine what he'll do when he finds me here with you."

For my own part, I could, and with blinding clarity. In a flash, I foresaw the whole scene in glorious Technicolor—the confrontation, Elaine's hysteria, the melee as Nevil struck me on the bugle and drew claret, the constabulary's arrival in full fig. Then our visages spread across the *News of the World,* implemented by succulent detail and climaxing in a divorce whose outcome was predetermined: I should have to do the gentlemanly thing and espouse Elaine. The injustice of my plight, so bitter an expiation for an altruistic phone call, hit me like a blow in the solar plexus. As Holmes observed of his death grapple with Professor Moriarty at the Reichenbach Fall, so rapidly does the brain act that I believe I had thought all this out and managed to emit a bleat of self-pity before Elaine tugged my sleeve.

"Wait," she said uncertainly. "I'm not sure it's Nevil after all; I can never tell people apart without my contact lenses. Is he tall and sort of devil-may-care?"

I swiveled about and took a good look at the man. Far from resembling Rex Harrison, he was somewhat under five feet tall, had olive skin and glittering black eyes, and wore an Existentialist beard. While he was definitely serpentine, there was nothing about him either debonair or domestic. I exhaled slowly and arose. The time had come to sever, as delicately as possible, the Cupid's bowknot that had fettered my heart for three decades. Gracefully excusing myself, I slipped out to the coatroom and had a quick tête-à-tête with the attendant—a rather appealing French girl, by the way, with a cameo profile and a willowy figure. Three minutes later, she approached our table with a message from my publisher enjoining me to meet him in Herzegovina at once. I pressed a fistful of notes on Elaine to square the check, kissed her hand in Bosnian free style, and made off down Curzon Street on the double. For the balance of my stay at Peacock's, I emerged only at night and ate exclusively in butteries. . . . Oh, yes, I emerged once by day to dine with a French person I know, but that's another story. And sufficiently droll, not that you could ever tempt me to tell it.

Eine

Kleine

Mothmusik

The moths are beginning to eat. Even if the weather seems cool, this is their season for gluttony. Miss Rose Finkel, manager of Keystone Cleaners at 313 West Fifty-seventh Street, urges that these precautions be taken:

All winter clothes should be dry-cleaned, even if no stains are apparent. Moths feast on soiled clothes, and if a garment has been worn several times in the last few months, it should be cleaned.

Clean clothes may be kept in the closet in a plastic bag. It is safer, however, to send all woolens to a dry cleaner to put in cold storage.

Customers should check to make sure that their clothes are really sent to a cold storage and not hung in the back of the store.—*The Times.*

GAY HEAD,
MARTHA'S VINEYARD, MASS.,
JULY 14

Mr. Stanley Merlin,
Busy Bee Cleaners,
161 Macdougal Street,
New York City

DEAR MR. MERLIN:

I HEARD on the radio this morning before I went for my swim that the heat in New York is catastrophic, but you wouldn't guess it up here. There is a dandy breeze at all times, and the salt-water bathing, as you can imagine, is superlative. Miles of glorious white beach, marvelous breakers, rainbow-colored cliffs—in short, paradise. One feels so rested, so completely purified, that it seems profane to mention anything as sordid as dry cleaning. Still, that's not exactly your problem, is it? I have one that is.

Do you, by chance, remember a tan gabardine suit I sent in to be pressed three or four years ago? It's a very expensive garment, made of that changeable, shimmering material they call solari cloth. The reverse side is a reddish color, like cayenne pepper; during the British occupation of India, as you doubtless know, it was widely used for officers' dress uniforms. Anyway, I'm a trifle concerned lest moths get into the closet where I left it in our apartment. The suit isn't really stained, mind you; there's just a faint smudge of lychee syrup on the right sleeve, about the size of your pinkie, that I got in a Chinese restaurant last winter. (I identify it only to help you expunge it without too much friction. I mean, it's a pretty costly garment, and the nap could be damaged if some boob started rubbing it with pumice or whatever.)

Will you, hence, arrange to have your delivery boy pick up the suit at my flat any time next Thursday morning after nine-fifteen? He'll have to show before ten-twenty, since the maid leaves on the dot and would certainly split a gusset if she had to sit around a hot apartment waiting for a delivery boy. (You know how they are, Mr. Merlin.) Tell the boy to be sure and take the right suit; it's hanging next to one made of covert cloth with diagonal flap pockets, and as the Venetian blinds are drawn, he could easily make a mistake in the dark. Flotilla, the maid, is new, so I think I'd better explain which closet to look in. It's in the hall, on his right when he stands facing the bedroom windows. If he stands facing the other way, naturally it's on his left. The main thing, tell him, is not to get rattled and look in the closet *opposite*, because there may be a gabardine suit in there, without pockets, but that isn't the one I have reference to.

Should Flotilla have gone, the visiting super will admit your boy to the flat if he arrives before eleven; otherwise, he is to press our landlord's bell (Coopersmith), in the next building, and ask them for the key. They can't very well give it to him, as they're in Amalfi, but they have a Yugoslav woman dusting for them, a highly intelligent person, to whom he can explain the situation. This woman speaks English.

After the suit is dry-cleaned—which, I repeat, is not essential if you'll only brush the stain with a little moist flannel—make certain that it goes into cold storage at once. I read a piece in the newspaper recently that upset me. It quoted a prominent lady in your profession, a Miss Rose Finkel, to the effect that some dry cleaners have been known to hang such orders in the back of their store. You and I have had such a long, cordial relationship, Mr. Merlin, that I realize you'd never do anything so unethical, but I just thought I'd underscore it.

Incidentally, and since I know what the temperature in your shop must be these days, let me pass on a couple of hot-weather tips. Eat lots of curries—the spicier the better—and try to take at least a three-hour siesta in the middle of the day. I learned this trick in India, where Old Sol can be a cruel taskmaster indeed. That's also the place, you'll recall, where solari cloth used to get a big play in officers' dress uniforms. Wears like iron, if you don't abuse it. With every good wish,

Yours sincerely,

S. J. PERELMAN

NEW YORK CITY,
JULY 22

DEAR MR. PEARLMAN:

I got your letter of instructions spelling everything out, and was happy to hear what a glorious vacation you are enjoying in that paradise. I only hope you will be careful to not run any fishhooks in your hand, or step in the undertow, or sunburn your body so badly you lay in the hospital. These troubles I personally don't have. I am a poor man with a wife and family to support, not like some people with stocks and bonds that they can sit in a resort all summer and look down their nose on the rest of humanity. Also my pressing machine was out of commission two days and we are shorthanded. Except for this, everything is peaches and cream.

I sent the boy over like you told me on Thursday. There was no sign of the maid, but for your information he found a note under the door saying she has quit. She says you need a bulldozer, not a servant, and the pay is so small she can do better on relief. Your landlady, by the way, is back from Amalfi, because some of the tenants, she didn't name names, are slow with the rent. She let the boy in the apartment, and while he was finding your red suit she checked over the icebox and the stove, which she claims are very greasy. (I am not criticizing your housekeeping, only reporting what she said.) She also examined the mail in the bureau drawers to see if the post office was forwarding your bills, urgent telegrams, etc.

I don't believe in telling a man his own business. Mine is dry cleaning, yours I don't know what, but you're deceiving yourself about this Indian outfit you gave us. It was one big stain from top to bottom. Maybe you leaned up against the stove or the icebox? (Just kidding.) The plant used every kind of solvent they had on it—benzine, naphtha, turpentine, even lighter fluid—and knocked out the spots, all right, but I warn you beforehand, there are a few brownish rings. The lining was shot to begin with, so that will be no surprise to you; according to the label, you had the suit since 1944. If you want us to replace same, I can supply a first-class, all-satin quarter lining for $91.50, workmanship included. Finally, buttons. Some of my beatnik customers wear the jacket open and don't need them. For a conservative man like yourself, I would advise spending another eight dollars.

As regards your worry about hiding cold-storage articles in the back of my store, I am not now nor have I ever been a chiseler, and I defy you to prove different. Every season like clockwork, I get one crackpot who expects me to be Santa Claus and haul his clothing up to the North Pole or someplace. My motto is live and let live, which it certainly is not this Rose Finkel's to go around destroying people's confidence in their dry cleaner. Who is she, anyway? I had one of these experts working for me already, in 1951, that nearly put me in the hands of the receivers. She told a good customer of ours, an artist who brought in some hand-painted ties to be rainproofed, to save his money and throw them in the Harlem River. To a client that showed her a dinner dress with a smear on the waist, she recommends the woman should go buy a bib. I am surprised that you, a high-school graduate, a man that pretends to be intelligent, would listen to such poison. But in this business you meet all kinds. Regards to the Mrs.

Yours truly,

S. MERLIN

GAY HEAD, MASS.,
JULY 25

DEAR MR. MERLIN:

While I'm altogether sympathetic to your plight and fully aware that your shop's an inferno at the moment—I myself am wearing an imported cashmere sweater as I write—I must say you misinterpreted my letter. My only motive in relaying Miss Stricture's finkels (excuse me, the strictures of Miss Finkel) on the subject of proper cold storage was concern for a favorite garment. I was not accusing you of duplicity, and I refuse to share the opinion, widespread among persons who deal with them frequently, that most dry cleaners are crooks. It is understandably somewhat off-putting to hear that my suit arrived at your establishment in ruinous condition, and, to be devastatingly candid, I wonder whether your boy may not have collided with a soup kitchen in transit. But each of us must answer to his own conscience, Merlin, and I am ready, if less than overjoyed, to regard yours as immaculate.

Answering your question about Miss Finkel's identity, I have never laid eyes on her, needless to say, though reason dictates that if a distinguished newspaper like the *Times* publishes her counsel, she must be an authority. Furthermore, if the practice of withholding clothes from cold storage were uncommon, why would she have broached the subject at all? No, my friend, it is both useless and ungenerous of you to attempt to undermine Miss Finkel. From the way you lashed out at her, I deduce that she touched you on the raw, in a most vulnerable area of our relationship, and that brings me to the core of this communication.

Nowhere in your letter is there any direct assertion that you *did* send my valuable solari suit to storage, or, correlatively, that you are *not* hiding it in the back of the store. I treasure my peace of mind too much to sit up here gnawed by anxiety. I must therefore demand from you a categorical statement by return airmail special delivery. Is this garment in your possession or not? Unless a definite answer is forthcoming within forty-eight hours, I shall be forced to take action.

> Yours truly,
> S. J. PERELMAN

> NEW YORK CITY,
> JULY 27

DEAR MR. PERLEMAN:

If all you can do with yourself in a summer place is hang indoors and write me love letters about Rose Finkel, I must say I have pity on you. Rose Finkel, Rose Finkel—why don't you marry this woman that you are so crazy about her. Then she could clean your suits at home and stick them in the icebox—after she cleans that, too. What do you want from me? Sometimes I think I am walking around in a dream.

Look, I will do anything you say. Should I parcel-post the suit to you so you can examine it under a microscope for holes? Should I board up my store, give the help a week free vacation in the mountains, and bring it to you personally in my Cadillac? I tell you once, twice, a million times—it went to cold storage. I didn't send it myself; I gave orders to my assistant, which she has been in my employ eleven years. From her I have no secrets, and you neither. She told me about some of the mail she found in your pants.

It is quite warm here today, but we are keeping busy and don't notice. My tailor collapsed last night with heat prostration, so I am handling alterations, pressing, ticketing, and hiding customers' property in the back of the store. Also looking up psychiatrists in the Yellow Pages.

Yours truly,
S. MERLIN

GAY HEAD, MASS.,
JULY 29

DEAR MR. MERLIN:

My gravest doubts are at last confirmed: You are unable to say unequivocally, without tergiversating, that you *saw* my suit put into cold storage. Knowing full well that the apparel was irreplaceable, now that the British Raj has been supplanted—knowing that it was the keystone of my entire wardrobe, the *sine qua non* of sartorial taste—you deliberately entrusted it to your creature, a cat's-paw who you admit rifles my pockets as a matter of routine. Your airy disavowal of your responsibility, therefore, leaves me with but one alternative. By this same post, I am delegating a close friend of mine, Irving Wiesel, to visit your place of business and ferret out the truth. You can lay your cards on the table with Wiesel or not, as you see fit. When he finishes with you, you will have neither cards nor table.

It would be plainly superfluous, at this crucial stage in our association, to hark back to such petty and characteristic vandalism as your penchant for jabbing pins into my rainwear, pressing buttons halfway through lapels, and the like. If I pass over these details now, however, do not yield to exultation. I shall expatiate at length in the proper surroundings; viz., in court. Wishing you every success in your next vocation,

Yours truly,
S. J. PERELMAN

NEW YORK CITY,
AUGUST 5

DEAR MR. PERLMAN:

I hope you received by now from my radiologist the two X-rays; he printed your name with white ink on the ulcer so you should be satisfied that you, and you alone, murdered me. I wanted him to print also "Here lies an honest man that he slaved for years like a dog, schlepped through rain and snow to put bread in his children's mouths, and see what gratitude a customer gave him," but he said there wasn't room. Are you satisfied now, you Cossack you? Even my *radiologist* is on your side.

You didn't need to tell me in advance that Wiesel was a friend of yours; it was stamped all over him the minute he walked in the store. Walked? He was staggering from the highballs you and your bohemian cronies bathe in. No how-do-you-do, explanations, nothing. Ran like a hooligan to the back and turned the whole stock upside down, pulled everything off the racks. I wouldn't mind he wrecked a filing system it cost me hundreds of dollars to install. Before I could grab the man, he makes a bee-line for the dressing room. So put yourself for a second in someone else's shoes. A young, refined matron from Boston, first time in the Village, is waiting for her dress to be spot-cleaned, quietly loafing through *Harper's Bazaar*. Suddenly a roughneck, for all she knows a plainclothesman, a junkie, tears aside the curtain. Your delegate Wiesel.

I am not going to soil myself by calling you names, you are a sick man and besides on vacation, so will make you a proposition. You owe me for cleaning the suit, the destruction you caused in my racks, medical advice, and general aggravation. I owe you for the suit, which you might as well know is kaput. The cold-storage people called me this morning. It seems like all the brownish rings in the material fell out and they will not assume responsibility for a sieve. This evens up everything between us, and I trust that on your return I will have the privilege of serving you and family as in years past. All work guaranteed, invisible weaving our specialty. Please remember me to your lovely wife.

Sincerely yours,
STANLEY MERLIN

Where Do You

Work-a, John?

SAY, gang, pardon me if my voice gets a trifle reedy with excitement, but something really big's just taken place. Remember those bull sessions at your frat when the brothers used to start discussing Schopenhauer and Omar Khayyám and the true meaning of life? I mean one of those nights that fairly crackled with good talk, everybody puffing on corncobs and interrupting the other man, and—gee, I don't know, you had the feeling you'd stripped away all the pretense and sham and come somewhere near the core of things. And before you could say Oscar Fingal O'Flahertie Wills Wilde, the room was blue with smoke, the whole bunch of you were logy with near beer, and the first flush of dawn had appeared over the trees on the campus. Then someone, probably a senior or some cuss with more perspective than the rest, suddenly said "Applesauce" and threw open a window, and in came a cool, refreshing current of air that dispersed all the palaver and fakery. Remember the relief of it? Well, that's precisely what has happened. A man named George W. Reinoehl, executive vice-president of the Executive Furniture Executives' Guild—I may have one too many "executive"'s in there—has flung open a casement and introduced a new, revolutionary concept of artistic creation, or perhaps I should say re-creation. It's a bit early as yet to foresee its implications, but there's no doubt Reinoehl is a man who is going places, though it's a bit early likewise to foresee what places.

Under the trig and forceful exterior that Reinoehl presented in a double-spread advertisement in *The New Yorker* not long ago, it was clear to the most negligent reader that there dwelt a visionary. Crew-topped, bespectacled, and natty, flanked by a violin and a metronome, he stood encircling a bust of Beethoven with a familiar arm, his pose a mixture of camaraderie and ownership. The accompanying text, ratified by his signature, set forth his credo. "What I did for Beethoven, I can do for you!" he proclaimed ebulliently. "One afternoon as I sat all alone listening to Beethoven's Ninth, I got to thinking what sheer genius the man must have had to accomplish so much under such primitive working conditions—handicapped by clutter, poor workspace, drafts, noise and bad lighting. So . . . I picked up my sketch pad—just for fun—and designed the poor fellow an office *worthy* of his greatness, with every detail as personal as his scrawl on a manuscript. Ludwig, I think, would have been happy here. But— let's talk about *you.* Why not let me develop for you, through your Executive Furniture Guild member dealer and his staff, an office worthy of your position," etc., etc.

So enraptured was I by Mr. Reinoehl's smuggling himself into Parnassus aboard the composer's coattails, his blissful intimation that he had helped to accouche the Ninth Symphony even *post factum,* that I was forced to lie down. Unluckily, the office in which I read his *affiche* contained nothing but a desk and chair, a rather grubby bookcase, and several hundredweight of yellowing newspapers, and I had to recline on the floor until equilibrium returned. As I lay there, it struck me that, in a curious way, the very things that had hampered Beethoven—the litter, the drafts, the medieval lighting—also shackled me. While admittedly less sheer, my own genius might conceivably flower in more congenial surroundings. The sensible course, manifestly, was to pose my situation to Reinoehl, or, better yet, to someone of his ilk I could afford. The Yellow Pages of the directory, ever a beacon to the perplexed, turned up a firm of experts on office décor who responded vibrantly to my quandary. Their consultant, a Mr. Morninghoff, had instilled harmony into the lives of innumerable folk, from scientists to sonneteers, whose names were available on request. He would drop by the next morning to make a survey; the only payment he asked was a chance to aid me in realizing my creative potential. It sounded like a bonanza offer.

At eleven the following day, my doorbell rang peremptorily and a hatless young man with a globular head and a portfolio under his arm—only the portfolio under his arm, to be exact—ascended the stairs. He wore a dark-blue trench coat of the type affected by Italian black-marketeers, and his manner was rather more cavalier than I had expected of a friendly diagnostician. It was, in fact, tinged with unmistakable peevishness. "Is this supposed to be an office building?" he demanded as he reached my landing. "I smelled cooking in the lower hall."

"That's the Moroccan who runs the travel bureau," I said. "He's probably making a pilaf or couscous down there—you know, with pine nuts and rice."

"You needn't explain," he rejoined haughtily. "I've been in all those places. Fez . . . Marrakech . . . Do you know Ouedi-bel-Youfni?" I shook my head, and a scornful smile creased his lips. "Well, if you don't know Ouedi-bel-Youfni, you don't know North Africa," he said. "It's the place everyone who's anyone raves about. Just a tiny, sun-drenched oasis with a few Berbers, but the only view of the dunes that makes any sense. Cocteau discovered it."

"Is that so?" I murmured. "Must be pretty special if he lives there."

"Oh, he pulled out long ago," my caller said, with disdain. "The whole area's overrun with Philistines. By the way," he went on, turning in the doorway, "Toby Morninghoff, who was scheduled to do you over, is laid up with an impacted hip. I'm Eveninghoff, his second in command."

I courteously assured him that my problem was unworthy of his stature (an opinion he showed no inclination to contradict), and disembarrassed him of his coat. He threw a disparaging glance at the contents of the small antechamber—the tableful of discarded books, the spavined coat tree, and the miscellany of photographs helter-skelter on the wall. "That's my high-school class," I volunteered as he paused to inspect one of them. "I'm the sensitive-faced kid, third from the end, in the Mackinaw."

"Hmm," he said, cocking his head critically. "You should have gone on wearing those bangs. They softened your features."

I withheld a riposte that would have seared him if I had been able to think of it, and followed him into the office. Candidly, it had never looked less prepossessing. A half-empty coffee container awash with cigarette ends topped an accumulation of mail on the desk; crumpled newspapers overflowed the wastebasket; and grime impenetrable obscured the windows. Mr. Eveninghoff made a slow, deadly inventory of the premises that finally included me.

"Unspeakable," he said, at length. "I don't mind a challenge, but this— It's frightening."

"Isn't there some way to liven it up a little?" I appealed. "I thought maybe we could stipple the walls—hang up some bead curtains . . ."

"You mean like those gypsy stores on Sixth Avenue where they read your palm?" I noticed that he habitually lifted one eyebrow in an ironic, quizzical fashion—a trick clearly gleaned from looking at old stills of Rod LaRocque. "I understood from my call sheet that you wrote something or other here—TV commercials, or advertising jingles."

"Er—not exactly," I said. "Puppet plays for colleges, in-

spirational verse for trade papers—that type of thing. I haven't
hit the jackpot yet—"

"You will, you will," he said encouragingly. "But you'd
better get one thing straight, my friend. You're defeating yourself. Nothing worth while ever came out of a hole like this." He
raised his hand before I could answer. "I know," he said.
"You're going to bring up Edgar Allan Poe, or John Keats in
his garret. Very well, then, have a look at this." He reached into
his portfolio and handed me a color sketch. It portrayed a spacious book-lined library some eighty feet long, with a massive
fireplace and a variegated-marble floor. The teak-paneled walls
were hung with abstract paintings, the deep club chairs upholstered in pastel tints of glove leather, the avant-garde desk
flanked by a unit containing a dictaphone, playback, and television screen. "That's where Keats would have written 'The
Eve of St. Agnes' if I'd had anything to say about it," he informed me. "And furthermore, the air-filtration system would
have doubled his life span. Think how long Edgar Guest survived under modern conditions."

"I often think of it," I confessed.

"Here's another one," said Eveninghoff, reopening his portfolio. "Ever heard of Thoreau? He was an eccentric who wrote
nature stories up in New England. A brilliant talent, but he, too,
stymied himself working in a distasteful environment. This is
how I redesigned his shack at Walden Pond." The interior he
presented could have housed the entire community of Yaddo, all
its members functioning harmoniously. Indoors and out had
been blended in an airy decorative scheme broken up by ban-
quettes and rattan screens; end tables served as storage space for
electric typewriters and encyclopedias; and the sun deck beyond
displayed every diversion from Crokinole to hi-fi.

I swallowed. "Old Henry would have flipped, and that's for
sure," I said, employing the only idiom that seemed to fit the
circumstances.

"He did anyway, but he would have flipped in comfort,"
Eveninghoff returned complacently. "We décor engineers are like

Houdini—we remove the handcuffs from the creative mind. Now, take this place of yours, for instance. The first thing I'd do is rip out the windows and substitute glass brick.''

"But I *like* to look at the clotheslines," I objected. "The wash is so snowy and crisp, and those gingham frocks dance in the wind—"

"Then as regards floor space," he went on, unheeding. "We could pick up a good twenty feet if we broke through that side wall. Don't interrupt," he snapped as I tried to mime the pants factory that lay behind. "You and your landlord can work it out—I'm not a real-estate broker. What I'm questing for is a furniture mood to express your personality. . . . Let's see, puppet plays. It ought to smack of the theater, the world of tinsel and make-believe . . . shadows, contrasts. . . . Wait—yes, I've got it!"

"What?" I asked, checking myself lest I be swept away by his fervor.

"Try to visualize it as I block in the tones," he commanded, forefinger extended and eyes narrowed in concentration. "Turkey-red carpeting and ebony walls—not coal black, charcoal relieved by tiny gold accents—with, of course, candelabra sidelights to match. At the far end there, an Empire sofa, covered in lime-and-silver stripes, between a pair of broken columns." I thought of my Latvian handmaid flicking her feather duster, and cringed. "In this area, a Renaissance coffee table—or, rather, the memory of a coffee table—surrounded by Swedish-modern chairs."

"Not Latvian?" I interposed. "I say that because—"

"You're right," said Eveninghoff graciously. "Chairwise, the Latvians have done some very arresting things lately. And now your work sector—for, after all, we mustn't forget that this is where you create, must we?" He gave me a flash of teeth—or, rather, the memory of teeth—that failed to captivate. "I see a gigantic refectory table here—modified Jacobean, in cherry wood simulating walnut—with a desk set of tooled Florentine leather. You dictate your things, I suppose."

"Not as a rule," I said. "I—ah—generally write in longhand with a quill pen, and shake pumice over the manuscript to dry it."

"Good—then you won't need recording equipment," he approved. "I loathe the mechanized feeling it imparts to one's *ambiance*. However, for illumination I don't think we should cleave to period. Do you insist on wax tapers? . . . I'm glad. Fluorescence it'll be, and much more contemporary. Well, now," he concluded, wheeling toward me, "how does it strike you?"

"Between the eyes," I admitted. "There's just one thing, though. You don't feel the black walls are a little—well, Aubrey Beardsley?"

"Is he using them this season?" Eveninghoff queried. "I never look at other decorators' work—I don't want to be influenced. Still, if black stifles anything in you they can always be changed to rust, or a subdued plum."

"No, sir, they cannot," I said emphatically. "They're the keystone, the very essence, of your whole design. Without them it's meaningless. I'm sorry, Mr. Eveninghoff," I added, trying to palliate my words, "but I guess it's not for me."

"But look here," he said, plainly chopfallen. "I'm not inflexible. We want the client to fulfill himself. If you'd prefer monk's cloth . . ."

"No, no," I said, herding him toward the door. "I'd sooner ask Pan to abandon his pipes or Krupa his drums than have you give up black. I won't compromise, and it would degrade me to force you to."

Eveninghoff's lips puckered as though tears were imminent. "Well, if you feel that strongly . . ."

"I'm afraid I do," I said regretfully. "Goodbye, old man. Watch out for rice on the stairs."

As the door closed behind him, I re-entered the office, got out the directory, and thumbed through the Yellow Pages. Then I dialed the number of a place on Third Avenue. "Mr. Pandora?" I said. "Could you have a look around your box? I need a pair of bead curtains."

Is You Is or Is You

Ain't, Goober Man?

I RECKON that anybody around here familiar with *This Side of Paradise* will recall the man in the brown sack suit, a phantom who recurs during the course of the novel to harass Amory Blaine, its central character. Everyone of normal sensitivity, I daresay, has been afflicted with similar hants on occasion. In 1934, for example, I went through a phase in Hollywood where I saw (or thought I saw) Clyde Fitch, a playwright celebrated circa 1900, at every buffet supper I attended. The vision was always the same: Fitch, in vintage evening dress with grosgrain lapels and boutonnière, and looking very much as though he had stepped out of a serial by Amélie Rives, had just raised a turkey leg to his lips and was studying me across it with a sly, half-accusatory grin that froze my marrow. Since I knew the man not at all apart from having read *Captain Jinks of the Horse Marines* in boyhood, and had never plagiarized any turkey from him, I had no basis for guilt. What upset me about the revenant was his transparency—I could see right through his shirt front to a damask spread laden with cold cuts, and, beyond that, to Bella Spewack helping herself to wild rice. Eventually, the obsession became so pronounced that I left Hollywood, retaining an agent to handle it for me. He writes that he still sees Fitch from time to time.

A few nights ago, in Times Square, I almost thought that something of the sort was again overtaking me. I was en route to a documentary at a nearby newsreel—an exposé of conditions at a nudist colony in Passaic—when a curious figure barred my progress. The upper half of his body was a gigantic peanut, with ostensibly human features, that sported a silk hat and a monocle. His spidery extremities, encased in funereal black, terminated in white gloves and spats, and he flourished a cane in a jaunty, raffish fashion that stiffened my scalp in horror. Whether he was preparing to engage me in badinage or direct my attention to the Planters Peanut showroom that lay alongside, I never learned, for in a flash I twisted past him, thrust my pennies through the wicket, and fled into the peepshow. The significant, the macabre element of the visitation was not meeting the thing face to face (if you could call it that) but, rather, the fact that it was our second encounter within a week. A scant five days before, traversing the Garden State Parkway with a poodle, I had reined in at a neo-Georgian roadside stand for a bag of cashews to absorb the humidity in our living room. When I regained the car, I found the identical apparition leaning inside, silk hat, monocle, and all, and trying to woo the dog with baby talk. Tartuffe, it went without saying, adopted the only dignified course; head stiffly averted, he sat staring off at the Watchung Mountains and refusing to encompass the existence of anything so improbable. The moment we careered back onto the highway, of course, his jangled nerves struck back and he burrowed under a seat, where I gladly would have joined him had I been able to unclench my fingers from the wheel.

By subsequent inquiry in certain quarters (not necessarily medical), I derived this reassurance, at least: The manifestation I saw is general, is sponsored by you know whom, and is said to have hypoed sales, except, as I can attest, among standard poodles. My two fleeting contacts with Mr. Planters Peanut, however, have left a slight residue of curiosity. If you could get under his shell, so to speak, what sort of a cuss would he prove to be? A thwarted actor? A bookie supplementing his precarious income? An English remittance man? How does he spend his time outside working hours? Is he a hail fellow well met, active in fraternal organizations, or a seclusive bachelor brooding over Mme. Blavatsky in his Y.M.C.A. cubbyhole? The best way to adumbrate these questions, obviously, is to seek him out in his habitat, which I somehow envision as a suburb akin to Plandome, Long Island. Let's don our invisible cloak, therefore, and insinuate ourselves, with a maximum of stealth, into the residence of Rolf and Capricia Trubshaw.

SCENE: *The Trubshaw kitchen, shortly before dusk. As the curtain rises, Capricia, a lackluster blonde with a patent air of disillusion, has just finished tidying up. She strips off her apron, extracts a pencil from a clip board, and begins scribbling a note, unaware that her husband has entered behind her clad in his working clothes—i.e., peanut carapace, black tights, and silk hat and spats. He tiptoes forward, seizes her in an embrace.*

CAPRICIA (*wheeling in alarm*): Why, how dare— Oh, it's *you.*
ROLF: Who'd you think it was?
CAPRICIA: Listen, I've told you already—I don't like people sneaking up behind me. One of these days, you're liable to get a saucepan over your sconce.
ROLF: I don't do it to anybody else.
CAPRICIA: I should hope not. They'd drop dead of fright.
ROLF (*in an aggrieved voice, slightly muffled by papier-mâché*): You act like nobody ever saw this costume before. What if I told you that hundreds of greeters like me are dispensing good will across the country?

CAPRICIA: Well, dispense it at the store. You don't have to goof around here in that outfit.

ROLF: What are you—ashamed of my calling, or something?

CAPRICIA: Er—of course not, dear.

ROLF (*with dignity, adjusting his monocle*): You may not know it, but we're doing pretty valuable work in these troubled times—amusing the passersby, helping them forget their cares—

CAPRICIA: Sure, but you never wore your Good Humor uniform after hours. Or your surgical smock when you were demonstrating pens at Gimbel's.

ROLF: The psychology is altogether different. In these togs, I feel relaxed, like an actor in makeup. I have a sense of importance.

CAPRICIA: Well, at least take off that undertaker's hat while you're in the house. (*He complies grudgingly.*) I was just leaving you a note. Myrtle Turtletaub and I have a date to play bingo. Your dinner's on the table there.

ROLF (*lifting the napkin that shrouds it*): Peanut-butter sandwiches again?

CAPRICIA: You're always telling me how much you adore them.

ROLF: I know, but I work around the stuff all day. A fellow comes home at night, he likes a change.

CAPRICIA: I can't keep up with you men. O.K., there's a licorice salad in the icebox, and those French fries from last Tuesday. By the way, somebody called you this afternoon—an old man. Claimed he was your uncle from Australia.

ROLF: I haven't any uncle in Australia.

CAPRICIA: Search me—that's what he said. . . . Anything new at the store?

ROLF: No, not much. We're having a fall clearance on pralines—two for a quarter.

CAPRICIA: How much are they usually?

ROLF: Three for a quarter.

CAPRICIA: I don't see where the saving comes in.

ROLF: That's what I told Mr. Fortinbras, but he's stubborn.

Oh, yes, a strange kind of thing did happen today. A guy drove in with a stuffed poodle in his car.

CAPRICIA: You mean a real dog, like in a taxidermist's?

ROLF: No, a toy made out of plush. I tried to talk to it, but it wouldn't turn its head. What was peculiar, though—as the car was pulling away, I could've sworn it jumped down and hid under the seat.

CAPRICIA: You spend too much time in that blister of yours— your brain doesn't get enough oxygen. Well, I have to go.

ROLF: See you later. (*As she exits, he crosses to table, props up a paper, and begins feeding a sandwich through an aperture in the peanut, as one mails a letter—a bit of stagecraft that may tax the ingenuity of the costume designer. A pause, followed by a knock at the door. Rolf, absorbed, pays no heed. A wizened ancient in pepper-and-salt tweeds hobbles in, bent over a blackthorn. He peers about mistily.*)

OLD MAN (*falsetto*): Is this the home of Mr. Rolf Trubshaw?

ROLF (*springs up, startled*): Eh? What's that?

OLD MAN (*focusing on him*): My mistake—sorry. Must be the place next door.

ROLF: No, this is the house. What did you want to see him about?

OLD MAN: I'd rather talk to him personally.

ROLF: That's all right, you can tell me.

OLD MAN: Are you a friend of his?

ROLF: Yes, I'm—er—his brother-in-law. We're very close.

OLD MAN (*suspiciously*): I don't know whether I ought to trust you. Your face looks—well, dissipated, like a playboy.

ROLF: I beg your pardon?

OLD MAN: Now, don't take offense, young man. We Australians are a plain-spoken lot. None of your fancy airs and graces.

ROLF: Oh, you're his uncle! The one who phoned a while back.

OLD MAN: The same, sir—Quintus Trubshaw, of Woolloomoolloo, New South Wales. You can ask anybody down under about old Wattles Trubshaw. I'm a pretty substantial personage in those parts.

ROLF (*electrified*): Is that so? Here, have a chair. . . . You look tired. . . .

OLD MAN: Well, I'm not as spry as I used to be. (*Taps his middle*) And besides, these confounded money belts weigh a man down. You wouldn't think gold dust could be that heavy.

ROLF (*all sympathy*): I know, I know. Why not rest it awhile on the table here? I'll be glad to help you unbuckle—

OLD MAN (*warding him off*): Never mind, I'm quite comfortable now. When do you expect my nephew?

ROLF: He's—ah—he's just getting up.

OLD MAN: How's that? Is he one of those roisterers who sleep all day?

ROLF: No, no—he works nights. He's a steady, conscientious fellow—a real family man. Never touches a drop.

OLD MAN: Humph—a goody-goody, I'll be bound. I don't take to those sanctimonious, mealymouthed characters. Always scheming underneath.

ROLF: Ha-ha, not him. He's as straight as a die, Rolf is. Just wait till you meet him. . . . You were saying that you—ahem—did well in Australia?

OLD MAN: Aye, not too badly. I've about two million acres in sheep, half a dozen mines and mills, and a couple of banks. But I'm getting on in years, confidentially, and as I've neither chick nor child, I've decided to bequeath it all to Rolf.

ROLF (*crowing*): Well, that sure will come as a surprise to him, but he's got one for you, too. Watch! (*He fumbles open a network of zippers and pulls off his casque, revealing a rabbity visage and, below it, a torso garbed in an undershirt.*) Howdy, Uncle Quint!

OLD MAN (*backing away*): Eh? What's all this?

ROLF: Welcome home, sir—I'm your nephew, Rolf!

OLD MAN: You are? Then who was the other chap that was here a second ago?

ROLF: Oh, that wasn't anyone. I mean, that was me in my business clothes. You see, Uncle, I— Well, it's rather specialized work I do. I go around in disguise for these people I'm affiliated with.

OLD MAN: Hmm. Kind of a Secret Service job?

ROLF (*eagerly*): Yes, only much more delicate. Sort of public relations on the consumer level, if you understand me.

OLD MAN: What do you do—gumshoe about and peer into keyholes?

ROLF: Oh, not at all, sir. I impersonate a peanut to gain our patrons' confidence. I mingle among them informally, ingratiate myself with their pets, and cunningly tickle their risibilities in such wise as to unlock their purse strings.

OLD MAN: I see. Well, young man, if that's the case, you don't get a stiver out of me. Not a blessed farthing.

ROLF (*his face falling*): Wh-why not?

OLD MAN (*violently*): Because I won't have any kin of mine behaving like a bloody popinjay, insinuating himself into the graces of decent folk and deceiving their animals. You're unworthy of the name of Trubshaw, sir. For shame!

ROLF: But, Uncle Quint—

OLD MAN: Don't try to soft-soap me. I've dealt with rascals of your stripe before. Let me pass.

ROLF: Just one moment. Is that your last word?

OLD MAN: All but one. Goodbye.

ROLF: Then you listen to me. (*With spirit*) I'm only a cog in a mighty machine, Mr. Trubshaw, but I'm proud of my calling. Someone has to lift those bales of cotton; someone's got to merchandise those nuts. Dub me visionary, dreamer, idealist, if you will—my company's stockholders are depending on me to put this quarter's earnings over the top, and, by the eternal, I won't let them down!

OLD MAN (*unexpectedly*): Bravo, my boy—spoken like a true Planters man! (*As Rolf reacts to his sudden Yankee accent, Trubshaw straightens up, peels off his white wig and eyebrows, and reveals Marty Fescue, the far-northeastern-district sales manager of the organization.*)

ROLF: Mr. Fescue!

FESCUE: The same. For the last fortnight, Trubshaw, we top-echelon execs have been conducting an undercover survey of the loyalty of our pitchmen. Needless to say, you've passed the acid test with flying colors. (*Extends hand*) Congrats, old man, and don't be keeled over if you are eventually tagged to head up the raisin-cluster-and-chocolate-coated-Brazil section. (*He exits. As Rolf stares after him incredulously, Capricia enters—ideally, through a closet door, in order not to collide with the departing Fescue.*)

CAPRICIA: Well, I've played a lot of bingo in my time, but that was tops. (*Exhibiting a sheaf of bank notes*) Get a load of these winnings—well in excess of thirty-seven thousand clams!

ROLF: Yes, this is indeed a red-letter day for the both of us. (*He fills her in rapidly on the cascading developments of the past few minutes.*)

CAPRICIA (*nestling in his arms*): Oh, Rolf, hold me close. When have two mere groundlings e'er tasted such happiness?

ROLF: Not in mortal ken. Thanks to our free-enterprise system and phenomenal advances in marketing, we now stand on the threshold of an era when the American palate, stimulated by delicacies formerly reserved only for a Maecenas, will one day hold aloft a gustatory torch for the entire world. (*As he adjusts his monocle and their lips unite in a kiss—*)

CURTAIN

Dial "H" for

Heartburn

"MOTHER, DON'T FORGET TO TELEPHONE THE OVEN!" *Pittsburgh, Pa.*
To "telephone" your oven—or for that matter, any electric appliance—
may appear as a fantastic dream, but it's not. In fact, engineers of
Westinghouse Electric Corporation have made it possible today. Chris J.
Witting, vice president, consumer products, said the company has
developed a method of operating electric household appliances, cooling
and heating equipment, and other electrical devices in the home by
dial telephone from any location in the United States.

"As an example," he pointed out, "you are about to take a jet flight
from New York to Los Angeles. You step into a telephone booth—make
a call—and in a matter of seconds the air conditioner you turned off
last week will be turned on, and your house will be cool upon arrival in
a few hours. . . ."

The Westinghouse executive explained the system as follows: When
the owner of the equipment leaves the home, he turns the equipment to
automatic. Then from any dial telephone in the United States he can
call his home number. Next, he dials the code connecting him to the
relay box. Another code number connects him to a specific appliance or
device he wants to control. One more number selects the point at which
the setting is to be made, like operating the oven, turning off a light,
turning on an air conditioner, or defrosting a refrigerator.

—*Westinghouse news release.*

ALL RIGHT, so call me Miss Cliché of 1960, but the thing about the married ones that always spooks me is how sweet and attentive they are at first, when they're on the prowl. Here, sweetie, let's put your stole under my attaché case where it won't get mussed. Bawling out the captain because the lady distinctly ordered a Gibson. Is the sauce *Bigarade* prepared to your taste, my dear? I was passing Constance Spry's and just happened to remember you liked freesias. The weird part, like my girl friend says, is that you know the whole bit and yet you go along with the gag. They sit there all spaniel eyes, gushing over your new hairdo and that exciting perfume so typical of you, and inside a couple of months they wouldn't react if you wore turpentine. The pattern's the same every time—hearts and flowers for openers, they're a boy of sixteen again, then the stifled yawn and the Kodachrome of the twins in Pocatello or Soot Falls. The minute I looked up that afternoon in the Drake Bar and saw Jack Ribaldry give me a cool, calculating stare, I could have predicted the plot. But I certainly goofed. I never figured to get involved with an electrical Bluebeard.

How I met him, I was on my way home, beat out from nine hours' posing for this hair-spray commercial, when I decided I had to have a fast Daiquiri or else. You try standing around under those lights with a lot of grips, makeup people, and agency men nattering at you and see how glamorous it is. Sure, it's bread, and nobody can afford to turn up their nose at the residuals. Still, you do build up the most ghastly tension with all the takes and the coffee in between, and I simply had to unwind. Well, anyway, no sooner had I knocked one back then I began intercepting Junior's signals. The Drake isn't exactly the Carnegie Delicatessen, the bulbs they use, but from what I could see he was a dark, rather attractive character on the plump side, with a widow's peak, pin-striped suit, and good accessories. No Cesar Romero—a solid citizen, kind of a younger Eugene Pallette with overtones of the garment center, if you dig. Ordinarily, I'd have told him to get lost, except that while I was ignoring him my stole slipped off onto the floor and he very sweetly retrieved it. I suppose basically that there are times in every person's life when she feels a great need to be cherished. I was so weary of casual, fly-by-night friendships—weekends at some joker's in Rowayton that his wife is away in Europe, Ivy Leaguers in madras coats who don't know whether they're in love with their mother or their Porsche—that I just wanted a shoulder to lean on, a home instead of a kitchenette. I wanted an oven, though not the kind I got.

We had dinner at Spurio's that night, and he turned out to be Charlie Candid, the type that spills everything down to his Social Security number in the exposition. He *was* in the rag trade, like I guessed, though miles from Seventh Avenue; he ran a plant near Chillicothe, where he manufactured these hook-and-eye clasps on women's dresses that never work. Kicked out of Tulane, Grinnell, you name it, had a big creative drive toward dentistry or hopscotch or something but wound up in the family business. Ranch-style house in the suburbs, a wheel at the country club, two lovely daughters who adored him, and, surprise, one wife who didn't. To recover from this bombshell, I accepted another Daiquiri and admitted that people sometimes outgrew each other. He became so grateful that he upset all his credit cards into the *gazpacho*. When he asked me what time Van Cleef & Arpels opened in the morning, I knew I had it made.

Well, his country club must have developed a hot journal box the next ten days, because their chief wheel was spinning in New York. You had to hand it to Jack Ribaldry; cornball though he was, he cut a wide swath. He may have been Harry Hypotenuse, the sum of the squares, but his spending arm never flagged. We played so many matinées at Hattie's and Bergdorf that the help began setting their watches by me, and Kilgallen wrote that the night we passed up the Pavillon, Soulé tried to slash his wrists. (Or maybe it was her wrists—I forget.) Anyhow, he was a real mortgage-lifter for a working girl, and, to tell the truth, I got a teeny-weeny bit fond of him, in spite of myself. I guess what did it was my voice. He had a quite good ear and said I reminded him of Merman before she fell apart, which it gave him this inspiration. As a pure business investment, he very generously offered to subsidize me to a coach, special material, and a flat large enough to accommodate a piano, so I could practice. That way, he'd also have a spot to freshen up whenever he popped in from Ohio, thus saving hotel bills. I mean, it would work out to both our advantage.

And it did, the whole first month. Through my girl friend, I found a divine spot in the Seventies, a sub-lease from a party who'd been studying ballet at the Delehanty Institute until her husband looked up the curriculum. It was only a little bijou place, three rooms done in modified French Provincial with mirror accents and white wall-to-wall carpeting—a wee underfurnished, but I added some foam chairs covered in fake zebra and a fun coffee table made from an antique set of bellows. The bedroom was terribly feminine—pink ruffles and curtains to match; Jack said it made him feel like a bull in a china shop to walk in there, so he mainly sat in the dinette. I and he couldn't argue over that, for the kitchen was the room that appealed to us most. There was every appliance you'd find at Hammacher, including an electric schlemmer: blenders, percolators, casseroles, toasters and roasters, a refrigerator like a jukebox—God knows what. We used to get a charge out of eating in during those first few weeks. We'd have our cocktail, then a Cornish hen and stuff from the Vendôme that he heated up—I wasn't too expert at this cooking jazz, so he took over—and afterward he'd read *Playboy* while I watched Jack Paar.

"Man, this is it," he often said. "Think of those poor bastards out in Chillicothe playing bridge with their wives. I'd flip if I didn't have someone gay and uninhibited like you to pal with."

Well, shortly after, I went up to Utica to do an industrial for the Grotesque Towel people, one of these cockamaney musicals they stage at their dealers' convention. You know, old standards and routines plugging the company's product, like "I See Your Facecloth Before Me." You die, but they pay you three bills and it's a chance to sing to an audience, even if you have to block a pass or two on the runway. When I got back to the flat, there was a whole brand-new range in the kitchen—the stove of tomorrow the housewife dreams of along with Burt Lancaster, more dials than a B-52, and a big fuse box on the side. I ruined a nail stripping off the cellophane and the fancy blue bow, and inside was a card from Jack reading, "Relax, gorgeous. From now on, the Bell System and I do all the work." The *Bell* System, I thought—this guy must be off his rocker. It's my own fault for going so domestic, I analyzed, measuring out coffee into the Chemex; his next milk run it'll be strictly the Four Seasons, the Copa, and no dishes. Just then the phone in the bedroom rings, a long peal I could swear was a toll call, but the line was clear when I picked up. So I hustle back to the Java, and there I get my first kick in the head. Someone has switched on the unit under the Chemex. Don't ask me who, how, why—the plate was red hot, glowing, and I hadn't even touched the knob, that I'll guarantee. You may think it was kookie of me to panic over such a little thing. I couldn't help it, though; I flopped down in the dinette, trying to rationalize, figuring maybe I accidentally brushed it with my sleeve. . . . Then the vacuum cleaner shot out of the closet and I really blew my stack.

O.K., you say it was imagination, and that's your privilege. Exhaust fans and televisions, sun lamps and record-players don't go on by themselves, either, but mine did, all of them together, like the big Dorsey band. The whole joint was jumping—the mixer buzzing, the hair dryer blazing, the oven baking away. Anybody else would have blacked out, but a TV model that works with appliances learns how to handle them. (And studio electricians, too—some of those TV juicers generate more voltage than Grand Coulee.) I poured a shot to steady myself, disconnected the main fuse, and pondered what to do. There was probably a short in the wiring, but why should I put out for a major repair on Jack's hideaway? On the other hand, if I called Chillicothe and dumped it in his lap, the wife or a snoopy secretary might be listening. The best plan was to park at my girl friend's till he checked in. I was halfway to the phone when voom, the door flies open and there's Prince Charming.

"Hiya, doll!" he said. "Is dinner ready?"

"What dinner?" I said, glaring at him. The nerve of the creep, barging in as if it were Stouffer's. Besides, I was all set to flag a standby date I had in reserve, and I resented being caught off balance.

"Why, I telephoned the oven from LaGuardia," he said, with this annoyed expression. "Didn't the code function? Or didn't you think to look?"

I'm half Scotch-Irish on both sides, and when I lose my temper —brother, I go. I gave him an earful about crashing the pad without warning, practically told him to shove his foolish fixtures, and turned on the waterworks. Eventually, we both calmed down and I made a trifle sense out of his double-talk. The whole *tzimmas* with the current was due to the range, which it operated by dial phone from anywhere, and so did the other appliances.

"Hold on one second, Sarnoff," I said to him. "You mean that some grease monkey in Sausalito is liable to call a wrong number and sunburn my nose?"

"Not in a million years," he said. "The only combination that unlocks this circuit is right here in my little black book. Just think! Hereafter I can prepare your eggs without ever leaving my desk, or, if I feel like sea food before coming over, I can broil us a fish in advance."

That'll be the day, I thought, but I kept my mouth shut and took him to Perfidio's to restore his perspective. They're not actually a kickback place; the maître d' is a friend of mine and sends me a few stockings or a bottle of Joy every so often. After Jack saw the check, he lost his interest in cookery and let me alone for a while. I got a kind of a wounded, bleeding-hearts letter from him, grexing how selfish I was and couldn't appreciate a man's craving for home and fireside. It sounded as if his wife had wooed him back with a new recipe for peach shortcake, and that was hunky-dory with me. I had a couple other irons in the fire.

Then, around the middle of November, he comes to life again. My phone starts ringing at odd hours, the heat and the lights go on and off, and all the utilities fight me. Twice, when I was dead from a late night at Morocco, the clock on the radio woke me up —at nine-thirty, for God's sake. If I hooked up the iron to press some intimate garment—a slip, for instance—half the time Mr. Buttinsky out in Ohio would scorch it. The worst headache was the electric blanket. An electric blanket is a very personal thing, like your preference for a light or heavy Scotch, and you don't want some goon a thousand miles away dictating your body heat. He and his goddam remote control drove me so wacky that one morning I finally got fed up and decided to shove off. Just as I was gathering these oddments of Jack's to send to the thrift shop —cuff links, his watch, and a couple of suits—the doorman totes in a huge air-express package. It's from the old gourmet himself, natch. An eleven-pound frozen turkey and all the fixings—cranberries, yams, even a mince pie. Oh-oh, said a little voice in my head, you better cut out of here before he begins basting the bird from the airport. Famous last words—I'd hardly put my face on when I heard him stomp in the foyer. As far as he was concerned, the napkin was already tucked under his chin.

"My, that smells good!" he said romantically, sniffing toward the kitchen. "I bought a big gobbler so we'd have plenty of leftovers. How've you been, sugar?"

"Great," I said.

"And you look it," he said. That disposed of the courtship. "Wasn't this a hell of an idea—a cozy Thanksgiving feed, just the two of us?"

"Jack, I might as well level with you—" I began.

"Listen," he broke in. He was so used to giving orders, to lousing up everyone's life and their appliances, that my dialogue didn't matter. "I left for here in such a hurry I didn't get a chance to shave. Is my electric razor in there?" He doesn't even wait for an answer, lams into the *excusado,* and starts singing an aria in that off-key bass of his. All of a sudden, it stopped and he came out holding the razor.

"Something's wrong with my Beardmaster!" he snapped. "Has anybody else been using it?"

"Only the doorman," I said. "He picks the lint off his uniform with it."

"Don't clown around with me," he said. "It was in A-1 condition the last time . . . Wait a minute—now I remember. I must have forgot to dial the right code number. Where's my little black book?"

"How do I know?" I said. "I have enough to do without—" Then I saw him turn the most awful beige color, as if he'd been sapped. "Jack—what's the matter?"

"Right under her nose!" he said, almost sobbing. "I laid it on the dresser while I was changing my pants, and she always keeps her bridge there. Oh, my God, what'll she do?"

Well, she didn't keep him in suspense very long. He was ranting away like Maurice Schwartz, raving about his adorable daughters and the country club, when the long-distance phone rang. It started the razor, the blender, the dryer, the oven, and the juiciest testimony the tabloids printed in months. But I wasn't there to see any of it. I was in Montego—with this Ivy Leaguer, his mother, and his Porsche.

Small Is My Cinema,

Deep My Doze

THE hands of the clock pointed to one-thirty the other day, and my own, more flaccid than vermicelli, dangled inertly beside the dental chair as Dr. Yankwich shoved aside his drill, fired alternate rounds of compressed air and raspberry shrub down my throat, and straightened up. "There—wasn't it a breeze?" he asked gaily. "Let me help you off with that apron." He whisked off the plastic cocoon enveloping me and vigorously scrubbed at the dried foam on my chin. Mumbling several gutturals that sounded like Burmese participles dipped in Novocain, I groped my way out of his cubicle to the anteroom. The right quadrant of my face, from nose to ear lobe and including a tongue unaccountably enlarged to the size of a bolt of brocatel, was frozen solid, and I looked forward bleakly to an afternoon of prickly, reluctant thaw. I couldn't have been more mistaken. I had extricated my trench coat—or what I thought was mine—from a rack festooned with them, and, pulling it on, had headed toward the bank of elevators when, halfway down the hall, the afternoon took a totally unexpected turn.

The corridor, in my dozen years of traversing it, had been lined with a variety of humdrum enterprises—accountants, custom tailors, import-export firms, and the like. Today, however, I saw that the legend "Little Cinema Lyceum, Inc." had blossomed forth in boldface on a door that now stood open, surrounded by an animated crowd. Most of its number, I became aware as I reached the periphery, were girls cultivating a resolute bohemianism; their hair was disordered, they wore a minimum of makeup and a maximum of leotard, and a dustier flock of ravens had never postured around an espresso machine. The half-dozen young men in their midst, if equally liberated, were more colorful. They sported loud gooseneck sweaters, Breton fishermen's jackets, and, in one case at least, a single gold earring. All, to a man, had beards. The whole caboodle was chattering away nineteen to the dozen, everyone jockeying for position at the door, and despite my most strenuous efforts to get past, I was swept centripetally into the thick of the crush. Between the noise and the Novocain, I was like to founder when a forceful young Amazon, with braids on the order of Alma Gluck's encircling her head, loomed over me.

"Did you get your admission card?" she trumpeted, waving a handful of tickets. I tried to disclaim affiliation with the group, but all I could achieve was a few strangled monosyllables. "You signed up for the complete course—no?" she said with a bright, affirmative nod. "I remember you by that long vest you've got on." She thrust a card at me and plunged off. Perplexed, I glanced down and discovered with hot shame that I was clad not in my coat but its interlining, a sleeveless, maternity-type garment of tan shoddy that persistently refuses to stay buttoned to the exterior. Had I displayed myself in it on the Avenue, I would have been a rare figure of fun, but in this assemblage I was just another rebel; in fact, I detected a certain amount of covert admiration. In the same instant, it struck me that since Fate had fortuitously cast me into avant-garde film circles, I ought to glean whatever profit I could from the encounter. I accordingly trained my left, or unfrozen, ear toward two vestals engaged in colloquy directly behind me.

"It was called either *Bitter Berries* or *Wild Fruit*," one was saying *con brio*. "Gérard Philipe played opposite Danielle Delorme, or maybe it was Danielle Darrieux—"

"No, that was *Sour Fruit*, with Daniel Gelin and Dany Robin," the other contradicted. "Gérard Philipe wasn't in that one."

"He was too—he's in all of them!" the first declared vehemently. "It was about this passionate young peasant with a big bust who's married to an old tyrant in a Provençal village, and she despises him, and one day she finds a tempestuous swineherd named Niedou in a haystack."

As I was passably familiar with the plot under discussion, having drowsed through endless stereotypes, I shifted my attention elsewhere. Everybody within earshot, I found, was advertising to his fellows his profound expertise on European films, the more obscure the better. Quoted in evidence were Greek and Scandinavian pictures so experimental that nobody was quite sure of their content, except that all had the same glorious denominator of cuckoldry. The real phenomenon, though, was the zeal with which my neighbors had steeped themselves in the classics of the medium. Some had seen *Mädchen in Uniform*, *Secrets of a Soul*, and *Le Chien Andalou* thirty or forty times, and one pedant even exhibited a lock of F. W. Murnau's hair surreptitiously shorn from the director's head, he asserted, during the production of *Tabu* in the South Seas.

My speech, lamentably, was still too furry to ascertain the purpose of our bivouac when the Amazon sang out orders from the doorway to enter. We filed through a passage into a schoolroom of sorts, dominated by a desk at which a gentleman of obvious pedagogic status was busy shuffling papers. There was no hint of aestheticism in his dress or bearing; plump, a shade dyspeptic, and visibly in need of a shave, he might have passed for a millinery wholesaler on the edge of receivership. He coughed daintily, and restoring the dry cigar he had been chewing, rose to his feet.

"Welcome, friends," he began. "For the benefit of those that didn't attend the first session, I'm Gabe Fagin. As I told you last time, it's our mission to train personnel for little cinema theaters, which many applicants don't realize the special requirements of the work in that it differs radically from a job in the first-run houses and the nabes. So today we'll break it down into the different categories and see if we can't give you some pointers—inside trade secrets—that'll fit you for the post you want. First of all," he said thoughtfully, "how many of you girls figure on being cashiers?"

"Five hands," the Amazon reported from the sidelines.

"Good," said Mr. Fagin. "Now, will that person in the second row stand up? That's right, miss—you." A neatly coifed brunette with wide eyes and vivid coloring arose. "Thank you. You don't mind if I use you for an illustration? . . . Well, then, let's talk cold turkey. This girl will never get to first base the way she is."

"She looks too healthy," a young man near me hazarded.

"Correct," acquiesced Fagin. "The chief requisite of the cashier in an art house is a sickly, jaded expression—a trace of the ghoul. Her hair should be long and unkempt, and no lipstick, remember—just rice powder. Furthermore," he continued, addressing his exemplar directly, "your attitude isn't half scornful enough. When the patron pushes his money through the wicket, you've got to learn how to lay aside your Baudelaire and sneer at him like he was a bindlestiff. Create the impression he'd be better off at a horror bill on Forty-second Street."

"But I like people," the girl confessed, with downcast eyes.

"Then find yourself another profession," Fagin snapped. "If it's love you're after, take up nursing. There's no room in the little cinema for humanitarians and do-gooders." Disconsolate, she subsided, and Fagin punctuated the point with his cigar for emphasis. "That goes double for the attendants in the lounge," he expounded. "Their job is harder, because they work in almost pitch-blackness dispensing the free coffee and cigarettes. Now, it's tough to be insolent there, because your natural impulse in the dark is to be clubby. So you have to evolve your own particular techniques for humiliating the customer, like spilling java on their lapel, lighting the filter end of the cigarette, et cetera. Once in a while, you get a golden opportunity; one of our trainees spotted a man in a celluloid collar and managed to set fire to it, but a chance like that don't come along every day."

"What about the murals?" a young woman inquired from the rear. "Sometimes people want to know what those spooky things with the urns and the cornucopias mean."

"A very good point," said Fagin approvingly. "The best way to handle these inquiries is to pretend the murals don't exist. The patron's already so dizzy from the gloom and the coffee that he starts doubting his own sanity, and by the time he reaches his seat you've sowed the seeds of a breakdown. And right there," he cut in, indicating the males in the audience, "is where you budding theater managers come in, you fellows who arrange the programs. A generation ago, this whole problem of what we call 'exacerbation' was hardly understood, but since then we've made great strides. Let's take the short subjects to start with," he proposed. "What type would you favor to bore your clientele beyond endurance?"

A goat-bearded stripling clad in chamois raised his hand. "Anything with caverns or stalactites in it," he declared. "Or the annual tulip celebration at Holland, Michigan, showing floral windmills and tots in wooden shoes."

"How about 'The Making of a Drum Majorette'?" another asked.

"Big-game hunting with bow and arrow," called a third.

Fagin nodded benevolently. "All first-rate," he said, "but you've overlooked the most reliable, the very cornerstone of the art cinema—skiing. No bill is well balanced without at least one short called 'Mile-a-Minute Antics' or 'White Wilderness.' To set the folks really squirming in their chairs, you add a Bugs Bunny, or Wabbit, cartoon not less than twenty years old. The other components, the newsreel and 'Coming Attractions,' are a mite tricky; they must be skillfully pruned to render them as deadly as possible. On the first, you retain the whole opening montage of troops in review, water sports, and annual Mummers' Parade as a teaser."

"But then give 'em only one news clip of a flood or mine disaster—right?" a voice behind me suggested cunningly.

"Precisely," agreed our mentor, with a twinkle. "You're catching on fast. With 'Coming Attractions,' of course, you don't show any footage at all—just a few static cards with one-word plugs like 'Arresting—*Tacoma News-Tribune*' or 'Saucy . . . libidinous—*Women's Wear Daily*.' Between the different novelties and Terrytoons, it goes without saying, you keep opening and closing the scrim wherever the chance presents itself. Finally, there's the question of the chaser. Some managers use a commercial film they get for free—'Water Power, Your Magic Genie,' or 'The Romance of Tuna,' made by this or that cannery concern. Myself, I prefer to turn up the house lights and play a good, dismal sound track of Chaminade, say, or Charles Wakefield Cadman." He paused, ignited his cigar, and looked about. "Any questions?"

"Yes, sir," a young man spoke up. "What about lovers in the audience—the couples with the tall hair that neck through the feature? How can they be placed so as to best interfere with the vision of those behind?"

"If your theater is properly constructed—that is to say, without any pitch at all—that'll take care of itself," Fagin returned. He cupped his ear to catch a query from somebody in the rear. What if a foreign import, with every expectation of failure, proved a surprise hit? "That's where your true showmanship, your flair for operating an art house, will emerge," he said instantly. "Pull it out and substitute *The Cabinet of Dr. Caligari*. . . . No other problems? O.K., then, until next week, when we'll discuss twenty ways to withhold ice water and to cheat on your air conditioning.''

That night, strolling off our dinner of South African rock-lobster tails, my wife halted suddenly as we came abreast of our local art cinema. ''Look, they're showing *Acrid Fruit,* with Gérard Philipe, Danielle Delorme, and Danielle Darrieux!'' she exclaimed. ''Jesse Zunser of *Cue* gave it five mangosteens! It's all about an eager, middle-aged woman with a tyrannical hus-band—''

''Which is the part I play,'' I broke in, hustling her past. ''And I'll tell you this much, puss: you won't get me into those grottoes for a while. Not even if they're showing Daniel Webster, Daniel Deronda, and Daniel Defoe.''

We rounded out the evening in a bowling alley, where I cracked a metatarsal flange, but despite it I came out ahead. At least, I didn't have to watch any Chinook salmon fight their way up-stream.

Gather Ye Rosebuds,

but Watch Ye Step

WHEN the *Times* recently braided the floral into the fiscal with a report that a Balkan government had deposited eleven hundred pounds of attar of roses, valued at eight hundred and forty thousand dollars, in a London bank, a good many people doubtless began hoarding petals and envisioning themselves on Easy Street. I, for one, was not among them; by a fortuitous circumstance that will presently emerge, I knew of the transaction a full year ago, and, at the risk of sounding melodramatic, I'll add that I was drawn into a pretty harebrained conspiracy as a result. For less enlightened readers, however, the dispatch went on to clarify the bald details. A basic ingredient in the manufacture of perfume, the attar—a heavy, pale-yellow oil stored in small metal drums— had been put up as collateral by Bulgaria, in lieu of gold, at the Moscow Narodny Bank, a Communist finance house for East-West trade. But, said a New York expert named Walker the *Times* consulted, who deals in such commodities, "any purchaser would have to be on the alert. There have been cases where the oil in the sealed casks proved to be diluted or otherwise inferior.'' The *Times* continued, ''He recalled one case, in the late Nineteen Forties, when his concern rejected attar offered at $1,000 a pound. Some time later, the company bought the attar at $2.50 a pound. At the time, Mr. Walker said, confidence men were more likely to try to sell diluted attar, because techniques to analyze the contents of the oil were not so sure as they are now. Today, for example, Mr. Walker's company would test attar purchases with such techniques as infrared spectrophotometry, or gas chromatography. 'But the final judge of the question is still the nose,' Mr. Walker said.''

Up to a point, my own embroilment with the treasure in the Narodny vaults was purest mischance; it stemmed from an accidental lunch in Covent Garden last October with Basil Scrymgeour, a British publicist. Scrymgeour and I had met originally in New York a couple of years before, during his brief tenure there for the B.B.C., and had dined on occasion at Lindy's, the cuisine of which appealed to us both. It was only natural, therefore, that when we collided in the Charing Cross Road that forenoon he should propose a like *ambiance* to signalize our reunion.

''Gastlich's, in Brewer Street, old man,'' he said, energetically linking arms with me. ''What, you don't know it? The best pastrami in London. A blintz fit for a prince. Luscious golden matzo balls. Rye bread that'll bring tears to your eyes.'' As we wove through the turmoil of the wholesale food district, perilously sliding over a carpet of soup greens, Scrymgeour worked himself into a dangerous frenzy. The chopped chicken liver at Gastlich's, he stated categorically, was the finest in the world. Nor was this merely his opinion, he added, summoning up a noble authority— the Marquess of Londonderry thought so, too. Why the hell the latter was qualified to pontificate on chicken liver I could not imagine, but the weight of royal precedent was clearly incontestable with an Englishman, and I displayed suitable awe.

Except for the insolence of the waiters, which compared favorably with any I had encountered on Second Avenue, Gastlich's proved as spurious as I had anticipated. The marinated herring was a desecration and the bagels a mockery, the much-vaunted rye bread the work of an unbeliever who obviously drew no distinction between sesame and caraway seeds.

"Look here, you don't seem very hungry," complained Scrymgeour, glancing up from his sandwich. "Liver a bit peckish?"

"Brackish, I'd say rather," I replied, and waved it into limbo. "Maybe I should have ordered sturgeon, too."

"Fatal mistake," he agreed smugly. "Mine's absolutely wizard. But then, I've a thing about sturgeon—can't get enough of it. Dead keen on the stuff; have been from boyhood. Know something? I'll wager if somebody gave me a whole sturgeon—"

"I beg your pardon, friend," said a voice in the next booth. "I couldn't help overhearing that." Startled, we turned and beheld a dapper character leaning over Scrymgeour's shoulder. Though he sported a luxuriant Guards mustache and a club tie, his accent was patently American, and his facile bonhomie reminded me somehow of George Jessel. "You New York boys?"

"Well, he is," replied my tablemate. "I was there—"

"I knew I'd seen you," the intruder said with triumph. "Around Lindy's. I'm Julie Cahoon. Mind if I sit with you?" The question was already academic, for he was halfway into our banquette. Only Alfred Hitchcock, he declared effervescently, could have conceived so staggering a coincidence. He likewise was a sturgeon lover; had, in fact, just consumed a portion, and insisted on catechizing the waiter to prove it. Alarmed at our succumbing to a bore, or, worse yet, the victim of an *idée fixe*, I became restive, but Cahoon ignored me. As one aficionado to another, he told Scrymgeour, he felt obliged to reveal the existence in London of a veritable El Dorado, a Nibelungen hoard of Russian sturgeon and caviar to be had for the taking. "It breaks my heart to see it going to waste," he said, endeavoring to contain his emotion. "It's just laying there piled up to the ceiling, begging for someone to cop it."

"But what would I do with it?" objected Scrymgeour. "Why, damn it all, one fish that size'd last a man for months."

"Do with it?" echoed the other. "Sell it, of course—export it! Do you know what it'd fetch at Barney Greengrass's in New York, or Reuben's? I don't have much of a head for figures, Mac," he said, exuding more candor than a Shubert ingénue, "but this I'll put in writing—ten thousand per cent profit on your investment!"

"I thought you said this stuff was free," I corrected. I sometimes pretend to be naïve about business, but, deep down, the proposal didn't sound kosher to me.

"Refrigeration, shipping charges," he said evasively. "Also a little matter of hush money in the right quarters. Which I feel I ought to explain."

The feeling was general, the explanation more so. Unknown to the laity, certain European governments had latterly taken to depositing recherché essences and comestibles as financial security in a London bank. The coffers of the Moscow Narodny, swore Cahoon, literally bulged with ambergris from Norway, Bulgarian attar of roses, afflatus (the Hungarian indispensable in the manufacture of strudel), and various *zakuska* (finny delicacies from the U.S.S.R.) beyond catalogue. Sole guardian of the treasure was an outwardly dedicated young member of the Comsomol named Boguslav.

"Boguslav my eye," our informant sneered. "He ought to shorten it to Bogus. He's a crooner from Altoona—Nick Sauerwein. I knew him in the Army, up in Frankfurt, and then the other day I ran into him here at the races. At first he made like a muzhik—the deadpan bit—but after a few beers he broke down. The guy's a mad horseplayer and he's lost his shirt. Also he's mixed up with this zook, an actress in the West End, that she's taking him to the cleaners. Get the picture?"

Scrymgeour blinked at him. "You mean he's been dipping into the assets?"

"What else?" asked Cahoon. "He borrowed a pail of attar

here, a couple of sturgeon there, and now he's paralyzed that the auditors might check up. That's where we come in. If I slip him a couple of hundred to square the bookies, he'll glom enough fish out of the strong room for us to fly them to New York and make a quick turnover.''

"He'd still have the auditors on his back," I contended.

"That problem I already solved," he said, with a dazzling smile. "There's some papier-mâché tunas in a Japanese kite store he can substitute for the time being, till the heat is off. Well, gents, how does it sound to you? Better talk fast if you want in.''

"Mmm," said Scrymgeour dubiously. "Don't you think we should meet this—er—Bogus fellow, just to insure he's not pulling the wool over our eyes?''

"He wouldn't dare, not with what I got on him," returned Cahoon. "Besides, it's too risky, a contact between him and you. The bank's watching him every second. One false move—well, you know those Russkies.'' He flicked a finger across his throat in a graphic gesture, then rose abruptly. "I tell you—mull it over in your head and call me tonight at Claridge's. The lobby," he specified. "I'm working out of there while they find me a suite. Abbadabba.''

I must say that for a person of his experience and worldliness Basil Scrymgeour is one of the most artless men I know. Cynical though he can be of pretense, alive to the humbug of his industrial and show-business clients, he nonetheless proceeded to display a fatuity about the project that appalled me. I pointed out that Cahoon was visibly on the muscle and his story a tissue, that to involve oneself in an international fish-running scheme was to court disaster, but he doggedly rejected my plea. These were piping times, he retorted, and it behooved a chap to feather his nest if he could. Perhaps, he said—and I confess I bridled a bit— I tended to regard Cahoon as a spiv because we sprang from the same general background. Realizing that further admonition would only impair our friendship, I washed my hands of the affair.

"Ah, well, I don't propose to get down on my hands and knees," said Scrymgeour, with the clear imputation that I was an ignatz. "But I do expect one favor. Will you look after my interest—act as my factor, so to speak—when you're back in the States?"

"I most certainly will not," I started to say, but then I forbore. On reconsideration, I felt, Scrymgeour would inevitably perceive the folly of his design and abandon it.

I couldn't have been more mistaken. A fortnight later, a garbled phone message at the hotel announced that certain marine goods were in transit overseas, regarding which instructions would be wired to me on my return there. Pursuant to the principle that if you ignore something it ceases to exist, I busied myself with other concerns—I had come to London primarily to buy some Newmarket boots and a mask for pigeon shooting—and in due course flew on to New York. The cable I found waiting from Scrymgeour, while discreetly worded, left no doubt of the mandate he was issuing to me. A deal had been successfully effected with one Monroe Langsam, at the Moby Dick Delicatessen on Amsterdam Avenue. I was to rendezvous with him, employing the pseudonym Marty Torment, collect payment as agreed, and telegraph it forthwith to the partners at Scrymgeour's flat. Claridge's, I deduced, was still unable to find Cahoon a suite.

The exterior of the Moby Dick Delicatessen, on the raw autumnal morning I approached it, gave little token of the intrigue flourishing within; a hand-lettered sign advertising fresh belly lox flapped disconsolately from the steamy window, and behind it I saw the usual dusty display of roast chickens, stuffed olives, and Miss Rheingold. A burly individual with a voluted nostril, attired in a surgical gown and straw hat, was unpacking bloaters at the counter as I entered. He surveyed me indifferently as I sat down at a rear table and unfolded a newspaper. After a moment, he sauntered back, hands enveloped in a towel. "Yes, gentleman?"

I pretended to be absorbed in my paper. "Imported sturgeon sandwich and a glass of tea," I murmured.

"Sturgeon, you said?" His languor yielded to watchfulness on the instant. "We don't handle it, Mister."

"I hear different, Langsam," I said, looking up quietly. "In fact, I'm told you received a big fat invoice of it a few days back."

"Who—who are you?" he stammered. "How did you know me?"

"It's my business to know things like that, bud," I said. "What does the name Marty Torment mean to you?"

"Sh-h-h—quiet!" he besought me, and cast a panicky glance toward the street. Then he bent forward. "England?" he asked furtively. "Julie Cahoon?"

"Check," I said. "Here's their cable to show I'm legit, and I'll take the money in small bills—unmarked, if you don't mind."

"You'll get it, don't worry," he promised. He slid into the chair opposite me, his voice aquiver with entreaty. "There's just one little minor complication, though, Mr. Torment. The shipment seems to be O.K., but I'm having it analyzed by an expert to make sure."

"How?" I demanded. "By infrared spectrophotometry? Gas chromatography? Some phony technique like that?"

"Nah, he just sniffs it," said Langsam. "The final judge of the question is still the nose. Tonight he brings me his report, tomorrow I bring you the gelt wherever you say. Fair enough?"

It was, I saw, manifestly futile to apply pressure in the situation, and after whispered debate we agreed on a circumspect locale for the payoff. Had anyone been loitering around the Akeley Collection at the Museum of Natural History the next afternoon, he might have observed a burly individual with a voluted nostril accost a trench-coated figure, the brim of whose hat was snapped well down over his eyes. Unless the spectator was alert, however, he would have failed to notice the packet, wrapped in oilpaper, that passed swiftly between them. Forty-five minutes later, at a Western Union office, I filled in the particulars of a money-order form, opened the packet to verify the contents, and discovered what any astute reader of police fiction could have predicted. Before me lay three dozen slices of flavorsome, micrometrically thin corned beef. Almost simultaneously, two inescapable facts struck me. First, no conventional bank facilities I knew of could possibly transmit such payment abroad, and, second, nobody familiar with exploits of this genre would bother to raise a hue and cry, for the presiding genius of the Moby Dick must long ago have flown. I therefore took home the *valuta,* placed it on deposit, and nibbled away at it until it disappeared. I feel a twinge every time I go into Lindy's, thinking I'll meet Cahoon, but, Lord, he wouldn't dare denounce me. Not with what I've got on *him*.

Portrait of the Artist

as a Young Mime

"Song Without End" features the highlights of Franz Liszt's life. . . .
The music was recorded by Jorge Bolet, one of America's foremost
pianists. . . . Most dramatic story behind the scenes of the making of
"Song Without End" was the coaching of Dirk Bogarde by Victor Aller
to enable the actor to give a flawless visual performance at the keyboard
to match Bolet's already recorded score. Mr. Aller, a master pianist,
also is Hollywood's best known piano coach for stars. Dirk Bogarde had
never played a note in his life! Not only did he have to learn how to
play the piano—he had to learn to play like genius Franz Liszt.

—*The Journal-American.*

THE day started off, as all mine do, at a snail's pace. I got to my
studio on Carmine Street about a quarter of ten, closed the skylight and lit the kerosene stove—oxygen, however essential to
aeronautics and snorkeling, is death to the creative process—and
settled down with the coffee and Danish I pick up every morning
en route from the subway. Then I emptied the ashtrays into the
hall and washed out a few brushes, meanwhile listening to

WQXR and studying the canvas I had on the easel. Shortly before eleven, I ran out of excuses for cerebration and began mixing my colors. That's inevitably the moment some nuisance takes it into his head to phone, and in this case it was the bloodiest of them all—Vetlugin, my dealer. His voice trembled with excitement.

"Did he call you? What did he say?" he asked feverishly. Good old Vetlugin, the Tower of Babble. He opens his mouth and out comes confusion; the man has an absolute genius for muddle. By valiant effort, I finally extracted a modicum of sense from his bumbling. Some Hollywood nabob named Harry Hubris, reputedly a top producer at Twentieth Century-Fox, was clamoring to discuss a matter of utmost urgency. Ever quick to sniff out a kopeck, Vetlugin, in direct violation of orders, had promptly spilled my whereabouts. "I figured it'd save time if he came down to see you personally," he cooed. "The precise nature of what he wants he wouldn't reveal, but I smelled there must be dough in it."

"Listen, you Bessarabian Judas," I groaned. "How many times have I told you never, under any circumstances, to divulge—" Like all arguments with leeches, this one was futile; muttering some claptrap about ingratitude, he hung up and left me biting my own tail. It was a half hour before I calmed down sufficiently to resume work, but I knew the jig was up when the doorbell rang, and one look at the character bounding upstairs confirmed my fears. From his perky velvet dicer to the tips of his English brogues, he was as brash a highbinder as ever scurried out of Sardi's. The saffron polo coat draped impresario-fashion over his shoulders must have cost twelve hundred dollars.

"Say, are you kidding?" he exclaimed, fastidiously dusting a bit of plaster from his sleeve. "Those terrific abstractions of yours—you don't actually *paint* them here?"

"I do when I'm not interrupted," I said pointedly.

"Well, you're risking your life," he declared. "I've seen firetraps in my time, boychick, but this ain't for real. If I showed

it in a picture, they'd say it was overdone." He stuck out a paw.
"Harry Hubris," he said. "I guess you've heard of me."

Other than feigning an attack of scrofula, there was no escape
now that Vetlugin had crossed me up, so I motioned him in.

He made a quick, beady inventory of the décor. "Go figure
it," he said, with a shrug. "It always kills me an artist should
hole up in a fleabag to conceive a masterpiece. Still, everybody
to their own ulcer. Zuckmayer, I want you to know I consider you
one of the nine foremost painters of our time."

"Indeed," I said. "Who are the other eight?"

"Look, pal, don't get me started or I'm liable to talk all night,"
he said. "I've got maybe the most important collection in the
Los Angeles area—five Jackson Pollocks, three Abe Rattners,
two of yours—"

"Which ones?"

"I can't remember offhand," he said irritably. "A houseful
of paintings, you wouldn't expect me to recall every title. But
let's get down to basics. What would you say if I offered you
two thousand bucks for an hour's work?"

"I'd be even more suspicious than I am now, which is plenty."

"A blunt answer," he approved. "Well, here's the dodge, and
you needn't worry, it's strictly legit. Did you perchance read
Irving Stonehenge's biography of John Singer Sargent, *The
Tortured Bostonian?*"

I shook my head, and he frowned.

"You're the one guy in America that didn't," he said. "In my
humble opinion, it's going to make the greatest documentary-
type motion picture since *Lust for Life*. Just visualize Rob Roy
Fruitwell in the leading role and tell me how it could miss."

I visualized as best I could, but, never having heard of the
man, got nowhere. "Who is he?" I asked.

"Rob Roy?" Hubris's scorn for my ignorance was Olympian.
"Only the biggest potential draw in pictures today, that's all,"
he affirmed. "Properly handled, Fruitwell can be another Kirk
Douglas, *and*," he went on, lowering his voice, "I'll breathe you

something in strictest confidence. After he has his dimple deepened next spring, you won't be able to tell them apart. My immediate headache, though, and the reason I contacted you, is this. The kid's a born actor and he'll play the hell out of Sargent, but thus far he's appeared exclusively in horse operas—Westerns. What he requires is a little coaching from an expert—a professional artist like you."

"My dear Mr. Hubris," I said. "If you think I can transform a numskull into a master in one lesson—"

"For crisakes, smarten up, will you?" he implored. "All you got to furnish is the pantomime. Show him how to hold a brush, what a palette's for, which end of the tube the color comes out. Remember, this lug don't know from beauty or the Muse. Two years ago he was a busboy in Fort Wayne."

"But I've never dealt with actors," I objected. "I haven't the faintest clue to their mentality."

"Mentality's one problem you won't have with Rob Roy Fruitwell, brother," Hubris guaranteed. "He's got none. He's just a matzo ball, a sensitized sponge that'll soak up the info you give him and delineate it on the screen."

"Well, I'd have to think it over," I said. "I'm assembling a show at the moment—"

"So your dealer mentioned," he said. "And believe me, Mr. Zuckmayer, I feel like a rat pressuring you, but the point is, we're in a bind. You see, in view of the fact that we start shooting Friday, I had Rob Roy sky in from the Coast last night solely on purpose to huddle with you."

"Then you can jolly well sky him back," I began, and stopped short. After all, if this gasbag was aching to shell out a fat fee for an hour of *expertise,* it'd be downright loony to stand on dignity; my anemic budget could certainly use a transfusion. Obviously sensing I was tempted, Hubris threw in the clincher. Not only would he raise the ante another five hundred, but he was prepared to hand over a check on the spot provided I saw Fruitwell that afternoon. "Well-l-l, all right," I said, overborne.

"Have him down here at four o'clock and I'll see what I can do."

"Attaboy!" chortled my caller, whipping out a pen. "You mark my words, Zuckmayer—this may be a turning point in your career. Once the critics dig your name up there in the credits— 'Artistic Consultant to the Producer, Harry Hubris'—the whole industry'll be knocking on your door!"

"Don't bother to freeze my blood, please," I said. "Just write out the check."

Hubris made no pretense of concealing his umbrage. "You're a strange apple," he said. "What makes all you artists so anti-social?"

I knew why, but it would have been too expensive to reply. I needed the money.

I was tied up at the framer's after lunch, discussing a new molding of kelp on tinfoil for my show, and didn't get back to the studio until four-fifteen. There was a big rented Cadillac parked outside, the driver of which, a harassed plug-ugly in uniform, was standing off a mob of teen-agers screeching and waving autograph books. We had a dandy hassle proving I was kosher, but he finally let me upstairs to the unholy trinity awaiting me. Fruitwell was a standard prize bullock with a Brando tonsure and capped teeth, in a gooseneck sweater under his Italian silk suit which kept riding up to expose his thorax. His agent, a fat little party indistinguishable from a tapir, had apparently been summoned from the hunt, for he wore a Tattersall vest and a deep-skirted hacking coat. The third member of the group, a bearded aesthete dressed entirely in suède, flaunted a whistle on a silver chain encircling his throat. "I'm Dory Gallwise, the assistant director," he introduced himself. "We had to force the lock to get in here. Hope you don't mind."

"Not at all," I said. "Sorry the place is such a pigsty, but— well, you know how bohemians are."

"Oh, it's not so bad," he said graciously. "Of course, as I was just explaining to Rob Roy here, the studio he'll occupy as

Sargent will be a lot more imposing. The size of Carnegie Hall, in fact."

"*Natürlich*," I said. "Now, before we commence, Mr. Fruit-well, do you have any questions about art? Anything you'd like me to clarify?"

Immersed in contemplation of a torso on the wall, the young man did not respond at once. Then he lifted his head sleepily. "Yeah, this thing here," he said. "What's it supposed to be—a woman?"

I admitted I had embodied certain female elements, and he snickered.

"You really see that when you look at a dame?" he asked, with a quizzical smile. "Bud, you need therapy. Don't he, Monroe?"

His agent shot me a placatory wink. "Well, I wouldn't go *that* far, Rob Roy," he temporized. "Mr. Zuckmayer reacts to the world around him in a particular way—through the intellect, shall we say? He embodies certain elements—"

"Don't give me that bushwa," the other retorted. "I've dated Mamie van Doren, Marilyn Maxwell, and Diana Dors, and take it from me, pappy, they don't have any corners like that. This moke's in trouble."

"Ha, ha—who isn't?" Gallwise put in with wild gaiety. He cleared his throat nervously. "Listen, boys, let's not hold up Mr. Zuckmayer—he's a busy person." Snapping open his dispatch case, he drew forth a smock and a beret. "Here, Rob Roy, slip these on so you'll get used to the feel of 'em."

"Wait a second," said Fruitwell, clouding over, and wheeled on Monroe. "What the hell are we making, a costume picture? You said I wear a sweat shirt and dungarees."

"In the love scenes, baby," Monroe specified, "but when you're sketching, and like dreaming up your different master-pieces, why, they got to blueprint you're an artist. It establishes your identity."

"Sure, the way a sheriff puts on a tin star," said Gallwise.

"Or a busboy his white coat," I added helpfully.

Fruitwell turned and gave me a long, penetrating look. Then, evidently concluding his ears had deceived him, he surlily donned the habit, and for the next quarter of an hour submitted himself to our charade. I soon perceived that Hubris's depiction of him as a chowderhead was rank flattery. Totally devoid of either co-ordination or the ability to retain, he lumbered about upsetting jars of pigment, gashed himself disastrously with my palette knife, and in a burst of almost inspired clumsiness sprayed fixative into Monroe's eyeball, temporarily blinding the poor wretch. While the latter lay prostrate, whimpering under the poultices with which Gallwise and I rushed to allay his torment, Rob Roy leaned out of the skylight to mollify his fans. Since, however, they had dispersed meanwhile, his largess was wasted, and he was in a distinct pet by the time Monroe was ambulatory.

"You guys through playing beatnik?" he fretted. "Come on, let's blow. If the dauber's got any more dope, he can phone it in to Hubris, or I'll get it from research, on the Coast."

"Rob Roy—honey," pleaded Gallwise. "We'll spring you in two shakes, but just co-operate ten minutes more. I want Mr. Zuckmayer to check on a couple of scenes—you know, to make sure you don't pull a booboo. Here," he said, forcibly planting his charge in a chair. "Run through the situation where Vincent Youmans tries to win you back to your wife."

"Hold on," I protested. "How does *he* come into this?"

"A dramatic license we took to justify the score," he said hurriedly. "He's a young music student at Harvard that Sargent befriends. Can you remember the lines, Rob Roy?"

Fruitwell contorted his forehead in a simulation of deep thought.

"Never mind—spitball some dialogue to give the general idea," said Gallwise. "Go ahead, I'll cue you. I'll be Youmans."

"Hello, Youmans," complied Fruitwell, in a monotone. "Where you been, man?"

"Oh, just studying my counterpoint over in Cambridge," said

Gallwise. "But you certainly are a storm center these days, John Singer. All Beacon Hill is agog the way you threw up your job as stockbroker and abandoned your family. Can a pair of saucy blue orbs underlie this move, as wagging tongues imply?"

Fruitwell uttered a cynical hoot reminiscent of a puppy yelping for a biscuit. "Women!" he scoffed. "I'm tired of those silly little creatures casting their spell on me. I want to paint—to paint, do you hear? I've got to express what I feel deep down inside me! The agony, the heartbreak!"

His agent, who was following the recital from behind a crumpled handkerchief, sprang forward and embraced him. "Lover, don't change a word, a syllable," he begged. "Do that on camera and I personally—Monroe Sweetmeat—promise you an Academy Award. What about it, Mr. Zuckmayer?" he inquired anxiously. "Does it ring true from the artist's point of view?"

"Frighteningly," I agreed. "You've caught the very essence of the creative urge. I have only one criticism." Gallwise stiffened expectantly. "Mr. Fruitwell's got his smock on backwards. The audience might conceivably mistake him for a hairdresser."

"How could they, with that dialogue?" he demanded.

"That's what I mean," I said.

"Well, it's a point to watch," ruminated the director. "Remember that, Rob Roy. Now the key scene, where you get your big break from the hotel manager. The plot point here, Mr. Z., is that Sargent's down and out in New York. It's Christmas Day, the landlord's shut off the gas, and he's starving."

"Tell him about the onion," Monroe giggled.

"A bit of comedy relief," Gallwise explained. "He's so hungry that he finally has to eat this still-life of an onion and a herring."

"What, the canvas itself?" I asked.

"No, no—the objects he's painting," he said impatiently. "Anyway, just at his darkest hour, in comes Tuesday Weld, the coatroom girl at the St. Regis that's been secretly in love with him. She's persuaded the manager to let Sargent paint a mural of King Cole for the men's bar.''

"Using the pseudonym of Maxfield Parrish," I supplemented.

"God damn it," burst out Fruitwell, "I've got an eight-man team of writers from the New York *Post* waiting to interview me! Let's do the *scene!*"

Gallwise recoiled as if from a blast furnace. "Uh—on second thought, maybe we don't have to," he stammered, a muscle twitching in his cheek. "I only wanted to corroborate one small detail. Halfway through the action, Mr. Zuckmayer, as Sargent holds Tuesday in his arms, he suddenly stumbles on the idea for his greatest composition, 'The Kiss.' How would a painter react in those circumstances? What exact phraseology would he employ?"

"To herald an inspiration, you mean?" I pondered. "Well, I always smite my forehead and use a simple Greek word—eureka."

Fruitwell ripped off his smock and flung it at his agent. "And for this you fly me from the Coast, you muzzler," he snarled. "Any coffeepot could of told you that!" Suffused with outrage, he stalked to the door, pulverized me and my artifacts with a glance, and was gone. Monroe scampered after him, his face stricken.

Gallwise stood immobilized an instant. Then, swallowing painfully, he folded the smock into the dispatch case like a somnambulist and crossed to the threshold. The crucified smile he turned on me was purest Fra Angelico. "Temperament," he apologized. "But don't be afraid, Mr. Zuckmayer—there won't be a trace of it on the screen. The kid's a great trouper."

It was such nirvana, standing there tranquilly in the dusk after he had left, that I let the phone ring for a full minute. I knew who it was, and my parfait was complete without a Bessarabian cherry, but I also knew Vetlugin's tenacity. I picked up the receiver.

"It's me, Tovarisch." He spoke in such a conspiratorial

whisper that for a moment I had trouble distinguishing him. "Look, which painting should I give Mr. Hubris?" he asked breathlessly. "He says he deserves a big one, on account of the publicity you'll get from the film. I claim—"

"I'll settle it." I cut him short. "Call him to the phone."

"But I said you were working—I had orders not to disturb—"

"I've finished," I said. "It's catharsis time."

And it was.

Monomania,

You and Me Is Quits

My IMMEDIATE REACTION when a head studded with aluminum rheostats confronted me over the garden gate last Tuesday morning was one of perplexity. That it belonged to a courier from outer space was, I felt, improbable, for nobody of such transcendent importance would have chosen a weedy Pennsylvania freehold to land on. Its features, moreover, were much too traditional for an interplanetary nuncio; instead of the elephant ears and needle-sharp proboscis that science fiction had prepared me for, the apparition exhibited a freckled Slavic nose and wattles ripened by frequent irrigations of malt. In the same instant, as I straightened up, giddy with the effort of extricating a mullein from the cucumbers, I realized that the spiny coiffure was in actuality a home permanent and the bulging expanse of gingham below it the rest of Mrs. Kozlich, our current cleaning woman.

"I hope I didn't scare you," she said tremulously, "but I thought I better drive over and speak to you personally. Something funny happened while you and the missus were away last weekend.'' She cast a quick, nervous glance about the surrounding eighty-three acres and lowered her voice. ''A man burned a chair on your place Friday night.''

''Yes, I know,'' I replied. ''I meant to call you so you wouldn't be alar—''

''I was so frightened I almost fainted,'' she pursued, unheeding. ''My niece Kafka and I were washing your upstairs windows around five o'clock when this station wagon came up the lane. I figured it was yours.''

''It was mine, Mrs. Kozlich,'' I gentled her. ''Listen to me, will you? I made a special trip back from the city—on purpose— to *burn* that chair. Do you understand?''

It was obvious she didn't, or, even if she did, was determined not to be denied the opportunity of a dramatic recital. The car, she went on breathlessly, had traversed a long field adjacent to the barn, parking by the gulch where I file old paint cans, leaky gutters, and window screens for future reference. The driver (who bore a striking resemblance to me, the ladies decided from their distant vantage point) had then unloaded a large black easy chair, systematically disemboweled its upholstery, and, while they watched spellbound, set fire to it. ''Go back there and look, if you don't believe me,'' she challenged. ''The springs are laying all over the ground where he kicked them. After he drove out, I sent Kafka up and she found a couple of scraps like horsehide or something. It must have been a leather chair.''

It was indeed, but what Mrs. Kozlich had witnessed, and what I prudently decided not to spell out for her, was the end of a dream—a romantic quest that began some twenty-two years ago. Just when or how my yearning for a tufted black leather armchair originated I cannot remember. Perhaps some elderly member of the Rhode Island medical profession, which I supported singlehanded as a boy, had one in his consulting room, or I may have seen the prototype, spavined with use, in the professorial chambers at Brown. At any rate, among the fantasies I nurtured into manhood—a princely income and a sleek, piratical schooner for cruising the Great Barrier Reef, to mention only two—was a clear-cut image of my ideal study. Its appointments varied from time to time; on occasion the walls were book-lined, or hung with rare trophies like Mrs. Gray's lechwe or a sitatunga, or again bare except for a few gems of Impressionist painting. The focus, the keystone of the décor, nonetheless, never varied—a capacious, swollen club chair, well polished, into whose depths one sank and somniferously browsed through the latest English review. There might be a revolving mahogany bookcase alongside, but I wasn't sure. I was afraid it might detract from the rich, baroque impact of the chair.

By the time I had acquired my own inglenook in the mid-thirties, though, and started prowling the auction rooms for my fictive *fauteuil*, I discovered it was a chimera. Curiosities of that sort, dealers pityingly confided, had vanished with the buffalo lap robe and congress gaiters. They offered me substitutes that awoke my outrage—knobby monstrosities of red plastic that tilted at the touch of a spring, slippery leatherette abstractions that pitchforked one into prenatal discomfort inches off the floor. The more I insisted, the more derisive they became. "Look, Grover Cleveland," one of them finally snapped at me after my third approach. "Harmoniums and water wings, diavolos and pungs we got, but Victorian easy chairs—*nyet*. And now, excuse me, will you? I have another nudnick here wants a round table like King Arthur's."

The first intimation that my will-o'-the-wisp, however unattainable, did in fact still exist came in 1938. Yawning through a Tim McCoy Western at a rural cinema in our township, I was suddenly electrified by the furnishings of the sheriff's office. Beside the period roll-top desk stood a voluptuously padded armchair, not only covered in black leather but (tears rose to my eyes) its outlines accented by brass nailheads. I whipped to my feet. "That's it! That's it!" I fluted, my voice gone contralto with agitation. "That's my chair!" I was so overwhelmed, to be candid, that it required the intervention of the manager to persuade me to resume my seat, and subsequent accounts, gleaned by my wife from local tradespeople, hinted I had succumbed to a Holy Roller seizure. Undaunted, I took care to note the production details of the film against some future visit to Hollywood, and chancing to be there shortly, at once proceeded to track down the chair. It was relatively simple. In a matter of minutes, Columbia's art department disclosed the name of the warehouse that supplied such props, and, cramming my pockets with enough rhino to vanquish any obstacle, I pelted over. The manager of the enterprise, a foxy-nose with a serried gray marcel that mounted like a linotype keyboard, was the soul of courtesy.

"Of course I remember the piece," he acknowledged smoothly. "This way, please." The freight elevator discharged us in a shadowy loft on the sixth floor, where furniture of every conceivable epoch lay stored. He dove into the maze and yanked aside a dust cover. "There," he said. "Is this the one you mean?"

An inexpressible radiance suffused me. The chair was so much more beautiful than my cinematic memory that speech was inadequate. It was a haven, a refuge; I saw myself lolling in it, churchwarden poised, evolving new cosmogonies, quoting abstruse references to Occam's razor and Paley's watch. "Oh, God," I choked, extracting a fistful of bills. "I— You've made me so happy! How much?"

"How much what?" he asked woodenly.

I explained that I was prepared to buy it, to buy the whole warehouse if necessary. He uttered a sharp, sardonic hoot and bade me wipe my chin. "Not for sale, buddy," he said, replacing its shroud. "You know what this thing brings in every year in rentals? Why, last month alone it worked in *Addled Saddles, Drums Along the Yazoo—*"

Short of manacling myself to the chair, I used every inducement I could marshal to obtain it, including bribery, pleas of medical need, and threats of legal duress, but the chap was intractable. I retired so crushed in spirit that I inclined to be somewhat paranoid about the subject over the ensuing decade. The world supply of tufted black leather, I frequently told my friends, was being manipulated by a small ring of interior decorators, men who would stick at nothing to bilk me. I was telling it to one of them, an advertising nabob and self-admitted expert in arranging the impossible, at a Turkish bath, when he brought me up short.

"Wait a minute," said Broomhead imperiously. "Outside of Hollywood or the Reform Club, are any of these chairs still extant?"

"Yes, in Washington," I said. "They've some honeys in the Senate corridors—the real McCoy, so to speak—but nobody could ever wangle—"

He produced a solid-gold pencil the diameter of a needle from his towel and scrawled a note on a masseur. "Relax," he commanded. "Your worries are over. I happen to know a politico or two down there who'd go pretty . . . far . . . out of his way to accommodate Curt Broomhead."

I automatically dismissed the assertion as bluster, until his secretary phoned me a month later. A certain Mr. X, whom it was inadvisable to identify, in an equally mysterious government bureau, was laid up with croup. On his recovery, he would promptly expedite the item requested by Mr. Tuftola, which, she whispered, was the pseudonym her boss had adopted for the transaction. While elated at the news, I experienced a vague malaise. It bothered me that some fine old lawgiver, a chivalrous Southerner out of George Cable, with a white imperial and arthritis, might be unceremoniously deposed from his chair because of my whim. I was also positive that I had heard a muffled click during our phone conversation, as though the line were bugged. Before I could cry peccavi and tout Broomhead off, however, the affair took on juggernaut momentum. Telegrams and messages proliferated, warning me that Mr. X's favor was in transit, and I received unmistakable assurance from a Chinese fortune cookie that destiny was arranging a surprise. A fortnight thence, two orangutans in expressmen's aprons dumped a formidable crate on the sidewalk outside our New York brownstone. After an ugly jurisdictional squabble, they departed, leaving the handyman and me to wrestle the shipment up three flights; after an uglier one, we did so, and he departed, leaving me to open it. I was ablaze with fever and salivating freely as I hacked through the excelsior wrappings, but I cooled off fast enough. Inside was a stiff and dismal board-room chair, welted with tacks, that belonged in a third-rate loan shark's office. The sticker on the reverse, however, implied otherwise. It read, "Property of U.S. State Dept."

To adduce proof that the husky, straw-hatted young man in gabardine who tailed me the whole next month was an F.B.I. operative is impossible, nor can I swear that my mail was fluoroscoped during that period. I do know that for a while I underwent all the tremors of a Graham Greene character on the run, even if it had no purificatory effect on my religious views. When my funk abated sufficiently to donate the chair to a charity bazaar, I arrived at a decision. The only way I could possibly attain my ideal was to have it custom made, and to that end I embarked on a secret layaway plan at the Coiners' and Purloiners' National. Early last summer, I took the accrual to a wholesaler friend in the Furniture Design Center, along with a steel engraving that embodied every curlicue I lusted for. He examined it tolerantly.

"It's your money, Sidney," he said, "but if I were you, I'd look around the auction rooms—"

I flung my hat on his showroom floor and stamped on it like Edgar Kennedy. "Stop!" I screamed. "Duplicate that chair and keep your Goddam advice to yourself! If I need advice, I'll go to a shrinker!"

"You're overdue now," he observed, picking up a hassock to ward me off. "Okey-doke. It'll take six weeks. And don't call for it," he added quickly. "We'll deliver."

The result was not a masterpiece, as one applies the term to a floral group by Odilon Redon or the mosaics in the Naples Museum, but it ran a close second. It was a paragon of cozy chairs, a marvel of the most intricate tufting, a monument to the upholsterer's art. You sank into its refulgent black bosom and were instantly permeated with *douceur de vivre* such as you had never known. Apothegms worthy of La Rochefoucauld tumbled from your lips, full-fashioned epigrams pleading to be encased in boxes in *McCall's* and *Reader's Digest*. True, it was a difficult chair to slumber in; at the beginning, its magnificence overawed me and I sat gingerly in it, holding at eye level a copy of Sir Samuel Baker's *The Albert Nyanza* in crushed levant. I then tried browsing through the latest English review, but somehow couldn't get past the pictures of Ovomalt and thermal underwear. At last, I found the key in Max Lerner's windy periods, and, lapped in his peristaltic rhetoric, slept like a baby. Once inside that chair, Lerner in hand, I was as remote from hypertension as from the Asiatic capitals where he bombinated.

When Buddha smiles and all is cotton candy, though, it is axiomatic that one edges toward the nearest cyclone cellar. Following a blissful week, my wife and I motored off to Willimantic to pick up a few spools of vintage thread. En route, she informed me that in our absence a new domestic had been instructed to give the flat a thorough cleaning. The place fairly gleamed when we tottered in the door; the rugs had been shampooed, the silver was burnished to diamond brilliance, and the furniture sparkled with a million highlights. As I stood openmouthed, like one of the carp at Fontainebleau, my wife issued from the kitchen, brandishing a note and a clotted paintbrush.

"A treasure! A dreamboat!" she chortled. "Guess what that girl did! She shellacked all the tables, even the breadboard and the stepladder! She worked two whole nights—"

"W-why is that sheet draped over my comfy chair?" I quavered.

"To protect it, stupid," she said impatiently. "I'm going to double her salary tomorrow, sign her to a lifetime contract—"

I leaped past her, whisked away the sheet, and was presented with a spectacle beyond description, beyond contemplation. The leather was piebald, marbleized with a scaly armor plate of orange-and-gray shellac bonded onto its surface for eternity. Never, even among the tortured vinyl-and-zebra abominations in the lowest borax showroom on East Eighth Street, had I beheld anything so loathsome. With a great cry, I sank to my knees, and, nuzzling one bulbous armrest, burst into racking sobs. Half an hour afterward, I slung a five-gallon can of kerosene into the rear of our wagon, unmindful that it splattered the aspiration of a lifetime. Then I slammed up the tailgate and headed grimly downtown toward the Holland Tunnel.

Any Purple

Subjunctives Today?

WHENEVER metropolitan life tends to pall, as it often does, I like to emulate Lieutenant Brackenbury Rich, late of the Indian hill wars and the Adventure of the Superfluous Mansion, and court the adventure lurking behind the city's prosaic façade. On one occasion I may perch my fedora at a rakish angle and, flaunting a pair of fierce mustaches executed in charcoal, invade the purlieus of Little Italy, disguised as a basso. On another I plunge into Yorkville in rough pea jacket and fatigue cap, a saboteur in quest of shelter. It was in this venturesome mood that I descended at Sheridan Square the other afternoon and struck out boldly into the Village. The bearded sculptors and their grisettes thronging the sidewalk gave me no second glance; my portfolio and Windsor tie admitted me instantly to their freemasonry. Occasionally, to strengthen the characterization, I held up a pencil to some passing model and exclaimed, "What foreshortening! What impasto! Could I but limn those classic contours!"

After several mishaps of no consequence to the present narrative, except that I was treated with every consideration in the emergency ward at Bellevue, I returned to my compound bearing a remarkable handbill thrust on me by an urchin. In language as ornate as any that ever appeared in the *Yellow Book,* the broadside celebrated the jewelry obtainable at the Studio of Sam Kramer, at 29 West Eighth Street. Never having seen it, I cannot vouch for the work of this downtown Cellini, but here is his own evaluation:

FANTASTIC JEWELRY for People Who Are Slightly Mad. This is vital and challenging stuff—these pieces of laced and beaten silver—real adventures in personal decoration. TORTURED AND MASSIVE. Some of the things have a morbid feeling: tortured and massive, they almost cry out with hysteria. Some are mild or wicked satires; many are tantalizing abstractions. NEITHER UNCOUTH NOR OUTRAGEOUS. And yet, there are pieces too, which are neither uncouth nor outrageous, but just distinguished and appealing . . . ideal gifts. BUYING IS DEFINITELY DISCOURAGED. People who come to the studio of Sam Kramer are never pressed into buying. In some cases buying is actually discouraged. . . . HOW DO YOU TAKE YOUR BLASPHEMIES? If you're a cynic with an appetite for subtle blasphemies . . . or if you're a woman in a black gown with a sense of what is stark and dramatic . . . or a man with a ring-finger going to waste for want of something heavy or amazing—or if you're someone sick through and through of being anyone in a crowd . . . IF YOU'RE ANY OF THESE PEOPLE or if you just like jewelry—particularly original hand wrought jewelry—why then you must surely come to the STUDIO OF SAM KRAMER.

Well, Sam, I wish I could get down there, but, to tell the truth, I've been laid up with some kind of word poisoning, so I'll just have to visualize what's going on in my absence:

(Scene: The Studio of Sam Kramer, a spacious atelier decorated with blood-red velvet drapes and modernique furniture. Skyscraper bookcases, one of them a model of the Bush Terminal Building so faithful that it even has tiny office workers scurrying in and out. The paintings are largely tantalizing abstractions—an egg balanced on a cone, an erg balanced on a bone, a hag

balanced on a roan. Along one wall a showcase displays a variety of hysterical but inexpensive brooches, priced from five to ten dollars.

At rise, eight or nine persons are discovered chatting animatedly over cocktails. They include Blount, a dealer in literary curiosa and thrice indicted by the postal authorities; Moira Bland, an intense minor poetess in hoop earrings and Paisley; Dennis O'Toole, a publisher's assistant who is single-handedly sponsoring Russia; Beatrice and Donald Ogden Larousse, the dictionary people; Diego Satchel, a Mexican muralist often mistaken for Orozco; and the Korngolds, two plain people who are simply sick of being anyone in a crowd. As Sam Kramer has been called out of town unexpectedly, Orestes Munn, his chief apprentice, is busily circulating a tray of canapés.)

BLOUNT (*to Mrs. Larousse*): You mean to say you never read the memoirs of Fanny Hill? Why, it's one of the great experiences!

MRS. LAROUSSE: What is it—some kind of a historical work?

BLOUNT: No, it's more a true-confessions type thing. I'll mail you a copy tomorrow in a plain wrapper.

MRS. LAROUSSE (*archly*): Do I have to read it in a plain wrapper?

BLOUNT (*inflamed*): I got a closetful of fancy ones. Come up to my place and we'll read it together.

LAROUSSE: Look here, you little greaser, are you trying—

BLOUNT (*dodging*): Excuse me, I have to correct some proofs. (*He hastily joins Diego and Moira Bland.*)

DIEGO: The trouble with MacDougal Alley is it has only two dimensions. The people over there is strictly a lot of cheap crumbs. Now, in my home in Guadalajara—

MOIRA (*transported*): Guadalajara. The echolalia of that word. It's so—so tarred with the bright black brush of authenticity.

DIEGO: You see what I mean?

MOIRA: Oh, I do, I do!

DIEGO: Then you must be crazy. (*He turns away, nearly upsetting the tray Orestes Munn is proffering O'Toole and Mrs. Larousse.*)

O'TOOLE (*taking a canapé*): Thank you.

ORESTES: How do you like the Korngolds, Mrs. Larousse?

MRS. LAROUSSE: I think they're the most delicious little things I've ever eaten. (*Confidentially*) Tell me, are you related to Ector and Mrs. Gurnee Munn?

ORESTES: No, but I'm always getting their mail. Isn't it maddening?

MRS. LAROUSSE: Isn't what maddening?

ORESTES: Always getting their mail.

MRS. LAROUSSE: I don't know. I never got any of it.

O'TOOLE (*seeking to conceal her gaffe*): What do you hear from the Princess Chavchavadze?

ORESTES: Dear Katya! She never writes. (*He moves toward the Korngolds, who are embroiled in a domestic argument.*)

MRS. KORNGOLD (*bitterly*): A clasp. That's all I'm asking you for—a lousy little clasp. You wouldn't part with five dollars to make your own wife stark and dramatic.

KORNGOLD: Leave me alone. If you're dying for something tortured and massive, go feed the elephants in the Zoo.

ORESTES (*entering*): Well, how you folks getting along? Everything O.K.?

MRS. KORNGOLD: Lovely.

ORESTES: You've made a conquest, Mrs. Korngold. Mr. Blount was just saying that your body had the clean, soaring sweep of Brancusi's "Bird."

KORNGOLD: The brain, too.

ORESTES: Your face suggests strange scarlet sins. If I were your husband, I know the very thing I'd buy you.

KORNGOLD: A muzzle.

ORESTES: No, that ring there—the big one with the filigree. The original belonged to Lucrezia Borgia.

MRS. KORNGOLD (*grimly*) : What I want is the original poison from it.

KORNGOLD : That was obvious when you made me double my insurance.

MRS. KORNGOLD (*convulsively*) : Why, you soapy *schmegeggie*—

ORESTES : Er—pardon me. (*As he backs away, he collides with a man who has entered and is looking around uncertainly.*)

MAN : I'm sorry. . . . Say, bud, is this the right floor for the jewelry?

ORESTES (*carelessly*) : Yes, we have a few paltry arabesques from fabled Samarkand and Cathay. May I show you a frothy chaplet of centaurs and Nereids prisoned in chalcedony?

MAN : Well, no, I—

ORESTES : Then how about a ribald locket from storied Cockaigne, peopled with the antic creatures of Branch Cabell? Or a panache of star dust to rival the promise in your sweetheart's eyes?

MAN : Not this minute. I tell you, Jack, what I had in mind—

ORESTES : Something grave yet gay? A locket as demure as a May morning, fashioned with a cunning spring which opens to reveal the drolleries of Aretino? Or mayhap a ponderous silver amulet that graced but yesteryear some lordly rover of the Spanish Main?

MAN : Gee, that sounds perfect, but look—do you handle key rings?

ORESTES (*freezing*) : I beg your pardon?

MAN : You know, some kind of a gimmick so the change and the keys don't get mixed up in my pants.

ORESTES : How did *you* get in here?

MAN : Why, through that door over there. I saw a sign outside—

ORESTES (*clapping his hands peremptorily*) : Take him, Wing Fat! (*Wing Fat, a giant Cantonese with soft brown noodles, fiercely loyal to Munn, emerges from behind the arras, pinions the intruder.*)

WING FAT: Him velly bad joss. Plenty bobbery along him. (*He draws his finger significantly across his throat.*)

ORESTES: No—just a skulking jackal sent by Black, Starr & Gorham, Inc., to mulct us of our most cherished designs.

MAN (*weakly*): Competition is the life of trade.

THE OTHERS: Hang him, hang him!

ORESTES: No. Go now, but tell your scheming masters that if they ever come below Fourteenth Street, we'll present them with a necklace made fashionable by Judge Lynch!

(*As all acclaim his words, Wing Fat removes the captive, Blount resumes pinching Mrs. Larousse, and the Korngolds take a No. 19 bus to West End Avenue.*)

CURTAIN

Dry Run–

Everybody Down!

. . . Warner financing was arranged for the movie [*The Old Man and the Sea*], and Hemingway was given an advance of $175,000. The author suggested that Peter Viertel, whose work he knew, write the screen play. Hemingway wanted Viertel, as part of his conditioning, to live for a while in a primitive Cuban fishing shack and to spend an equal amount of time handling a native fishing dory, single-handed, against the turbulent currents and under the blazing 120-degree summer sun of the Gulf Stream. Viertel surprised everyone (except, perhaps, Hemingway) by surviving this tropical ordeal, and, later, completed the script in New York.—*From an article by Halsey Raines in the* Times.

OILSKINS AGLEAM, his orangutan eyes glittering at the prospect of baksheesh, the doorman of the Ganymede bent forward into my taxi, plucked me from it like a walnut meat, and expertly tilted his umbrella to funnel the maximum of rain down my collar. "Great weather for ducks," he whickered, all greasy bonhomie. I rewarded him with a smile negotiable at any frozen-food locker and circled past into the lobby. At the desk, a sallow ramrod in a regimental necktie that could have denoted His

Majesty's Seventh Imperturbables mantled his forehead in disdain when I asked for Mort Schrift.

"Would he be expecting you, perchance?" he inquired, struggling to master his incredulity. I examined his cravat as though it were a lizard, and said briefly that I was a client of the man. "Suite 647," he disclosed, producing a small box, "and you might take along this parcel from Dunhill's that just arrived. It's his special mixture—I happen to know he needs it quite urgently."

"Gee whillikins!" I said. "I hope he can hold out till I get there."

"That I'll guarantee you," he returned spitefully.

Shriveling him to ash with a glance (though I daresay he may have twitched spasmodically for a while), I stalked toward the elevators. The other occupants of my car were a pair of tall, willowy thoroughbreds apparently checking in from Oshkosh, for they were flanked by luggage, the color of a weathered skull, of every conceivable size. From the scorn they evinced, I sensed that they were unaccustomed to persons bearing packages, so I receded as far as I was able into the costly woodwork. The coryphee who opened the door of Schrift's antechamber, a Dresden-china shepherdess with scallops of blue-black hair framing her face, looked like the secretaries he generally used on his lightning visits from the Coast—more adept at disengaging a zipper at the Copa than at shorthand. She uttered a happy squeak at the sight of the parcel.

"You finally brought it!" she cried. "We were calling up all morning! Here, wait till I get some change—"

I explained, rather frigidly, that I was no delivery boy but a business associate, who, at Schrift's entreaty, had trekked from the Pennsylvania bush in a torrential downpour, and that unless given instant audience I had other fish to fry. "Is he up yet?" I demanded.

"Well—er—I think so," she said evasively. "I mean, he didn't get in till four. He hosted a party at Neuralgio's for our new

French author, Claude Nasal-Passages, and then everybody went on to the Twelve Apostles.''

''In that case,'' I growled, but rhetoric withered on my lips. Clad in primrose-yellow pajamas the breast pocket of which bore a large fleur-de-lis and his initials in soutache, Schrift leaped from the bedroom and caught me in a hammerlock. So emotional was his welcome and so astringent his cologne that I was nearly undone. After all, it was almost two years since he had become my agent in Hollywood, and while he had never earned me even a picayune, I still viewed him as my genie in embryo. ''I had a hell of a time getting here, brother,'' I revealed when we had finished trading insincerities. ''I hope it's not the usual wild-goose chase.''

''Pops,'' declaimed Schrift, one hand on his soutache and the other raised like Richelieu, ''this much I'll tell you. We stand on the threshold of such loot that it frightens me. Piastres—yellow doubloons—the wealth of the Indies! But first there must be coffee,'' he said, spinning toward his odalisque. ''Don't stand there—bring coffee, toast, the papers! And get John Huston on the phone.''

''In Galway?'' she queried uncertainly.

''Galway,'' he groaned. ''He was in Galway *yesterday;* today he's in Cuzco. Wait—on second thought, never mind; I'll see him Thursday at Klosters. Here, baby,'' he said, turning back to me, ''come in the bedroom while I dress. Larry Olivier's waiting for me at the Pavillon, and you know how he hates to be hung up.'' I didn't, but I realized that to expect preferential treatment over a knight would be absurd, especially since I had lost face with Schrift by hastening to his summons, and I complied meekly. Dispersing the hillock of galley proofs and playscripts on a twin bed, my genie bade me sit, and vanished into a closet. To judge by the bounteous wardrobe he had imported for his forty-eight-hour visit, he evidently planned to run the social gamut. Even the mantelpiece, I observed with wonder, held a quartet of sports caps in various arresting tweeds, all cinctured at the brim by minuscule leather belts. A moment later, Schrift reappeared in a striking pair of undershorts, with vertical stripes like French wallpaper. "Now, for openers," he began, extracting the trees from a pair of suède chukker boots, "did you read this new best seller *Valuta*, by Waldemar Knobnose?"

"Only the first eighteen pages," I admitted. "The woman whose copy it was got off the bus at Altman's."

"Well, you missed a great literary experience, catharsiswise," he said. "It's going to make the hottest picture in the annals of the industry, and you, lover"—he stabbed his index finger at me forcefully—"are going to adapt it for the screen. At a prince's ransom."

"Sounds tempting," I said, making no effort to conceal my skepticism, "but there's one detail you forget—censorship. A romance between a nine-year-old bank auditor and a female cashier six times his age? Show me one Hollywood producer who'd dare to make a movie of that."

"O.K., wisenheimer, I will," chortled Schrift, in triumph. "I closed a deal for it at three o'clock yesterday with Jerry GeWald himself! Four hundred and thirty thousand smackers, plus eight per cent of the gross!"

"And he intends to follow the story just as it stands?" I asked doubtfully.

"Down to the smallest financial and emotional *drehdel*," he swore. "The audience'll see every Goddam roll of pennies she steals—they'll quiver with him as he strives to reconcile her debits, as their totals accidentally brush, as passion is born. Then the midnight orgies around the adding machine in the deserted cage, where she plies him with drugged brownies, and their cross-country flight through the entire banking system till she loses him to that little blond tramp of a C.P.A. Yes, sirree, GeWald's going to film it all, and he's hungry for you to do the screenplay, regardless of fee."

"Then what's the hitch?" I demanded, mindful of the worm that lurked somewhere in his golden apple.

"Look at this shirt!" exclaimed Schrift, with sudden irrelevant fury. "Specially made for me by Thresher & Glenny in London—it cost more than you probably spent on coal last winter. If I told 'em once, I told 'em a hundred times—I want the monogram in Old *English*, not roman type! What do they think I am—a letterhead? No wonder the British Empire's falling apart."

"Getting back to *Valuta*," I reminded him gently, "who does GeWald have in mind for the leads? Now that Freddie Bartholomew's shaving, there may be trouble casting the boy auditor."

"Ah, we don't have to stick to the book too literally," he said carelessly. "I'd buy any good juvenile in the part—like Donald O'Connor, say, or Paul Newman. Then your cashier, I see her as a little younger dame—a Julie Newmar, or Cyd Charisse with a silver rinse. The main thing is to preserve the *spirit* of the novel, which is why Knobnose, the author, wants you to work in a bank first. GeWald's set up the whole thing for you, the job and everything—"

"One sec," I interjected. "You mean I have to take a fiscal to qualify for the assignment?"

"Don't blow your stack, for crisake," implored Schrift from the depths of the pullover he was squirming into. "It's just to condition you—to help you dig the psychology of the characters. You merely go and spend a month or so behind the wicket, handling bills of different denominations, chaffing depositors, and like that. It's a friendly little family bank in Sphagnum, New Jersey—the Peculators' & Predators' National."

"It isn't going to be all that simple," I demurred. "To really steep myself in the boy's point of view, I'd have to live the role—dress the way he does, play with trains, even contract measles."

"Nah, just put on knickerbockers and get rid of the mustache," he advised. "Those squares over in Jersey'll never tumble—their kids look like old men anyway. Well," he said, knotting a Paisley kerchief under his blazer, "I'm glad you kindled to the idea, and I know you'll do a sensational script if I can sell Olivier on you."

"Olivier?" I repeated. "Where does he fit into the picture?"

"He doesn't yet, but he will when we get through lunch," predicted Schrift confidently. "It's a terrific vehicle for him. Can you imagine a marquee reading '*Valuta*, with Sir Laurence Olivier'? Man, would that bring in the people!"

"Even in a rainstorm," I agreed, rising. "And, speaking of bringing in people in a rainstorm, the next time you dare to call me and suggest—"

As oblivious as though I were speaking Urdu, Schrift whisked up the phone, cuddled it in his shoulder, and fired a volley of orders at his handmaiden off-scene. They involved a multiplicity of names of such theatrical luster—Moss and Noël, Leland and Abe, George and Josh—that my grievance trailed off into a peevish whine. Capping his monologue with a command to rush Marlene a dozen orchids and break their dinner date, Schrift swung about peremptorily. "What's it doing outside?" he barked.

"Why—er—I—I guess it's still teeming, Mort," I said, in an unexpected falsetto that was deeply humiliating.

"Hmm," he observed with a frown. "Good thing I brought my rainwear from the Coast." He plunged into the closet and emerged with an armful of mackintoshes, slickers, and waterproofs of various weights. Selecting a heavy rubberized garment ideally suited to the Brazilian rain forest, he slipped into it and crossed to the mantelpiece. For a moment, he stood indecisive before the array of tweed caps; then, donning one scarcely larger than a wheat cake, he tightened its surcingle and threw me a crisp nod. "Come along," he commanded. "You can walk me down the lobby."

Our descent, somnambulistic as any of Beebe's to the ocean floor, was devoid of incident except for one moment at the elevator. As the doors clashed open to admit us, I was confronted by the same patrician couple, surrounded by their osseous luggage, with whom I had risen earlier. They had apparently stood there, transfixed and endlessly levitating, the whole time—unless, of course, they were waxworks arranged by the management to lend chic to the premises. Schrift, immersed in a wad of cables and correspondence, paid them no heed, merely emitting an occasional yelp of gratification or anguish at some coup or setback.

Once on the sidewalk, he suddenly recollected my existence and seized my hand in a grip so convulsive that it almost brought me to my knees. "Keep in touch, now," he rapped out, "and whatever you do, stay near the phone. The way this deal's developing, I may need you in the middle of the night." He nimbly sidestepped a basset hound that had wound itself about his ankles, and, with a wave, pelted off toward Madison.

I've eaten and slept by the phone ever since, but thus far no word. I suspect they've hired Peter Viertel for the post, and quite properly. Be it in quest of a marlin or a defalcation, he's twice the man I am.

DR. PERELMAN, I PRESUME,
OR SMALL-BORE IN AFRICA

I

This Is the Forest

Primeval?

ONE SATURDAY AFTERNOON early in January of this year, an individual who was neither sportsman nor scholar, poet nor peasant, but, in fact, a remarkable combination of all four arrived in Nairobi, capital of the East African colony of Kenya. As he descended from an airways bus before the New Stanley Hotel, the handful of loungers basking on the sidewalk stiffened to inattention. The stranger, patently, was a man accustomed to giving orders and having them disobeyed. His profile, oddly akin to that of the youthful D'Annunzio, bespoke a spirit as wild and free as the vultures circling above him in welcome. He wore a reach-me-down trench coat, three buttons of which had disappeared and been replaced with safety pins. Slung over his shoulder was a complex of cameras, binoculars, and first-aid kits bulging with every sort of nostrum—antimalarial compounds like paludrine, daraprim, and atabrin, tube on tube of molds and yeasts designed to combat blackwater fever, bilharzia, and tsetse fly, antivenins without number, embrocations, febrifuges, heat lotions, and sedatives—a pharmacopoeia, in short, to dazzle a Schweitzer. Perceiving that there was, however, no Schweitzer present to dazzle, the traveler picked up his satchels, entered the hotel, and fractured the laws of coincidence by affixing my name to the register.

"Your room's just being made up, sir," apologized the receptionist, a sparrowlike person resembling Mildred Natwick. "The painters just finished within the hour."

"Ah?" I returned pleasantly. "Redecorating it, are they?"

"Well, rather," she said, pursing her lips. "When those blighters got through with the last occupant, the place *was* a shambles. Goodness!"

I cleared the rust out of my voice and kept it as buoyant as I could. "I say, I'm just in from overshoes—I mean overseas," I said. "You weren't by any chance referring to the—er—Mau Mau?"

"Why, of course not," she said, her face suddenly wooden. "Whatever gave you that idea? Here, boy, take this gentleman's things up to three-seventeen."

"I—I believe I'll have a tup of kee in the lounge," I interposed quickly. "I feel a trifle giddy—the altitude, no doubt."

"Yes, it bothers everyone at first," she agreed. "Better not run up any stairs for a day or two—that is, unless you have to."

I promised to heed her advice and, disengaging my sleeve from the inkwell, headed toward the lounge. Halfway across the lobby, I heard my name called out. Turning, I beheld a gaunt young Englishman with a Mephistophelean beard and a falcon's eye, followed by a vision of loveliness in yellow Tootal.

"I'm Eric Mothersill of the tourist association," he introduced himself affably. "This is Xanthia, my wife."

"Enchanted," I said as our hands met. "From the luminous eyes and name, I gather that Madame is Greek?"

"Yes, but reared in Egypt," she replied, enslaving me with her smile. "Monsieur is very observant."

"O-oh, I've knocked about a bit," I admitted modestly.

"Good," said Mothersill. "Then you'll certainly enjoy the outing we've planned for this weekend. It's different." In the following few minutes, and with only gin-and-lime as anesthetic, I got a portent of what my East African sojourn might be like. This afternoon, it appeared, there was merely time for an hors d'oeuvre—a quick circuit of the suburbs, the Ngong Hills, the Rift Valley Escarpment, a sisal farm or two, and the Kikuyu Reserve—followed by an informal dinner party *chez* Mothersill. Early next morning, though, we were leaving by motor for Tree-tops, the lodge in the Aberdare Range where one eavesdropped on rhino, elephant, and similar big game. "By the way," went on Mothersill, obviously a master of the *arrière pensée,* "I forgot to mention that it's in the heart of the Mau Mau country."

"It's *where?*" I asked, recoiling.

"Now, there's no reason whatever for apprehension," he soothed me. "Xanthia and I'll both be armed, and, moreover, the hotel's promised us a convoy for our walk in."

There was a brief silence while I fought to free my tongue, which had somehow become lodged in my epiglottis. "Look here," I said, oozing more nobility than one of Landseer's dogs, "you two have gone to a lot of trouble planning this holiday, and the last thing you want is an extra man along. I'm a married man and I know how married couples are." I maundered off into a long, woolly discourse on matrimony, reminiscent of a women's magazine, that brought tears to my eyes but failed to stir anyone else. Before I could rally, the two of them had pinioned my arms and propelled me through the door to the curb. With a sinking heart, I crawled into the rear of their convertible and prepared to sell my life as cheaply as possible.

Some eight hours later, I entered my hotel room and collapsed on the bed. My skin was intact enough, but I retained only a blurred, kaleidoscopic memory of the interval—the herds of wildebeest and zebra in the Nairobi National Park, the omnipresent roadblocks manned by the King's African Rifles, a coffee plantation near Limuru with a stable yard lifted straight out of

Devonshire, the groups of philoprogenitive Hindus picnic-bound in consumptive jalopies, the detention camps placarded with the winning understatement "Protected Area," and the cryptic chitchat around the Mothersills' dinner table. A fatigue pervaded my bones as profound as if I had gone without sleep for three nights, which, indeed, I had. And just to compound matters, I recalled with sudden heartburn, tomorrow I was being thrown to the lions in the middle of a holocaust—I, a peaceable, flabby burgess who had never even shot a chipmunk. The full anguish of my plight was more than I could bear. Burying my face in the bolster, I burst into long, racking sobs.

Toward noon the following day, a Humber saloon covered with red dust slued into the driveway of the Outspan Hotel at Nyeri, a hamlet about seventy miles north of Nairobi. Its khaki-clad chauffeur, a Kipsigis with ears nattily twisted into rosettes in the characteristic fashion of his tribe, reined in under the porte-cochère and, whipping open the door with a flourish, handed down our threesome. To the Mothersills, inured to East African roads, the four-hour trip had been trivial, but it had reduced me to library paste. Mile on mile, we had jounced over a corduroy highway devoid of traffic but full of hairpin bends ideally suited to ambush. Every now and again, the driver would point out some inglenook where the Mau Mau had butchered a party of Europeans or been surprised in turn, and once, when the car stalled momentarily in a wooded divide, I closed my eyes and sat mutely intoning the serial number of my insurance policy. My hosts, contrariwise, never lost their sang-froid. Except for pronounced facial tics and a tendency to reach for their heaters every time the engine missed, they betrayed not the slightest awareness of danger.

"Well, you must admit it was worth the trip," observed Xanthia later, as we dawdled over tea on the veranda. "Isn't this a heavenly place? I haven't felt so relaxed in years."

"Yes, it's certainly a bit of all right," Eric assented. "Look at

the weaverbirds in that golden acacia tree." We both followed
his eyes, bewitched by the jeweled flash of wings. It was, indeed,
a superb vista—flowering quince against a background of mango,
jacaranda, and flamboyant trees, and, beyond, the sun glinting
on the masses of barbed wire surrounding the hotel. At intervals
all too infrequent, a pair of gaily plumaged sentries, with car-
bines on their backs, supplied a vivid accent to the scene.

"When do we make this—ah—excursion to Treetops?" I inquired, with a bright musical-comedy smile that would have
sickened my intimates.

"Right after lunch tomorrow," said Eric. "I understand
there'll be eight in the party. A safari car takes us to the forest
edge, where we'll rendezvous with our guards. Actually, it's a
very short trek to the lodge—only a third of a mile—but it's
fairly thick cover and it *could* be sticky if we ran into the odd
rhino or a terrorist patrol."

I casually extinguished my cigarette in the wild-currant jam.
"That place you spoke of, up in the tree," I said. "I presume
we stay there only an hour or two?"

"Quite the opposite, old boy," he replied. "We stay the night.
At night is when you see the really wizard stuff milling around
the salt lick. Imagine—elephant and buffalo right under one's
feet! Fantastic, what?"

"Now, darling, don't spoil it for him; he'll expect too much,"
Xanthia chided. "Anyway, it's time we were dressing for dinner.
See you in the bar *tout à l'heure?*"

The shadows were lengthening as I went meditatively to my
room to change, but it was still light enough to make an interesting
discovery. The French windows at one end, which opened into
the garden, were secured by an absurdly flimsy catch that could
be unfastened from outside. The room also seemed to have a
plethora of closets, all of them just large enough to hold a man
nursing a grievance. I took a shower and dressed hastily, though
trying to get into my pants with one foot braced against the
bathroom door impeded me somewhat. By the time the Mothersills

rejoined me, I had managed to fortify myself for the evening, and it passed off agreeably. Around one-thirty, when nobody appeared willing to stay up any longer, I turned in and, having made a rapid tally of the closets, dossed down with the poems of Anais Nin.

Just as I was dropping off, a bloodcurdling crash, unmistakably caused by someone hammering on the door with a *panga*, or African machete, echoed through the room. I jackknifed upward in bed and, completely forgetting where I was, called out "Come in!" Simultaneously, I realized the folly of my words; if it was the visitors I suspected, there was no need for fulsome hospitality. I awaited developments, but none came. After a bit, the anvil blows in my pulse subsided, and I worked out a hypothesis. Somebody in the room overhead must have dropped his pipe on the tile floor—rather a large pipe, as I visualized it. In fact, it might even be one of those Turkish pipes—a hubble-bubble or a chibouk or whatever they called it. I fell asleep with a smile, musing over the odd crotchets one encounters in foreign lands. The next morning, of course, I discovered there *was* no room overhead, but by then the sun was shining and birds were clamorous.

It was an assorted lot that piled into the safari car after lunch—an elderly British noblewoman, a Canadian couple, a pair of young matrons from Rhodesia, the Mothersills, and myself. The mood of the party was definitely one of nervous bravado; as each of us signed waivers absolving the hotel of responsibility for breakage, it was greeted with hollow giggles and japes of a mortuary turn. The route into the Aberdare National Park led through precipitous terrain overgrown with scrub evocative of New Jersey at its most dismal. Less than a mile inside was the staging point for our hike. The quartet waiting there to escort us was as lethal as anything ever assembled outside a comic book. Mr. Oakeshott, the manager of the hotel, and Colonel Bagby, a retired white hunter, displayed side arms and express rifles, and two chunky subalterns, on leave from the Royal Devons, were fondling Sten guns. While our African bearers finished packing linen, blankets, and food into sacks, Mr. Oakeshott outlined the plan of march.

"We'll go up the path in single file," he said. "Please keep your voices low so that we don't—ahem—attract unnecessary attention. Here and there, you'll notice ladders on the trees. We probably shan't encounter game of any size, but if we do raise a stray buff or rhino, just nip up a ladder until he clears off. Are there any questions? . . . What? . . . Oh, I thought the gentleman there with the green face said something. Righto, then, let's get started."

To survive the hazardous next ten minutes, I fell back on an expedient that has pulled me out of many a tight corner. Emptying the air from my lungs, as one would from an old pair of water wings, I not only kept pace with the others but several times almost outstripped them. The twelve of us snaked through the bush at a gait midway between a shuffle and a squirm that would have taxed the powers even of Eleanora Sears. Once, I cautiously turned to appraise the scenery, but my neck gave off a creak like a New Year's ratchet and I hastily withdrew it into my shell. When we finally gained the giant fig tree containing the lodge, most of my companions were pink with exertion, whereas I, curiously enough, was hardly breathing. Indeed, as we toiled up the gangway that led to our leafy aerie, I was in a state of such tranquillity that I could barely count the spots before my eyes.

The lodge, on investigation, proved to be a two-story structure about thirty feet square, partitioned off into screened porches, bedrooms, and a dining alcove. Twelve or fifteen yards below its far side was the salt lick and water hole where the game congregated nightly. At the moment, only a family of baboons was visible, but with the onset of dusk, Mr. Oakeshott explained, various quadrupeds large and small would be arriving.

"By the bye," I observed offhandedly to Mothersill, "d'ye

suppose those Mau Mau chaps know we're up here?" I thought he might have overlooked the possibility, and it would be churlish not to bring it to his attention.

"Of course they do," he said. "They've an incredible communications system. Probably watched us every foot of the way in."

"But listen," I said in an urgent undertone, trying not to alarm the rest of the group. "What prevents them from, say, setting fire to this tree and smoking us out like a nest of bees?"

"Quite, quite," he agreed. "A very feasible idea. I certainly hope it doesn't occur to them. However, no use borrowing trouble. Here, do try one of these rock buns—they're frightfully good."

I declined, my appetite having been under par all day, and, borrowing his field glasses, beguiled the afternoon watching the forest for any suspicious movement. Outside the racket of the baboons and an occasional squadron of planes roaring overhead to bomb the terrorist hideouts nearby on Mount Kenya, the landscape was as peaceful as a country vicarage. Shortly after sunset, however, half a dozen wart hogs materialized below, rooted about noisily in the salt, and departed. They were succeeded by several gazelles and waterbuck, who yielded the stage, just before dark, to a herd of fifteen giant forest hogs. The adults of the troupe, fearsome swine well over four feet high and exhibiting wicked tusks, held a brief conference, evidently trying to decide whether to gnaw down our perch, but cooler heads must have prevailed, for they soon retired. By now, it was pitch black outside and impossible to distinguish anything on the salt lick, though we ourselves had plenty of light within. In fact, as I felt constrained to point out to Colonel Bagby, we were brightly silhouetted against the windows for any snipers who happened to be mousing about.

"You're dead right, old man," he said warmly. "Some night those wretched sods'll pick one of us off and there'll be a proper dustup. Still, it does lend a certain zest to the occasion, what?"

This Is the Forest Primeval?

It was roughly half an hour after dinner—a capital tureen of chicken pie warmed up on a Primus stove—that the rhino began moving in. An amber spotlight simulating the full moon had been turned on, and it made the beasts seem even more antediluvian than normally. One by one, seven bulls and cows, a couple of them suckling calves, detached themselves soundlessly from the darkness and circulated about underneath us. They were plainly in a bilious humor—engendered, I was told, by their favorite diet of thorns—and they kept chivying each other and rumbling like Frenchmen in a street altercation. Once in a while, a jackal or bushbuck would drift into their orbit to browse, but the rhino ignored it and, with a tact worthy of Emily Post, confined their spleen to their kinsfolk. Absorbing spectacle though it was, I found after a couple of hours that an element of tedium was creeping in. A headache induced by eyestrain clove my skull, I was *hors de combat* with laryngitis from conversing in whispers, and my teeth chattered with cold. Waiting until the Mothersills relaxed their guard, I stole off to a rear bedroom, gulped down some nirvana powder, and curled up in a blanket. All around me an awesome nocturnal symphony was tuning up—leopards coughing, hyenas and monkeys howling, the whole jungle awakening to life. As the Demerol slowly took hold, the realization smote me that I was missing one of the experiences of my life. I rolled over and slept like a baby.

I awoke with a horrid start; someone was shaking me violently, but it was too dark to see his face and I was too addled to make out what he was whispering. Luckily, before I could scream— which I had every intention of doing—he identified himself by clapping his hand over my mouth.

"Sh-h-h!" he hissed. "It's Eric! Come quick—elephant!" I rose groggily and, clutching his arm, blundered out to the porch. Below it to the right stood a gigantic hulk, its ears fanned out and its trunk lifted, facing an animal with tremendous, heavily bossed horns less than forty feet away. Though it bore no more resemblance to our bison than a barracuda does to a smelt, I knew instinctively that it was a buffalo. Mothersill was palpitant with joy. "Great Scott, man, this is the rarest sight in Africa!" he babbled into my ear. "They're deadly enemies—it'll be a massacre!" As he spoke, the elephant let forth a shriek that loosened the bark on every tree within a nine-mile radius, and charged. The buffalo stood his ground, saving face until the last possible moment. There were scarcely five yards between them when he wheeled with incredible speed and vamoosed, his adversary hot on his heels. In the distance, we heard apocalyptic sounds of branches being rent and the elephant trumpeting in fury. Several minutes passed, during which a sizable dew condensed on everyone's forehead, and then the elephant reappeared. In the manner of a British constable assuring himself that all was tickety-boo, he made a slow, majestic circuit of the salt lick, and melted into the night.

A couple of weeks later, in Nairobi, I was having a glass of sherry with an Iowa chick named Ruby Querschnitt, a member of an American all-girl safari that had recently arrived in a blaze of flash bulbs. She had asked me, as an old Kenya hand, to vet her itinerary, and since she was friendless and a rather appealing little thing, I consented. It was an ambitious program —a fortnight's shooting in Tanganyika, a tour of the coast, a motor trip through the eastern Congo, and a journey by launch to Murchison Falls.

"What I really wanted to see was Treetops," she said disconsolately, "but they've closed it till the emergency's over. It's supposed to be awfully dangerous."

"Balderdash," I said, smoothing my mustache. "A bit tiresome, if you must know. It gets a chap down, rather—nothing but Mau Mau and elephant mucking about."

"Gee, some people are certainly blasé," she said. "Tell me, is it true that out of the party you went with, only twelve came back?"

I allowed myself a fatalistic shrug. "That's Africa, lassie," I said. "One gets used to it in time."

"Well," she said pensively, "just the same, you must be pretty brave."

"Think so?" I said. "Say, let's have another one of these. . . . Wait, I've got an idea. Have you ever tried a gin-and-lime?"

II

To Count the

Cats in Zanzibar

"WELL," said Mr. Fortescue, jovially raising his gimlet, "here's confusion to the enemies of the Crown." I piously echoed the toast, and, lowering my glass, cast a discreet look around the bar of the Belgrave Hotel. The half-dozen types who, like us, had taken refuge from the afternoon heat of Mombasa were unremarkable—a couple of angular British mems in flowered chiffon, several Teutons masquerading as Swiss and festooned with light-meters, a pair of turbaned Hindus. A barefoot waiter, clad in the voluminous white *khanzu* and scarlet fez commonly worn by East African servants, dozed upright against a wall, overtaken by the general inertia. Mr. Fortescue had loosened his cravat and was busily sponging his wattles. He was a large, dropsical gentleman in the mid-sixties, with a Courvoisier nose and a quarter-deck manner, who had spent most of his life in the Royal Navy and now devoted himself to fostering tourism in coastal Kenya. His mood at the moment was one of vast relief, which he took no pains to hide. "By God, sir," he wheezed, "when you told me this morning you wanted to sail to Zanzibar on an Arab dhow, I thought at first you were deranged—absolutely crackers."

"What changed your opinion?" I inquired.

"Nothing," he said. "I still think so, but I've reconciled myself to it. Obviously," he went on, "if you're determined to wallow around the Indian Ocean with a boatload of vagrants and expose yourself to the Oriental cockroach, logic isn't going to deter you."

"Precisely," I agreed. "Look, Mr. Fortescue, this isn't any sudden whim—it's the realization of a childhood dream. When I was eleven years old, someone gave me a copy of *Sinbad the Sailor* illustrated by Howard Pyle. Right then and there, I made up my mind—"

"Yes, yes," said Fortescue impatiently. "Touching devotion to an ideal—must mention that to the press when your signet ring turns up inside a shark. But let's get back to the *modus navigandi,* as it were. I've interceded with the chief Arab official here, the Wali of the Coast, and everything's in order. You're sailing at daylight tomorrow." He consulted an envelope crisscrossed with notes. "The dhow you're booked aboard is a ninety-ton vessel named the *Hamidullah*. She's been ten weeks in transit from Sur, on the Persian Gulf, with a crew of twenty-nine and a mixed cargo of dates, maize meal, dried fish, and simsim oil. Needless to say, there are no cabins, but for a consideration of thirty shillings you'll be allowed six feet of afterdeck to sprawl on. The sanitary arrangements can be described in one word—horrifying. That's about all, except it's a hundred and thirty-five miles to Zanzibar and these smaller dhows average five knots. You're going to need plenty of Keating's powder."

I drew a long breath, arose, and steadied myself against the roll of the bar. "Sir," I said emotionally, "I don't know how to repay you, but if you're ever in the States and you want anybody's loyalty checked or his arm broken, just give me a call."

"Thank you, lad, and *bon voyage*," he said. "Where are you off to now?"

"The nearest ship chandler's," I replied. "I've got to lay in a few stores—you know, bully beef and hardtack, a hogshead of grog, that sort of thing.''

''Yes, and take along some Arab delicacies as well,'' advised Fortescue benignly. ''You and your shipmates might like to nibble on a sheep's eye whilst you're rolling around those long, greasy swells. *Salaam aleikum.*''

As I walked purposefully down Kilindini Road, past the rows of Indian shops full of brummagem—the ivory knickknacks, fly whisks, and musical chamber pots that called up nostalgic memoirs of Sixth Avenue—my nerves tingled with exultation. It seemed incredible that when the sun rose again, I would be skimming before the southwest monsoon, part of a great annual hegira dating back three thousand years. In my euphoria, I bought a number of obvious superfluities, like bouillon cubes, a plum pudding, and a lotion warranted to counteract barnacles, but by the time I regained the hotel, I was prepared for any contingency. Right after dinner, I shook down my kit to essentials, burned all but a handful of express checks so my pockets would not be overburdened, and wrote two or three farewell notes couched in a rather grandiloquent style. I then burned those, and, with the satisfaction of work well done, fell peacefully asleep.

The stars on the eastern horizon were paling, and an insubstantial breeze, freighted with the light, spicy odor of drains, whispered through the alleys of the Old Port, heralding the advent of dawn. I descended the steps of the customs jetty and paused uncertainly. Except for the lights of a trawler moored nearby, the harbor was shrouded in darkness, and all I could hear was the rhythmic lap of water against the sea wall and the occasional strident cry of gulls. It suddenly came over me that for a man whose touchstone was Prudential, I had displayed a singular lack of prudence. Here I was, a lone foreigner with a mouthful of gold inlays, astray in a milieu where human life was reckoned in terms of gingersnaps. What was to prevent anyone from slipping a gunny sack over my head and a dirk into my ribs—I sprang aside with a convulsive gasp as a hand touched mine. A misshapen figure in a burnous, straight out of *The Thief of Bagdad,* had materialized at my elbow, and was jabbering something and gesticulating seductively toward the basin. I finally deduced that he was a boat wallah sent to conduct me, and, stifling my misgivings, clambered into his wherry. He bent to the oars, and presently several dhows loomed up ahead of us out of the murk. It was too dark to see them in detail, but they all appeared to have the same great lateen sail furled fore and aft, the lofty poop reminiscent of Spanish caravels and Macassar *praus,* and exaggerated bowsprits.

"Hamidullah this side?" I inquired hopefully of the boatman, indicating the largest of the group. With a contemptuous sniff, he jerked his thumb toward a craft that stood well away from the others. A chill of disappointment enveloped me as we swung under her lee. She was a ramshackle, dispirited scow, with none of the panache I had expected, but the ship's company, observing me over the side in the growing light, would have elated any casting director in Hollywood. If ever a crew was motley, they were it. Their faces, ranging in hue from *café-au-lait* to ebony, were lined with what I recognized as every evil passion, and while they wore no cutlasses in their teeth, they struck me as being the bloodthirstiest ruffians since the sack of Porto Bello. Before I could call down anathema on Howard Pyle, I was yanked up a rope ladder, whisked through a tangle of cordage and bales, and dumped on the afterdeck. Three or four of the bolder spirits clustered about me, peering into my face and fingering my garments curiously. I heard the word "Inglis" repeated several times, and there was a short, acrimonious debate, obviously concerned with the ultimate division of my effects. It was halted by a bellow from amidships; in a trice all had scattered and were busying themselves with preparations for departure. Under the

direction of a burly patriarch who looked as though he could drive a laggard through an oak plank with his fist, a longboat was unshipped, and manned by ten oarsmen and a couple of drummers equipped with tomtoms and bells. These then proceeded to fish up the anchor, and, to the accompaniment of a series of plaintive chanteys, towed us into the outer harbor for a final immigration and customs check. At this point, the captain, or *nahoda,* took charge. He was a grave, handsome stripling with a Vandyke beard—surprisingly immature for his job, I thought with a twinge of anxiety, and certainly no match for his men if they decided to throw me up for grabs.

The attitude of the port officials was equally disquieting. The senior immigration officer, a beefy Scot who had apparently had previous contact with romantics, grinned wolfishly as he returned my passport. "Heard about you from Piggy Fortescue," he remarked. "Got your Dramamine ready?"

I observed, with considerable hauteur, that I had smelled salt water before.

"Aye, but wait till the bilge starts rolling around this tub," he said with relish. "And, of course, there's always the off-chance she'll spring a leak. Ah, well, I'm sure you've taken all that into account. Good luck." He gave me a cheery wave and skipped over the side. I watched him chug away to his breakfast of porridge, bacon and eggs, and hot buttered scones, and I prayed it would stick in his throat.

All hands now collaborated in hoisting the sail to an obbligato of tympany effects, *accelerando con hysteria,* and the dhow edged slowly out of the harbor mouth into open water. At once, as the quickening monsoon filled the canvas, she developed the most extraordinary centrifugal lurch—a combination of roll, pitch, and stagger quite unparalleled in my past seafaring. It was not bothersome in any sense—just *outré,* so to speak—but it required study and management. By closing my eyes each time we dipped into the trough, and gritting my teeth, I soon became inured, if not passionately addicted, to it. Unfortunately, the incline of the poop deck was such that if I let go the taffrail an instant, I slid forward and became entangled with the steersman, visibly impeding his efficiency. To remedy this, as well as to accord a measure of hospitality, the captain ordered several carpets spread under me, and, ensconced on these, I felt very much of a pasha. The illusion was strengthened by the arrival of dates and coffee, small cups of which were ceremoniously offered to me and then circulated among the personnel. Nothing promotes racial amity like the knowledge that you have just communicated your diseases to someone or contracted his, and in a short time, despite the absence of any language tie, we were all purring like a basketful of cobras.

Throughout the foregoing, intense activity of some sort had been going on in the bow; small boys were being cuffed, wood chopped, and water fetched, and I finally teetered forward to see what was cooking. It proved to be two sizable fish, suspended over an open blaze that had apparently been kindled right on the deck. The sparks whirled about in every direction, for the most part into the sail, and it was abundantly clear that within seconds the whole dhow would be one single sheet of flame. Hastily retreating aft, I discarded my shoes and held myself ready to abandon ship if necessary. The precaution, luckily, was excessive; half an hour later, a reasonably edible curry was served up, followed by quantities of scalding mint tea. As a gesture of reciprocity, I broached my own provisions, and, to judge by the gusto with which the sweets were consumed, one could buy one's way into the caliphate with three pounds of Fanny Farmer. At the conclusion of the meal, everyone belched politely to signify he was replete, and sank down for the noonday rest. The sun was high overhead and the wind steady. The African coastline had receded to a blur, and as I lay under the canopy that shielded my dais, the overdraft clerk at my bank seemed very far away. When I subsequently checked up, I found he had been even farther away than I thought. He had absconded to Canada just about the time I reached Nairobi.

Sometime toward midafternoon, I was awakened by a gabble of voices; my fellow voyagers, genuflecting toward Mecca, were at their devotions, and, remembering my status of infidel, I did nothing to distract them. Another helping of dates was next pressed on me; the sight of them made me go all queasy, but to refuse, I knew, was tantamount to suicide, and I knuckled under. The captain had been tidying his sea chest meanwhile, and now produced for my admiration his ceremonial sword and curved, silver-mounted dagger. The instant I prepared to photograph him, the other Arabs, naturally, started importuning me to snap them, too. Nobody—at least nobody in his right mind—can resist the appeal of a man flourishing a scimitar, and it was twilight before we finished. The curry dished up for our evening repast was less toothsome, on the whole, than the original batch, dates having been added to give it body. Made cunning by desperation, I waited until an unusually heavy sea rolled the dhow over, and swept my portion into the wake. As darkness came on, myriads of stars appeared in the heavens, the wind grew steadily more intense, and it was manifest from the bustle around the mast as the crew shortened sail that we were in for a blow. Recumbent on the carpet, feet braced against a thwart, I gave myself up to somber reflection. I thought of other hotspurs who had tempted destiny too far—Phlebas the Phoenician, Captain Slocum, Richard Halliburton. I conjured up visions of Fortescue and the immigration officer in the Belgrave bar, swilling gimlets and cackling obscenely over my plight. Then I began to picture their shock on receiving the news of my heroic end, and I reveled in their abasement. The wilder the tempest grew, the more hopeless my predicament, the more I reveled.

How many hours we buffeted about would be difficult to conjecture, but eventually, in a disembodied way, I became aware that the dhow had stopped oscillating. The sail, as nearly as I could make out, was down, and we were bobbing idly in the trough, broadside to a diminishing sea. Suddenly a horrid possibility occurred to me, inspired, no doubt, by memories of Kipling's *Captains Courageous*. With no riding light aboard, let alone any kind of lamp, we were a cinch to be run down by one of the British India or Lloyd Triestino liners plying along the coast. Once I started thinking creatively, of course, all kinds of qualms presented themselves. Perhaps we had been blown off our course altogether, far outside the steamer lanes. The Indian Ocean was limitless; it was a cool four thousand miles eastward to Australia, and even though we had more than enough dates below to live on—a grisly prospect in itself—we would unquestionably perish of thirst. On the other hand, and worse yet, perhaps the *Hamidullah* was not adrift after all. Perhaps, while I slept, the crew had nosed her up some estuary, where I would be garroted with a silk scarf and my body disposed of. In a flash, I saw everything. The whole show of hospitality had been a blind to pinch my belongings—in particular the camera, which had obviously aroused cupidity. Months, years would elapse before my belt buckle or cardcase would turn up in a Kuwait bazaar to give a clue to my fate. A wave of such acute self-pity swept over me that I groaned aloud. To die like a dog in a mangrove swamp . . . unmarked grave . . . cut off in the prime of life, a mere boy actually . . .

I was so busy reading eulogies over myself that it was two minutes before I realized we were under way again. Down in the waist I heard the captain's authoritative voice, and the lugubrious singsong of the men as they hauled away at the lines. The *Hamidullah* began her old familiar undulation, but, it seemed to me, with a new purpose and assurance. Far off on the port bow, a dove-gray streak was spreading imperceptibly across the sky, deepening to rose at the promise of the sun. The man at the wheel swung about with a grin and beckoned me toward him. Pointing to a faint smudge on the horizon, no wider than a pencil stroke, he uttered the most melodious phrase that has ever fallen on the human ear.

"Liyatamajjad Allah," he said happily. *"Hunak yarkud Zanzibar."*

It was suffocating in the dining room of the Zanzibar Hotel the next morning, and the three other occupants of my table did nothing to make it less oppressive. One of them was a fat steamship agent from Dar-es-Salaam with a triangular smile that must have driven some poor woman mad, another a supercilious behemoth who gave the impression he was administering Kenya singlehanded, and the third a sallow, insufferable youth, all nose and R.A.F. mustache, who kept furtively wiping his cutlery. Inevitably, as we progressed through the kippers, they got onto mutual acquaintances along the East African littoral and, eventually, my whilom benefactor Fortescue. I pricked up my ears.

"Salt of the earth, old Piggy," the steamship man was declaring huskily. "One of the best. Matter of fact, we'd a couple together only yesterday at the Belgrave, in Mombasa."

"I say, how very extraordinary," drawled the mustache. "I saw him, too—at the airdrome this morning when I came away. Did he tell you about the smuggler chap—the Yank who led him up the garden path?"

"Rotten show," huffed the other. "Can't understand how the bleeder talked Piggy into helping him escape by dhow."

"Played on his good nature, I daresay," said the youth. "The swine was loaded down with hashish and pearls. Piggy's convinced of it, but he daren't go to the police, for fear of being implicated."

"Typical American trick," chimed in the administrative genius. "The bastards'll do it every time. I remember once up at Djibouti—"

I excused myself abruptly, taking care to emphasize the nasal twang in my voice, and flew down Portuguese Street on the double to the Cable & Wireless office.

The Indian clerk scanned the message I shoved through the

wicket, and blinked at me over his horn-rimmed spectacles. "You wish this sent exactly as written, sir?"

"As fast as you can work that key," I answered. "Why? Anything wrong with it?"

"Oh, not at all," he said quickly. "It's just— Well, forgive the liberty, sir, but I used to be stationed at Mombasa and I know Mr. Fortescue. Won't he be very offended?"

"Deeply," I said. "In fact, it may even cause him to fall down and foam at the mouth."

He leaned forward, his antennae aquiver with curiosity. "He behaved badly to you, sir?"

"On the contrary," I replied. "He did just what I asked him to—blast him."

"Ah, yes," said the clerk slowly. "Yes, of course." He watched me with a sad, puzzled expression as I pocketed my change and went out. He was dying to exchange confidences, and one day we will, when I revisit Zanzibar. I'd love to, if somebody'd only build a bridge.

Shoot, If You Must,

Past This Old Gray Head

SOME two hundred miles west of Nairobi, in the illimitable, baking waste of decomposed gneiss and thorn scrub called the Northern Frontier Province, which stretches across Kenya from the Ethiopian border, there is a remote British outpost on the Tana River by the name of Garissa. Fifty-eight miles downstream lies Bura, a dismal settlement of six mud-and-wattle huts clustered around an Indian store. Had you been strolling along the road that links the two of an afternoon late last January (a likelihood even more remote than either), you would have seen a sight guaranteed to freeze the marrow in your head; to wit, the present writer on safari. The present writer is now off safari and, unless wild horses are brought to bear, intends to stay that way the rest of his life. He has, in fact, taken to leaving rooms at the mere mention of the word, and faithfully promises to quit this one just as soon as he has poured out his woeful chronicle.

It began the day before in the Nairobi offices of Safariland, Ltd., an organization that furnishes custom-tailored hunting or photographic safaris to anyone who can pony up sufficient lettuce to indulge his whim. Through the blandishments of the local tourist bureau, the firm had been euchred into permitting me to join one of its clients—an American couple named Forepaugh—in the field for a week, and I was reporting for a final briefing and whatever gear was judged necessary. When I was shown in, the managing director, Colonel Brett, an engaging gentleman whose thirty-five years in the Indian Army had equipped him to cope with every sort of vagary including thuggee, had been up since dawn supervising the arrangements for a party of Mexican wowsers off on a big-game shoot through Tanganyika. In tones as honeyed as those of the shama thrush, he was entreating Her Majesty's excise officer over the phone to release fifteen quarts of tequila imported by the visitors.

"It's mother's milk to these chaps, Festering," he pleaded. "Of *course* it's for their own use—nobody else could drink the stuff. Word of honor, I wouldn't spray it on a tsetse fly. . . . Good Lord, they can't afford any such duty. That's more than the ruddy safari costs. . . . Very well, if that's your decision, but I warn you the United Nations will hear of this." He hung up and regarded me sorrowfully. "Bureaucrats," he said. "No compassion. Bowels of flint."

"Shame to haul it so far in vain," I said. "How will they manage?"

"The Mexicans?" asked Brett. "Oh, they anticipated it. Sneaked in thirty quarts in their baggage, I'm told. However," he said, briskly unfurling a map, "that's not your problem. Are you ready to push off? Good. Now then, at noon tomorrow you're being dropped off up here at Garissa by charter plane to rendezvous with the Forepaughs and Vyvyan Figgis, their white hunter. They've been working down through Isiolo and Kinya—this country to the northwest—looking for lion, and we'll alert them to collect you in transit."

With a pretense of being terribly casual, I extracted a gold-tipped Sobranie, struck a match, and applied it to my nose.

"These—ah—charter planes," I ventured. "It just stood in the morning paper where Mr. Ernest Hemingway cracked up in one over Murchison Falls."

"Yes, but his was larger than what you'll have," Brett replied comfortingly. "The smaller your aircraft, the safer. More maneuverable, don't you see? I mean, suppose your pilot finds he's heading into a mountain." He dipped his hand in a sickeningly graphic gesture. "Whooosh—he just lifts her up and over. But you needn't fret about mountains, old boy. You'll be flying so high you won't see a thing."

"I'm not clear about one point," I said after a tingling pause. "What happens if the Forepaughs and I don't connect? This Northern Frontier's five times the size of Arizona. The guidebook says it's a hundred miles between wells."

"Quite," said Brett. "And chockablock with mambas and those tiresome man-eating centipedes. Best sit tight in Garissa and don't stray off into the rough. Your group'll be along in a few days." All the Nimrods astir in East Africa, he went on to explain, tuned in nightly to a special safari broadcast from Nairobi carrying personal messages, emergency directions for the sick, and the like, and my whereabouts would be noised abroad repeatedly to avoid any mischance. With a parting injunction to shun rogue elephants, Brett commandeered a bedroll and mosquito bar from his supply depot and turned me loose. I was a good mile away, at a sporting outfitter's in Hardinge Street, trying on a jaunty double terai, when it hit me that I had stupidly forgotten to get any gen whatsoever on the Forepaughs. My stomach capsized at the oversight; for all I knew, they might be the most odious of companions—Texas oil tycoons or social butterflies from Pasadena or football enthusiasts: crashing bores of the kind who range the world solely in search of victims and whose *bavardage,* in our enforced week together, could easily unsettle one's reason. I became so agitated that the salesman made bold to ask if I were unwell.

"Oh, no, no—just a touch of paresis," I stammered. "Er—

about this hat, I was really looking for something I could drink from—you know, the way they do in the films. Wouldn't the water leak out of these air holes?"

"Where'd you plan to use it, sir?" he asked. I told him, and he smiled dryly. "No worry on that score," he said. "There isn't a bead of moisture in upper Kenya. The Tana River, of course, but that's alive with crocodiles."

"You don't say," I said, steadying the triple mirror to keep it from whirling around me. "Let's see, now. What do you have in the way of some sturdy leggings—wooden ones, if possible? Or even iron—I don't mind."

The flight to Garissa next morning mercifully was swift, and I made it swifter with a couple of oblivion tablets that beveled the jagged edges off the scenery. The pilot hospitably kept offering to show me various chasms at close range, and even to fly through them so I could study their unusual stratification, but that would have entailed removing my head from the tent of newspaper I had erected over it, and it was quite comfy there. Shortly before noon, the tortuous green belt of the Tana River materialized below us in the shimmering plain; we swooped down over a sprinkle of adobe houses, without, however, shearing off any of their tiles, veered away into the outskirts, and descended to an airstrip of scorched brown grass. Two sergeants of the Kenya police, all spit and polish, greeted me with word that I was to be billeted on the District Commissioner, and, piling my bedroll into their lorry, bore me off. The heat and the glare were catastrophic—so malevolent that conversation was minimal. From several veiled gibes, though, I gathered my escorts considered the D.C. a stinker, and when he strolled out of his weedy suburban residence to welcome me, I began to see why. He was a tall, intense cadaver with a black waxed mustache surmounting his vampire grin, a blood brother to Mr. Coffee Nerves in the advertisements.

"I'm Critchworth-Napier," he said, contemptuously eying

my ready-made desert boots. "You're the person who's meeting
the safari, I daresay."

"What? Has it shown up already?" I asked, elated.

"My dear sir," said Critchworth-Napier, with icy clarity, "the
Colonial Office does not employ me to keep track of displaced
sportsmen. I haven't the foggiest idea where your associates are,
but if you wish to shake down in that banda over there until they
arrive"—he indicated a hut nearby—"I have no means of pre-
venting you. And now, if you'll pardon me, I shall resume my
administrative duties, trivial in your eyes as they no doubt are."

What two or three days with this alkaline Lugosi would have
wrought paralyzes the imagination, but by some divine coincidence I was spared. An hour and a half later, the expedition
rolled into Garissa in its two vehicles—the Forepaughs and their
white hunter, Figgis, in a Land Rover, and, trailing them, fourteen Africans with a truckful of impedimenta. Our meeting at
all, it shook me to learn, was quite fortuitous. They knew nothing
of any broadcast about me, but a week-old letter from Nairobi had
mentioned the fact that I might be kicking around the district,
and since Garissa was the gateway to the lower Tana, they were
calling by to check. Dazed, and with the singular feeling of being
a needle plucked out of a haystack, I was boosted into the cab of
the truck, and we went jolting away to Bura in the wake of the
Land Rover.

It was a grueling trip, for the truck was heavily loaded, the
route bisected by frequent wadis, and the temperature hovered
ever upward into the nineties. My command of Swahili and the
driver's of English were on a par, and after a while we both gave
up trying. In the brief exchange of civilities with my hosts, it
had been difficult to classify them. Forepaugh was a short, beefy
man of late middle age, bald as an egg and rather snappish, who
looked like a prosperous hardware dealer from Utica. His wife
was a good bit younger, a foxy-nosed redhead with buck teeth
and an indefinable aura of show business. As for the hunter, he
seemed typical of those I had seen congregated around the New

Stanley bar—a professional smile of unlimited candle power, dimples he obviously regarded as irresistible, and a plunging neckline that revealed a shade too much masculine brawn. From time to time, I caught glimpses of the trio ahead in their jeep, with Mrs. Forepaugh coquetting fit to kill, and I was tempted to suspect romantic didoes in the Macomber tradition. Instinct warned me, though, against preconceptions, and in any case I was too intent on the quadrupeds I expected to see, and *their* horns, to brood about Mr. Forepaugh's.

By seven that evening, everything had come into clearer focus. We were encamped on the riverbank just outside Bura, and over the ritual gin-and-French, my companions freely identified themselves. My conjectures, it proved, could not have been less accurate. Forepaugh, a San Diego quack and the head of an establishment specializing in what he called "brain breathing," was also the founder of a new religion predicated on a massive intake of figs, and his wife, as nearly as I could determine, was high priestess of the faith. Her theatrical air, I learned, was a throwback to an epoch when she had demonstrated shampoo in movie lobbies. The pair had undertaken the safari to acquire trophies for their home, described by Forepaugh as a show place second to none.

"Cost me a hundred and fifty G's unfurnished," he said, leaning back expansively from the mess table. "The outside is Italian Renaissance, and every room's done in a different period— Empire, Jacobean, Biedermeier, anything you can name. The robing room is authentic Queen Anne. When I got the idea for the African playroom, I said, 'Verma,' I said, 'either it's the best or I don't want it. Every trophy I put in there has got to be a world's record.' That's why I won't shoot anything unless it's bigger than the stuff in the record book."

"What animals are you looking for here?" I asked.

Forepaugh hesitated, obviously nonplused, and Figgis chimed in smoothly. "Lesser kudu, Hunter's hartebeest, and oryx," he said. "Mr. Forepaugh's a perfectionist, bless his heart, but I guarantee he'll find superb heads in this area. By God, I'll stake my reputation on it.'' He glared around the tent, waiting for someone to dare him stake it, but nobody peeped. ''Well, folks,'' he said, ''time to feed. Better get cracking by five tomorrow morning if we're to see anything.''

It was still dark at that hour, when, after a hasty cup of tea, the four of us climbed into the Land Rover and, accompanied by a couple of gunbearers and a tracker, set off into the plain. As the light came up, we began encountering a variety of exotic creatures in the vegetation along the road—giraffe by the score, tiny dik-dik, the exquisite long-necked antelope called gerenuk, and birds in unimaginable profusion. There were hordes of vulturine guinea fowl and crowned plover, European and marabout storks, Brahmany kites, wood ibis, lesser bustards, hornbills, African goshawks, and all sorts of ornithological rarities like the nob-nosed duck, Montagu's harrier, the carmine bee eater, Burchell's glossy starling, and the white-faced whistling teal. None of these, however, interested Forepaugh in the slightest; after an interval of grumbling, he querulously started demanding action.

''For Pete's sake, Figgis,'' he rasped, ''this mileage is costing me a fortune. Where's all the game you were bragging about? We don't want a Goddamned sight-seeing tour—got all this junk in our zoo back home. Get a move on, will you?''

Figgis, whose role, it was becoming plain, was as much that of sycophant and courtier as guide, was evidently used to rough diamonds. He never turned a hair. ''Now, don't get fidgety, Forps,'' he advised, all dimples and cream. ''You're too impetuous—too ardent. Don't you find that so, Mrs. Forepaugh?'' he inquired slyly. I was just wondering how a neurasthenic bookworm had ever conned himself into bouncing through the African bush to listen to double-entendres before breakfast when Figgis brought me out of it. ''Keep the bwana's gun ready,'' he told the bearers. ''He's going to bag something special before long. I can feel it in my bones.''

As one temperamentally unsuited to blood sports, I should have recognized this as a signal that carnage was about to ensue, and returned to camp by shank's mare, but, like a fool, I let myself be swept along. In the next two hours, I witnessed one of the least edifying spectacles in my memory. Using a rifle only a shade less powerful than a siege gun, Forepaugh maladroitly slew a Hunter's hartebeest and a gerenuk, both of them a good eight inches under the world's record. It was a lengthy process and, to my prejudiced eye, as ennobling as what happens routinely in any municipal abattoir. The parallel seemed even more apt when I rode homeward in the back of the Land Rover with two gory carcasses buzzing with flies. Forepaugh, his ego inflated to balloon proportions by the exploit, treated us en route to a detailed post-mortem of his emotions during the stalk, and Figgis was loud with praise for his marksmanship and pluck, smearing the jap-a-lac as fast as his brush could fly.

For three mortal days, differing only in the fauna they cooled, Forepaugh and Figgis went through the same pattern morning and afternoon. Evenings and mealtimes afforded no respite, since the pair, with Boy Scout intensity, spent them analyzing each other's shooting technique and quarreling about ballistics. In desperation, I turned to Mrs. Forepaugh for stimulus, and found it on a lofty mental plane. Verma was a great reader, gifted with total recall; she knew the works of Mika Waltari, Ben Ames Williams, and Frances Parkinson Keyes backward, and she painstakingly recounted their plots that way. She had also written some lyric poetry, the sort of kapok that pads out the editorial columns of newspapers, which she was not at all averse to reciting. By the fourth day of my sojourn, I thought I had reached the nadir, but there was an enchanting surprise in store. Around five o'clock that afternoon, while the huntsmen were off reconnoitering a herd of fringe-eared oryx and Verma was reciting one of her madrigals to me in the mess tent, a jeep rattled into camp. A rather distraught young Briton sprang out and, directing his African boys to stand by, burst in on us.

"I say, have you seen anything of two Swedes who've been hunting crocs hereabout?" he fluted. "Stumbleblad and Maelstrom, some such names." We said we had not, and his face fell. "Bother," he said. "Where d'ye suppose the swine have gone? I did want to let them know, rather." Before we could learn what he wanted to impart, he sped back to the jeep, reversed it, and slammed it into gear. Then, patently as an afterthought, he leaned out and addressed us. "By the way," he said, "I have to warn you that twelve hard-core Mau Mau have escaped from the detention camp at Lamu, a hundred miles below here on the coast. They'll undoubtedly work their way upriver at night, so keep your eyes open, what?"

"Are they, so to speak, carrying any—how shall I say?— persuasive instruments?" I asked, suddenly conscious that my mucous membrane was coated with flannel.

"Yes sir*ree*," declared the young man. "Pangas, and sharp ones. However, they'll be looking for guns—they always do. Better lock up any you're not using. Cheerio."

As the sound of the jeep died away, I swiveled around slowly toward Verma, who was just then swiveling around slowly toward me. "I—believe Figgis left three rifles in our tent," I said. "Why don't you slip over and bring them in here?"

"*Me?*" she retorted. "Why don't you? You're a man."

"I am not!" I said hotly. "I mean I am, but do you expect me to walk all the way across that clearing? It's getting dark, and besides I don't know anything about guns."

"That makes two of us," she said. "Oh, well, the others'll be back soon. Meanwhile, listen to this sonnet. I call it 'Spume at Eventide.'"

How anybody could be so obtuse and self-centered in circumstances of such peril still evades me, but women are inexplicable, and, *faute de mieux*, I was forced to humor the poor daft creature. When, hours later, her husband and Figgis showed up, the strain of my vigil and the nails I had chewed were beginning to tell on me. It developed that they had heard the news earlier from a forest ranger, and after an extended discussion of the probabilities at dinner, Forepaugh announced his decision to break camp and move on to a safer area.

"Forgive me for putting my oar in, friends," I said. "I realize I'm merely a guest here, but I disagree." Everybody stared at me, confounded. "Personally, I'm for staying here and giving those Johnnies a sizzling welcome. Show 'em they can't intimidate *us*, by gad."

"Well, in that event—" began Figgis.

"And I would, too," I said, hastily overriding him, "if I didn't have to be back in Nairobi tomorrow. Orders from Sir Evelyn Baring, at Government House. They take precedence, you know." Fortunately, nobody dared question the statement, or perhaps nobody cared. It was portentous enough in any case to secure me a lift the next day back to Garissa, where I wangled a ride home from a locust-control officer. He was a sterling chap— a complete illiterate who had never heard of Mika Waltari or lyric poetry and who abhorred hunting anything except grasshoppers. Talked about them for seven hours straight and never once drew his breath. I did, though, over and over. You don't get much of a chance to when you're on safari. . . . Blast! There goes that word again!

DR. PERELMAN, I PRESUME,
OR SMALL-BORE IN AFRICA

IV

The

Artemisses

By the Saturday afternoon last winter when the sixteen American ladies publicized as the Artemisses, a hunting safari composed exclusively of girls, deplaned at Nairobi to begin their historic jaunt through East Africa, the tension around the New Stanley Hotel was such that you could have heard a pin drop. While awaiting their arrival there, I inadvertently dropped one, with which I was fastening some money inside my jumper, and the reverberations awoke the bellboys snoozing near the elevator. It was obvious that despite their pretense of indifference they, and indeed the whole male population of the colony, were keyed up to a fantastic pitch, for it was not every day that a galaxy of beauties understood to rival Rosemary Theby and bulging, in addition, with hard currency descended on the frontier metropolis. All over Nairobi, husbands were cooking up spurious excuses like toothache and overdue gas bills to hustle downtown for a dekko at the newcomers. From the bars frequented by the military, the upcountry settlers, and other technical bachelors there came the whiplike report of cuffs being shot and the sound of heavy breathing.

My presence in the lobby, however, was motivated by neither sensuality nor greed but altruism. Several months earlier in New York, prior to departing for Kenya, I had met the young person who conceived and organized the junket—a symmetrical titian-haired cupcake named Bella Parmechenee. Bella, a drumbeater, or flack, employed by a luggage corporation, had inserted in a fashion magazine a teaser ad calling for footloose and adventuresome maidens to join her in an African safari complete with white hunter, and the response had been overwhelming. As we nibbled our parfaits at Rumpelmayer's—for both of us, by a coincidence, were rigidly abstemious—I chose a bold means of cementing our friendship. Was there, I asked candidly, any foundation to the rumor that she had filched her idea from a project called the All-Girl Safari, which had been announced some months before? Her answer was forthright and uncompromising. With a spirited gesture of denial, whose imprint I can still feel on my cheek, she at once disposed of the canard and created an atmosphere of healthy camaraderie. After our second parfait, all shyness fled and she expressed trepidation at the loneliness ahead on the Dark Continent, the prospect of no friendly face to welcome her troupe. Reacting with instinctive gallantry, and perhaps somewhat dizzied by chocolate sauce, I offered to act as a one-man reception committee. Bella was ecstatic, so much so that she overturned her glass—that is, the glass the parfait was in. She insisted I accompany the girls on the last week of their tour—a motor excursion through Uganda and a voyage up Lake Albert to the Murchison Falls.

"But wouldn't it be—harumph—deuced unconventional?" I demurred. "One fellow alone with so many girls, without any chaperon. I'm not sure my wife would approve—"

"Oh, come on, be a man," she said impatiently. "You only live once. You don't want people to think you're a milksop, do you?"

The taunt decided me; rather than have Bella bruit it about

every sweetshop in Gotham that I was craven, I gave in, and we parted with a buoyant pledge to meet under African skies.

Now that our reunion was nigh, I resolved to be watchful. It would not do to cheapen myself, to let Bella and her charges fondle or caress me publicly. If they showed signs, as I feared they might, of being overcome by a kissing bug, I would suggest adjourning to some clubbier locale, where I could remonstrate with each individually and recall her to her senses. Suddenly, from the portico of the hotel I heard a confused uproar, like a flash flood approaching, and above it the babble of female voices. A moment later, a horde of the most extraordinary women boiled into the lobby, elbowing and tumbling each other aside in their anxiety to be first at the reception desk. They were all shapes and sizes, and, both en masse and singly, conveyed a staggering lack of charm. They were clad in tunics, whipcords, and jodhpurs that missed musical comedy by only a few sequins; their faces, which had been slept in on a series of flying machines, were putty-colored with fatigue and oversmoking; and they all moved in a fighter's crouch, girding their massive loins to battle for whatever perquisites they were entitled to. I circled the hillock of mink coats, cameras, ukuleles, and cosmetic kits they had discarded, and found Bella, in a state of near hysteria, trying to pacify several of the more clamorous.

"But you *have* to room with her, at least for tonight," she was pleading desperately. "I can't help it if she snores. . . . Darling, you couldn't have left your jewels in Cairo—we never stopped there. . . . Ask the clerk; there must be a place to get your hair done. . . . Well, if you think it's malaria, take an aspirin, take a drink—take arsenic, for all I care . . ."

From the blank stare my greeting evoked, I suspected Bella had forgotten our orgy *chez* Rumpelmayer, but a thimbleful of grenadine in the lounge soon restored her memory, and she proceeded to update me on the odyssey thus far. The women ranged in age from thirty to sixty-eight (with a preponderance in the late forties) ; all but four were married, divorced, or widowed; and—other than what they had gleaned from *The Snows of Kilimanjaro* and *King Solomon's Mines*—they were unhampered by any knowledge of African geography, woodcraft, or hunting. In fact, said Bella, she doubted that any of them had ever fired a gun—except, she added generously, at a husband. All sorts of feuds had been germinating en route; certain ladies felt that they had been overlooked by the photographers at the airports, others complained that they found the publicity demeaning and unpalatable. New cliques formed hourly, backbiting and acrimony were rife, and the forthcoming safari into Tanganyika, patently, was destined to be a sockdolager.

"Well, I'll see you when you get back from it—that is, if you're not gored by a buffalo," I said, endeavoring to lighten her mood. "Meanwhile, should you run into trouble or need help, I'll be on the headwaters of the Juba River, visiting a tribe ruled by a strange white goddess."

"How near is that to where we're going?" asked Bella.

"A thousand miles north," I said regretfully. "Beastly luck, isn't it? Oh, well, chin up—you're not dead yet." I sped out of the hotel by a side door and, during the remainder of the Artemisses' stay in Nairobi, managed to avoid any embroilment.

Our next encounter was a fortnight later, when Bella rang up to announce the expedition's return and invite me to inspect its trophies. Apparently, the trip had been a stimulating one, for her voice sounded breathless. "You'll adore Tanganyika," she burbled. "The most primitive country—real rugged tureen. And the animals! I can't wait to tell you."

Awesome as I found the five buffalo heads, the two dozen antelope horns, and the other meat products exultantly shown me, I was even more spellbound by the behavior of the huntresses. There was no bloody nonsense about manners in divvying the spoils; each snatched up whichever pelt or skull she thought would make the best souvenir, regardless of who had bagged it, and defended it with the virulence of a bobcat. One pair, indeed, got into so sulphurous a dispute over a zebra hide that a mule skinner standing near me crimsoned and left the premises. In the face of such open dissension, I supposed the group would disband now that the safari was finished, yet, oddly enough, the ladies seemed revivified. The following day, they whizzed off on a rubberneck tour of Zanzibar, and thereafter of the eastern Congo. Presently, I received a chit from Bella mailed in Ruanda-Urundi. Quoting my promise quixotically made over the parfaits, she besought me to meet her party at a whistle stop called Katwe, in westernmost Uganda. The decision was a trying one, and I paced the floor a whole night through. Could I betray the trust this fragile, copper-crested child with the alluring shape reposed in me? My chevalier's code held no alternative, especially since she was picking up the tab. When the sun was again at the meridian, I was winging over Lake Victoria.

Deep in the Queen Elizabeth National Park, Uganda's newest game reserve, I came to Katwe. It turned out to be a half-completed motel on a barren knob of ground overlooking Lake Edward, and the Artemisses' motorcade had paused there to refuel and change lipsticks. Enforced proximity and their intensive tourism had exacerbated my compatriots to a homicidal degree. Only two or three were still on speaking terms; the glances the ladies exchanged throbbed with hatred, and one after another drew me aside to pour out grievances. The fabled Watusi were not as tall as Bella had led them to believe, and the pygmies not as tiny, and evil-smelling to boot. The food in the Congo was inferior, the scenery insipid, and the gorillas nonexistent.

"And as for that *friend* of yours, or whatever she is," one of them said, glaring venomously at Bella and extracting the last possible drop of innuendo, "she's a two-faced, selfish, brazen, scheming—"

"Please," I said, with icy dignity. "As a guest of Miss Parmechenee's, I refuse to discuss her behind her back. Besides," I pointed out, to keep their boilers up to pressure, "it's such a pretty back, don't you think? So slim and willowy, unlike most.''

The three-day drive to the shores of Lake Albert that followed is possibly the most tedious journey in my recollection, which, if massaged, can yield up some pippins. I rode in the lead car of the caravan, with Bella, a garrulous matron from Cedar Rapids named Crabshaw, and an indigenous chauffeur dazed by protracted exposure to her voice. Mrs. Crabshaw had girdled the globe endless times—always at the captain's table, naturally— and anecdotes spouted from her lips in a geyser as unfailing as Old Faithful. Her reminiscences of General Douglas MacArthur, whom she doted on, whiled away many an hour as we ground up and down the foothills of the Ruwenzori Range. Our bivouac the first night was a hotel at Fort Portal romantically called the Mountains of the Moon. Dinner was a gay affair; our whole group sat at a long table—with someone at the head of it whose identity is his own business—and the sallies and backchat were audible to a whole roomful of starchy British colonials. Midway through the meal, a Mrs. Gonister created a diversion by wresting a plate of cold cuts from her neighbor. The management was able to subdue the two before they could plunge their forks into each other's eyeballs, but it was touch and go for a minute.

Our leave-taking next morning had a similar touch of drama. Just as we were embarking, Mrs. Spurgeon, a hyperthyroid Midwestern type who owned a chain of beauty shops, was overtaken by a *crise;* all her notes, the material she was amassing for a series of travel articles in her home-town paper, had disappeared. Since the bulk of her companions, so to speak, had like journalistic tieups, they were automatically suspected of swiping it, and even I was not excepted. Fuming like so many barnyard turkeys, the ladies paraded about, daring Mrs. Spurgeon to suggest they submit to a search. The air was thick with threats of hair pulling, of action for slander. Fortunately for us, if not for the newspaper readers of southern Nebraska, the missing diary came to light in a glove compartment, and the storm clouds passed over.

The objective that night was a place called Masindi, and we

reached it without any major lesions, although—thanks to the voluble Mrs. Crabshaw—somewhat nicked by flying ennui. Owing to overcrowded conditions in the hotel, I shared quarters there with an engineer in the Public Works Department, a strange, sunken-eyed zombie out of a Universal horror film. He had a waxen face, and a black spade beard like Edward Teach's, and was visibly piqued by the sight of my seraglio, as he assumed the Artemisses to be. He made all sorts of conversational feints, seeking to ascertain whether I was a Moslem, or the head of an obscure religious cult, or someone engaged in the South American export trade. I was really in no position to enlighten him. At that point, the outlines were beginning to shift and blur.

Twenty-four hours later, aboard the twin steam launches *Murchison* and *Livingstone*, we chugged out of Butiaba, on Lake Albert, toward the mouth of the Victoria Nile. The vessel I shared with eight of the nymphs, the *Murchison*, had achieved a certain dubious *réclame* shortly before, having borne Mr. Hemingway back from his epochal crash. Our feeling of glamour intensified when we entered the tortuous, reed-choked waterways interlacing the delta, for this was the locale of *The African Queen*, and the girls were inspired to frequent and comic impersonations of Katharine Hepburn. Luckily, the advent of millions of gnats drove them to their bunks after dinner, which gave Bella and me an interlude alone on the upper deck. I was amazed to find her an erudite, astute individual, not in the least giddy, as I had thought, but filled with an enormous and restless curiosity. To satisfy it under the conditions was clearly out of the question, as the captain was forever poking his snoot in on some trumped-up pretext; however, we did squeeze in an informal astronomy lesson, and a perusal of our palms that foretold events in no way germane to this narrative. That they subsequently failed to come true does not invalidate the science of palmistry. I feel that we in the Occidental world have much left to learn.

The hippos, elephants, crocodiles, and aquatic birds on the

riverbank were so numerous in the morning that it was difficult to moor, but we finally put in at a landing stage below the Murchison Falls and began the slow trek upward to the renowned cataract. The ascent, through a precipitous gorge and under a burning sun, was toilsome, and the ladies gave off a sustained peevish whine, like the skirl of bagpipes. It did no good for me to remind them that, apart from Bella, they were all overweight and shockingly flabby, and that if they aspired to catch a man, they had jolly well better put their backs into it. Their reaction was most disturbing. Panting, their faces mottled with fury, they reviled me—a typical instance of feminine ingratitude.

"It shows you how thin the veneer of civilization really is," I said aggrievedly to Bella. "Dash it all, I didn't come here to be abused. I accepted your invitation in good faith."

"I know—sometimes I wonder about human nature," she said with quick sympathy. "But try to bear with them, won't you? Whatever happens, you mustn't leave us now."

Frankly, the thought had never entered my head, as there was nowhere to go, and while the women were manifestly irresponsible, their sheer size protected one against marauding animals. With a steadfast assurance to Bella that she could rely on me, I spurred the column on, and at length, utterly spent, we gained the top of the falls. It was a prodigious spectacle, one of the truly rewarding sights of a lifetime. For minutes on end, I stood reverently contemplating the torrent as it thundered four hundred feet into the Dantesque abyss and trying to imagine the rapture Sir Samuel Baker must have felt when he first beheld it ninety years before. Then, mute with exaltation, I returned to the stunted tree under whose shade the ladies had congregated and were grumpily fanning themselves. They were in a baleful mood.

"An outrage, an absolute swindle," one of them snapped. "Dragging us all this distance for a lousy little trickle like that. I wouldn't give you two cents for it. Why, out where I come from, we've got a waterfall—"

"*I* thought it was going to be another Niagara," said Mrs. Crabshaw indignantly. "There isn't even a bench to sit down on, or an attendant. No wonder they don't get any tourists."

"Yes, and now we have to walk all the way back," chimed in Mrs. Gonister. "All but Her Highness, there, that is. She's got someone who's probably fool enough to carry her down."

I walked over to the rock where Bella sat, head in hands, and bowed. "Permit me, *querida*," I said, and swung her up on my shoulder. She wasn't as light as she looked, and the climb down almost killed me, but I figured it was worth it. They none of them addressed a word to me the rest of the trip, and that's the sort of thing money can't buy. I read an interesting piece in the paper the day they left—said they'd had a wonderful time and were all coming back next year, with their husbands. O.K.—I'll be waiting in the lobby of the New Stanley. A party of that size might be pretty unwieldy, of course, and one of us might have to drop out. Never mind who. Let's cross that bridge when we come to it.

V

Jet-Propelled

Turban

IF TRAVEL has taught me nothing more, and it certainly has, it's this: you never know when some trifling incident, utterly without significance, may pitchfork you into adventure or, by the same token, may not. A look across a smoky room, a chance word or gesture, and all of a sudden you're standing breathless before a bead curtain in Cairo or clinging to an outrigger in the Nicobars or pawning your cuff links at Simpson's. I for one never dreamed as I stooped to retrieve a hairbrush from under the washbowl of a Paris hotel room last December that I was taking the first step in a grotesque excursion across the Indian Ocean with that venerable mainspring, His Highness Seyyid Sir Khalifa bin Harub, the Sultan of Zanzibar. Could I have foreseen the complications in the offing, I probably would have brushed my hair with a toothbrush and let it go hang. But then, the toothbrush was under the basin, too. I'd had a couple of pousse-cafés the night before.

What happened was simple to the point of banality. After

ineffectually groping around under the sink, I miscalculated the amount of headroom over me and laid open my scalp as though it had been cleft by a yataghan. A pharmacist in the Rue de Vaugirard, absorbed in bottling leeches and obviously a figment of René Clair's imagination, paused long enough to patch me up grudgingly, and I went into a *brasserie* hard by for a restorative. There, staring meditatively across the zinc into the *patronne's* blouse, was an English sculptor named Noel Desuetude, who recognized me at once as an old companion of his Montparnasse days. Under other circumstances, I could have given the man an argument, but it was folly to be knocked down in my weakened condition, and I humored him. When he started reaching for the menu, however, I played my ace.

"Kenya?" he said, crestfallen. "You mean you're flying there this very noon? Damn it, I'd rather counted on your buying me lunch. Ah, well, another time. See here, though, you really must look up my godfather in Nairobi. He's the head of East African Airways—hellishly influential cove."

"Gladly," I said. "Jot down his name, will you?"

"I don't know it, to be candid," he said. "The fact is he's not my godfather at all, but we English are a clannish lot. I mean we're slow to make friends, but once we warm up, we can't do enough for you. Like, for instance, the way I'm sending you on to my godfather in Nairobi."

"Yes, and I'm deeply obliged—" I began.

"Now, don't start slobbering over me like a confounded sheep-dog," he said testily. "If you must show your gratitude, pay for these." He shoved a pile of saucers toward me. "Sorry to bolt, but I'm meeting a popsy the other side of Paris. *A bientôt.*"

Well, around a month later, at a supper party in Muthaiga, a residential quarter of Nairobi, I met a well-set-up chap named Sorsbie, keen as mustard—there was some on the tablecloth, so one could judge—who proved to be the head of East African Airways. Seizing an opportune moment when the conversation had turned on bogus godsons, I told him about my encounter. Though he pretended to be deaf, as your Englishman frequently will out of shyness, I could see he was engrossed.

"And you paid his score, did you?" he asked. "You know, you ought to have your head examined."

"I did, but they couldn't find anything," I said. "If there was porcelain in the brain, wouldn't I feel it?"

"Only time will tell," he said darkly. "These things take a while to show. I say," he went on, with a thoughtful frown, "in a way I feel morally responsible for what this sponge in Paris did to you, and I'd like to make amends. Ever hear of the island of Pemba?"

"Gee, I can't use any more real estate," I protested. "I've got a farm in Pennsylvania—"

"It's about thirty miles northeast of Zanzibar," said Sorsbie, rolling over me like a Juggernaut, "and part of the Sultan's domain. We're opening an airfield there day after tomorrow, and we're flying over the Sultan and some other bigwigs in a special plane to dedicate it. Why don't you come along, too? Fascinating old duffer, His Highness. You two should have lots in common."

Offhand, I couldn't guess what it might be, outside inordinate wealth, but Sorsbie's heart was set on our meeting and I acceded. Late the next afternoon, I flew to Zanzibar, where the junket was to originate, and, boarding an ancient tumbril at the airport, set off through the labyrinthine alleys of the town for the hotel. In the car was another bird of passage off the same flight, a corpulent, dynamic gentleman in white sharkskin, whose artificial choppers sparkled with veritable ingots of gold. His languishing sidelong glances told me he was perishing to make friends. The opportunity came when he saw me extract a packet of Bisodol tablets.

"An American!" he said delightedly. "From your aristocratic nose, I thought you were a Portuguese hidalgo. Permit me, sir," he went on, deftly plucking a tablet from my hand. "I never miss a chance to eat these when they are offered. You know, we

Greeks are authorities on heartburn—heartburn and women, ha ha ha. If you please—my card.''

I took it and learned that fate had thrown me with Constantine Tigris, domiciled at Arusha, Tanganyika, and styling himself an industrialist. He seemed so hurt at my inability to produce a card that I brought out my passport, which he studied with deep interest, nodding repeatedly, and then thrust into his breast pocket.

''Would you mind awfully returning that?'' I asked hesitantly. ''It isn't the intrinsic cost, but it's got sentimental associations—''

''Oh—oh! Forgive me, my dear fellow,'' he said, overcome with chagrin. ''Imagine being so absent-minded. There you are. By the way, if you want to sell this at any time, I pay cash and no questions asked.''

I promised not to dispose of it without giving him priority, and, secreting it under my toupee, withdrew into a marmoreal silence. As we were both registering at the hotel, though, the clerk gave me a verbal message that Bikinized Mr. Hubris. It appeared that a seneschal wearing a dolman and a gold hearing aid had left word requesting me to join the Sultan's party at eight the next morning at the airport. Mr. Tigris's jaw dropped, and he watched me ascend the stairs as if I were clothed in white samite. Throughout dinner, he kept observing me furtively from his table, and afterward pursued me into the lobby and insisted on standing me to a brandy.

''Why didn't you say you were a diplomat?'' he reproached me. ''I had no idea you were a friend of the Sultan—''

I cut him short and, without demeaning myself unnecessarily, explained I had no official status at the forthcoming exercises on Pemba. An indulgent smile clearly revealed his disbelief. Typical American modesty, chuckled Mr. Tigris, signaling the waiter to replenish my glass; he was certain I was the emissary of persons of the highest consequence in Washington, that grave decisions would stem from my visit. Then, with mastodonlike subtlety, he maneuvered around to the gimmick. A little group of philanthropists he knew was interested in establishing a casino in Zanzibar —a place where the natives could eat ices and enjoy classical music and, if they felt disposed, dally with a harmless game of stuss. If I could drop a word *en passant* into the Sultan's ear, the syndicate would be overjoyed to set aside a few shares of stock for both of us. . . .

There being no exact local equivalent for the word "shill," it took ten minutes and considerable vehemence to disabuse Mr. Tigris. He was pained at my obduracy but not daunted. Waylaying me at breakfast in the morning, he offered to appoint me an honorary director of the project and implied that, between us, we could flimflam the Sultan out of his stock. I literally had to peel him off me to embark for the airport; in his final frenzy he made a grab for my wristwatch, figuring, I suppose, that it was better than nothing. The agony on his face, as I last saw it through the bus window, was almost Promethean, though perhaps it was only the brandy pecking at his liver.

In the waiting room at the field was a racial fricassee comparable to the Tower of Babel; Indians, Africans, Arabs, Malagasy, Seychellois, and half a dozen other nationalities milled about, costumed as if for a Shubert musical and behaving with much the same incoherence. The majority, it was evident, had no connection with the tour beyond a desire to catch a glimpse of the ruler, who arrived with suitable pomp in a Rolls-Royce flaunting his dynastic red flag. He was a benevolent, patriarchal gentleman of seventy-odd attired in Arab dress, with a white beard and horn-rimmed spectacles, and I felt a wave of resentment at Mr. Tigris for assuming that I would ever whipsaw such a kindly old codger. When his entourage, and various British dignitaries, aviation officials, and similar consequential guests were finally stowed aboard the *Seyyid Said bin Sultan,* a DC-3 christened for the occasion after Zanzibar's earliest sovereign, we numbered eighteen souls. The flight to Pemba was idyllic save for a continuous grinding noise, which turned out to be the voice of my seatmate, an Indian businessman attached to the chamber of commerce. While his statistics on the decline of clove production were stimulating enough, the warm pressure of his lips on my ear ultimately gave me goose flesh, and I sought out another chair. The passenger next to me there, a well-set-up Briton and keen as horseradish, had an oddly familiar look. Putting two and two together, I decided it was Sorsbie, the chap who had invited me on the trip and who, obviously out of shyness, had given no indication he was going along himself. Just as I was framing an oblique reference to a mutual acquaintance of ours up in Paris, however, he excused himself abruptly and departed. It was one of those curious coincidences that occur nowhere but in East Africa.

Except that the speeches were in Arabic and Swahili and the audience more exotic, the ensuing ceremony at Pemba, held in a marquee pitched beside the runway, could have served equally to consecrate a supermarket in Los Angeles. An assemblage of several hundred sheiks, African elders, and Khoja Ismailis, liegemen of the Aga Khan, applauded vociferously as one after another of their spokesmen rose to hail the new era of prosperity and universal brotherhood that would attend regular air service. The rest of Pemba's male population—Mohammedan custom bars the presence of women at important functions—stood or crouched in the blazing sun, wilting under the interminable rhetoric but doggedly awaiting the refreshments scheduled to follow. At last, when everyone had run out of bromides, the Sultan's speech of acknowledgment in three languages was read into the microphone by his aide-de-camp, taking three times as long as a speech of acknowledgment in one language, and the tension abated. To the strains of that perennial Islamic favorite, "Easter Parade," rendered by a military band, a platoon of waiters distributed highly appropriate sweetmeats of molten Turkish paste, and steaming coffee. The visitors were now worshipfully directed to resume their places in the aircraft, so that it could proceed onward to Nairobi. As we did, the four or five ladies in the contingent, who had been concealed behind a stockade during the exercises, rejoined us, among them the Sultana and her lady in waiting. The two promptly immured themselves in the washroom to change their costumes, and thereby created a horrid dilemma for crew and passengers alike. The pilot, afraid it would be lèse-majesté to bang on the door, had to delay the takeoff until they reappeared, and we were all nicely parboiled by the time the plane was aloft.

My previous contact with royalty had been limited to two Asiatic playboys, in the persons of the crown prince of Johore and the ex-emperor of Annam, Bao Dai, neither of them monarchs to overshadow Charlemagne, and when my turn came to meet Their Highnesses, I was inclined to hang back. However, I reflected that they could hardly bite my head off, since their bridgework, like mine, must be immobilized by Turkish paste, and, assuming the expression of servility one uses on credit managers, I sidled up to them. The audience began a bit chaotically, for just as I made my curtsy, the plane hit an air pocket and threatened to catapult me into the Sultana's lap. Nevertheless, by flailing around briskly, I caught hold of a gentlewoman's chignon across the aisle and recovered my balance. Kaleidoscopic though it was, my first impression of the Sultana was glamorous. A gazelle-eyed matron clad in a filmy blue sari, she wore a necklace of emblematic gold coins and matching bangles, and a square-cut emerald approximately the size of a Congress playing card.

"Well, this is a red-letter day for yours truly, sir," I assured the Sultan, deciding to adopt a straightforward, democratic line. "Little did I think a month ago that I would be shooting the breeze with a real Arab potentate two thousand feet up in the air. Actually," I commented, with a smile, "it's kind of a switch, isn't it? Shouldn't we all be seated on a flying carpet?"

"What did the young man say?" inquired His Highness, regarding me in perplexity.

141

"Something about a carpet," his wife said uncertainly. "I think he's trying to sell us one."

"We don't need any," the Sultan replied, with unnecessary force. "The house is full of them. Tell him to go away."

Amused that they had mistaken me for a salesman, I went back to the very beginning in Paris and described how I chanced to be present, not omitting a friendly injunction to beware of Tigris and his dubious casino. To fix the details firmly in his mind, and at the same time demonstrate that I had his undivided attention, the Sultan closed his eyes. He was very much *au courant*, though, because the moment I concluded, they flew wide-open again.

"What happened? Who are you?" he demanded. "Why are you looking at my wife's ring like that?"

"I was only admiring it," I stammered. "I've never seen such a headlight before."

"We-ell, all right," he said suspiciously, "but don't get any crazy ideas, Jack."

The ease with which he had slipped into the vernacular startled me. "Your Highness is at home in the American idiom?" I queried.

"Oh, I dig it a little," he admitted, visibly flattered. "You may think we're squares down here, but we see *Variety* and *Down Beat* and all those publications. One of my sultanic whims is to keep up with the box-office grosses and the different pop tunes. You know," he went on reflectively, "to me there's nothing worse than a suzerain who becomes insular. Of course, if he's an insular suzerain like I to begin with, that's different, but I believe that a man which he is the spiritual and political leader of a heterogeneous flock had ought to keep his finger on the pulse of the common man."

"It figures," I concurred. "If memory serves, the fabled Haroun-al-Rashid ofttimes used to dress up in rags and mingle with his subjects in the bazaar. Does Your Highness ever do that?"

"I don't have to dress up, the way things are going in Zanzibar," he observed gloomily. "Would you like some lugubrious statistics on the decline of clove production there?"

I would have loved it, but the plane was already over the outskirts of Nairobi, and whispers of a reception at the airdrome were circulating through the cabin. Within a few minutes, we were standing on terra firma, our heads bared to a salute from a guard of honor. The group photograph in next day's newspaper identified only the Sultan and a couple of his Ministers, charitably ignoring the man behind them struggling to detach a passport from a toupee. I got a letter from Sorsbie shortly afterward with a bill enclosed from Tigris for six brandies. He asked what the devil it meant and begged me not to explain. Curious race, the English. Once they warm up, there's no telling what they'll do for you.

VI

Against the Grain

with Charlene Bozeman

WHEN, I can hear you ask, did I first hear of Lamu, that fabulous entrepôt of gold and ivory, spice and slaves, off the northeastern coastline of Kenya? (The only reason I can hear you is that my ears detect sounds inaudible even to dogs, and particularly semi-rhetorical questions about Lamu.) Well, it's rather uncanny you should bring it up, for I was just thinking that the first I ever heard of it was in London last winter, a fortnight prior to my arrival in East Africa. With an unerring instinct for the cul-de-sac, I reached the British capital at the worst of all possible times—on a Friday, when everyone I knew there had left for the weekend. If my name had been Alexander Selkirk, I couldn't have been more effectively marooned. After two days of eating in snack bars, conversing with doormen, and mooning into barred shopwindows, I was so *triste* that I snuffled when I sought directions from passersby, which I did merely for the brief companionship it afforded. Sunday evening, revolted at the prospect of one more fish-paste sandwich, I entered an elegant restaurant off

Shaftesbury Avenue, a great, echoing mausoleum with platoons of waiters in impeccable evening dress, and with pink side lights on the walls. The place was totally deserted except for one table-ful of diners, and the maître d'hôtel, instinctively sensing my need for sociability, placed me on the adjoining banquette. Per-haps the five-pound note I slipped into his hand was excessive, but, lacking a diamond the size of the Cullinan, I had no adequate means of expressing my gratitude.

The meal, of course, was ghastly—fried plaice smothered in cream sauce, the usual Brussels sprouts boiled beyond cognizance, and a soggy plum tart as fibrous as corrugated paper. Still, I consumed it with relish, hoodwinking myself into an illusion of gaiety by the proximity of my neighbors. They were four tanned and hearty chaps, the sort whose aquiline profiles and flashing teeth you see in advertisements for Eno's Fruit Salts and Abdulla Cigarettes, and they primed themselves freely with claret as they ate. In a while, they began exchanging reminiscences of colonial life in Assam and Nyasaland, and ultimately, to my delight, in Kenya, whither I was bound. The place above all that had cap-tured his heart, declared one emotionally, was an old Arab port two hundred miles above Mombasa, on the Indian Ocean. Of all the paradisiacal spots on earth, not even excepting Bali, Lamu was his choice.

"Gad, what I'd give to stroll along that quay at sunset again!" he told his companions. "Those feathery palms against the sky, the voices of the boatmen drifting across the water . . ." He went into a long dithyramb about the ease and simplicity of life in the town, the absence of tension, the nobility of the inhabitants. Whether my anchorite existence of the preceding two days had made me especially suggestible or whether it was all preordained, I can't say, but his words etched themselves on my brain. On the plane that bore me from Addis Ababa to Nairobi, I consulted the East African Yearbook & Guide, which added two highlights to his ecstatic picture. Lamu had once been a rival of Mombasa as an entrepôt of gold, ivory, spice, and slaves, and H. Rider

Haggard's brother, who was believed to have provided much of the background for the celebrated novels, had occupied the post of vice-consul there in 1884–85. That cinched it for me. If there was any way of getting there—and from my British spellbinder's context I gathered it was virtually inaccessible—I was going. Bullheadedness? Romanticism? No, just a man with an ingrained flair for entrepôts and no concept of his limitations.

Once I began airing my *idée fixe* around Nairobi, I discovered I might as easily have projected a trip to the moon. Nobody had been up to Lamu in years, said the wiseacres; there was no air service, unless one chartered a plane at a prohibitive fee, and the coastal road was washed out most of the year. To be sure, a native bus out of Mombasa carried passengers and mail in that general direction, but this form of locomotion was judged infra dig and altogether too rigorous for Europeans. None of these strictures, naturally, affected me in the least. I joyously accepted them as a challenge to my stamina and booked passage at once on the first plane next morning to the coast.

It was a splendid gesture of defiance, and I had lots of time to rue it. Contrary to my blithe expectations, the bus service from Mombasa to Lamu operated on a thrice-weekly basis, which meant an overnight sojourn in one of the hottest and least endearing cities on earth. It also threw me straight into the arms, figuratively speaking, of Mrs. Charlene Bozeman. I was dawdling through an outdated illustrated weekly after dinner at the Belgrave Arms, sipping a cup of coffee redolent of ether, when the night clerk of the hotel, a natty young Goan, sidled up to me. Did I know there was a fellow countrywoman of mine here whom I had known years before, a charming person who had recognized me and longed to renew our acquaintance? Shyness had prevented her from introducing herself—

"But what nonsense, my dear sir!" I exclaimed, jumping up. "I'm the most approachable of men! Your description of the lady tallies exactly with that of Jetta Goudal or Toby Wing.

Please tell her that I'd be enchanted to have her join me for an inexpensive cordial.''

Mrs. Bozeman had obviously been lurking behind the palms, scrutinizing my reaction, because she came hurtling out of the lobby before I could even blot the coffee from my tie. The instant I saw her, I realized, too late, that the Goan had led me into a quicksand. She was a stout, kittenish woman in the late fifties with formidable dewlaps and bleached hair—one of those unmistakably affluent types before whose letters of credit bank managers kowtow like Buddhists.

''I know you'll never forgive my boldness,'' she cooed, subsiding in a flurry of bracelets, ''but I just had to speak to you. We met during the war, in Pittsburgh. You were there on a bond drive for the Treasury Department, and you sat near me on the dais at our women's luncheon. How's Max Factor?''

''I beg your pardon?'' I said, bewildered. Though I dimly recalled the ordeal she alluded to, I couldn't remember any cosmetic expert in our troupe.

''No, no, that wasn't his name,'' she corrected herself. ''Bromfield—Morris Bromfield. The one who wrote *The Yearling.*''

''Why, fine, I guess,'' I said, deciding it was futile to puncture her fantasies. ''I haven't seen—''

''Of all places to meet again, Mombasa,'' she pursued. ''You don't live here now, do you?'' I explained I was in transit to Lamu, and, urged on by her rapt interest, incautiously expatiated on its beauty, heightening with a few touches of my own what I had overheard and read. She thought it sounded fascinating. ''That's just the sort of thing I've been looking for in Africa!'' she exclaimed. ''Off the tourist track—unspoiled. Do you know, I've half a mind to go along with you?''

''Yes, it's too bad you can't,'' I said hurriedly. ''However, the bus takes at least nine hours, and it's really primitive. Besides, on those tricky roads there's no guarantee it'll get through.''

''Then why don't we fly up?'' she suggested brightly. ''With two of us sharing expenses, the plane shouldn't cost very much. Look, let's ask at the desk—they're terribly helpful here.''

To handle a woman with a bee in her bonnet requires an apiarist far more nimble than I, and within a few minutes, dazed and shorn of initiative, I was submitting to a *fait accompli*. All the arrangements had been effected in a trice. A Piper Cub would whisk us up the coast the following morning, remain the night, and return to Mombasa the next day. In vain I protested against such a lightning schedule, pleaded with Mrs. Bozeman that we would get only the most cursory glimpse of Lamu. She kept begging me to understand, in the maddening tone one adopts with a child, that our pilot had some crop-dusting to finish and couldn't absent himself any longer. My selfish insistence that we dally at Lamu, she implied, was tantamount to plucking the bread from his dependents' mouths. I awoke in the middle of the night racked by turbulent dreams in which I was being engorged by a boa constrictor, and found I had torn down the mosquito net and rolled up in it like a cocoon. A suspicion, as yet nebulous, was forming in my mind that I should have been less trustful with Mrs. Bozeman.

Her behavior on the journey the next day was, by and large, unobjectionable; we were both somewhat numbed by the immensity of the Indian Ocean and the frailty of the aircraft, but Mr. Annixter, the pilot, a clerklike gentleman with bifocals and briefcase, was so mundane that our qualms soon abated. He betrayed no noticeable exhilaration about Lamu; indeed, when I solicited his opinion of it, he dismissed it as a scruffy little place, a remnant of its past glory.

''Dead as a doornail,'' he pronounced. ''Just a typical old Arab village with crooked streets, too many flies, and a handful of Europeans—remittance men, mostly.''

''How marvelous,'' said Mrs. Bozeman. ''The very opposite of Pittsburgh. That's what I came to this country to escape— progress. And believe it or not, all I've found here is resorts. Swimming pools and barbecues—people dressing for dinner.''

"You don't have to worry about that at Lamu," Annixter grunted. "Wait till you see the hotel. Four rooms and precious little plumbing. Hardly the sort of thing Americans are used to, I daresay."

"He doesn't seem to understand we're a pioneer people, does he?" Mrs. Bozeman remarked with amused tolerance, and went on to describe how, as a girl, she had rendered maple sugar, or it may have been chicken fat, in sub-zero temperatures on her grandfather's farm in Ohio. Too polite to dispute the word of a frontierswoman, Annixter shrugged and abandoned the topic.

About an hour after we had passed Malindi, the only settlement of consequence in the two-hundred-mile stretch of wilderness, a sprinkle of islands came into view, the largest of which, it developed, was Lamu. In the glimpse I caught of the town as we circled over it, it looked pretty ruinous, and my forebodings multiplied in the launch that bore the three of us from the mainland to the island itself. Apart from the exotic touch supplied by the half-dozen dhows in the harbor, the port and the moldering buildings that fringed the quay resembled a seedy Mediterranean fishing village. Amid stupefying heat, a reception committee of four pariah dogs watched us disembark at the jetty and escorted us along the sea front to a ramshackle two-story structure identified on its peeling façade as the Hotel Balmoral. Mrs. Bozeman, whose mood had grown visibly less ebullient, stared at the place in dismay.

"You're not serious?" she demanded of Annixter. "You mean this is where we're going to *stay?*"

"Not exactly Claridge's, is it?" he replied pleasantly. "We're probably the first patrons they've had in years. However, it'll do for the night, and you'll enjoy old MacMurdo, the proprietor. One of the great characters of East Africa—I hope he's still functioning."

His wish was granted; Mr. MacMurdo was very much in evidence, a garrulous octogenarian who, somewhere in his remote career as a white hunter, had been gored by a rogue elephant and survived to tell the tale. He was telling it to a couple of other gaffers—the remittance men, presumably—in the combined lobby and bar, and it was an aeon before we managed to communicate our desire for shelter. The old gentleman inexplicably got it into his head that Mrs. Bozeman and I were married, a complication that took hours to unravel, but eventually the three of us were staked out in a series of dusty cubicles separated by wallboard partitions and equipped with china washbowls. I made the sketchiest of ablutions, descended to the bar, and tried without conspicuous success to glean some information from our host about Lamu's notable past or personalities.

"Rider Haggard's brother?" he ruminated. "Bless you, lad, his house has been dust these thirty years. The foundation's next to the wireless antenna, if that's of any use to you."

"Is there a bazaar, or a mosque, or any historic site one can visit?"

"Well," he said guardedly, "in another six weeks they'll be loading mangrove poles for shipment to the Persian Gulf, but right now it's a bit slow. . . . Will your wife be joining you for tiffin? I'm afraid we've only one portion of tinned pilchard."

I decided to let Mrs. Bozeman work out her own salvation, and struck off through the network of alleys behind the hotel toward the center of town. Annixter's somber vignette proved accurate; the population, Arab interspersed with an occasional Indian shopkeeper or African, looked rachitic and verminous, and whatever putative glamour had invested Lamu had clearly long since vanished. The only noteworthy souvenir of its past still visible was a species of doorway characterized by carved flower patterns of considerable invention, but, having already seen these in Zanzibar, I was able to retain my equanimity. Within half an hour, I had traversed the principal streets, acquired enough trinkets to prove to skeptics back home that I had gained my objective, and was making for the Balmoral with sand in my psyche. The prospect of chewing the fat until bedtime with Mrs. Bozeman so unnerved me that I began considering desperate measures. I confected a heart-rending saga about an appendicitis seizure in the market place that required my instant return to Mombasa, embroidered it with dark hints that if we were to hesitate even momentarily, I might not survive the trip. . . . And then occurred one of those providential intercessions that scenarios and converts are made of. Just as I gained the portico of the hotel, I heard shouts in the distance. Turning, I beheld my companions pursuing me, their faces scarlet with exhaustion.

"Damnation, man, where have you been?" Annixter panted. "We've combed every inch of this bloody hole for you! Good show you popped up now or we'd have taken off for Mombasa without you."

I instinctively knew that if one was dealt a handful of trumps, it was obligatory to play them. I bathed Mrs. Bozeman in a look of the most profound disillusionment. "So that's how you treat your war buddies, is it?" I demanded bitterly. "First you whip-saw me into staying here only one night, and then, after scarcely two hours—"

"I know, I know." She cut me short, oozing contrition. "I feel simply vile dragging you away like this, and I wouldn't blame you if you never spoke to me again. Would you be offended if I paid the cost of the charter, since the plane was my idea?"

"Well, it goes against the grain, but if you insist, I suppose there's no way I can prevent you," I said, with a philosophic shrug. "O.K., I'll go upstairs and pack."

"You don't *have* to come with us, you know," Annixter put in, qualifying for the title of most hateful man of his generation. "You'd have time for plenty of sight-seeing here if you took the bus down day after tomorrow."

"Sorry," I said with dignity. "I accepted the responsibility of escorting this lady, and we Americans don't go back on our word. I'll see you here in five minutes."

"There, didn't I tell you he was a wonderful person?" I heard Mrs. Bozeman say to Annixter as I departed. I didn't catch his reply. Some kind of monosyllable, inaudible even to the pariah dogs lounging around the door.

I thought I'd seen the last of my Pittsburgh dreamboat when we bade each other adieu in Mombasa that evening, but we had one final encounter afterward, though she was unaware of it. Some three weeks later, dining with friends at the New Stanley grill in Nairobi, I saw her enter, ablaze with diamonds and leaning on the arm of a young guardsman whose mustaches would have transfixed Ouida. The pair had manifestly been consorting with the grape, for their eyes were glassy and they showed a tendency to upset chafing dishes. I froze as she wove unsteadily in my direction, convinced that a noisy reunion was imminent, but she betrayed no sign of recognition and reeled past.

"Hmm. Looks as if young Harringay's managed to feather his nest again," commented one of the party. "Who is she? Some wealthy tripper, I imagine."

"She'd damn well better be," said another. "By the time he finishes with 'em, they're lucky to have a passport left. Remember the Greek sweetmeat he picked up in Pretoria?"

"Come off it, you chaps. Our friend here isn't interested in local scandal," a fourth broke in, turning to me. "You'd just mentioned Lamu, I believe. Did you ever succeed in getting there?"

"Er—no," I said lamely. "Why, is it worth the trouble?"

He laughed pityingly. "My dear boy, it's the eighth wonder of the world," he said. "Mark you, I haven't been there myself, but I know people who have. Listen."

I listened. I must say he made it sound idyllic.

VII

The Importance
of Healing Ernest

PEOPLE who happen to know that I'm a onetime premedical student (Brown University, 1925) frequently buttonhole me and ask, "In your career as a onetime premedical student at Brown University, 1925, what subsequent achievement has given you the greatest satisfaction?" (People who don't happen to know it, of course, just stand there tongue-tied, plucking at my buttonhole.) Well, take one thing with another, I'd say that my outstanding case professionally was the therapy I prescribed several winters ago for Ernest Hemingway after his dramatic plane crash in Africa. I don't want to sound chesty, but I think I was largely instrumental in delaying Hemingway's recovery by at least three weeks. Only a man of my stature, medically, and his, physically, could have survived the convalescence I helped him through. But I'll tell you this, cousin—it wasn't any picnic. It took a lot out of both of us.

The first inkling I received of Hemingway's aerial *dégringolade* was on a February morning in Nairobi, as I stood outside a tailor's shop in Hardinge Street trying on a broad-brimmed slouch hat. I was about to leave on my first safari into the bush and naturally wanted to look as sharp as possible, even though my audience would be mainly zebras and nomads afflicted with pellagra. The only decent mirror in the establishment happened to be in an outside foyer, and I was posturing there, with one foot raised as if it were resting on a slain buffalo, when I heard a surprised exclamation. Wheeling with a guilty start, I beheld Gerald Suppositorsky, the local Reuter's correspondent, who was hastening by. He stared at me dumfounded.

"Great Scott!" he ejaculated. "Who are you impersonating —Allen Quatermain?" I reassured him, asked where he was hurrying, and was given a preview of the news that was to agitate the world later that day. A report had been phoned in from Butiaba, in northeastern Uganda, that the Hemingways and their pilot had just cracked up over Murchison Falls. "Rotten show," he panted. "The grotesque part is, they've vanished into the weeds. Every game ranger around Lake Albert's been pressed into service. See you later—I've got to get through to London."

Well, you recall the ensuing drama: the night the party spent in the open, hurling rocks at marauding elephants, the second crash of the rescue plane, u.s.w. I was out of town the next ten days, confirming the existence of a bird named Montague's harrier, and, on my return, learned that Hemingway was recuperating at the very same hotel—right down the corridor, in fact. It struck me that as a former premedical student (Brown University, 1925) I was ethically bound to put what knowledge I had at his disposal. What if I *had* taken only half the Hippocratic oath, so to speak? I might be able to contribute some granule of misinformation that would crucially affect the struggle my colleague was waging for his life. The chit I sent around to him drew an immediate and hospitable reply. I betook myself to his room and found Hemingway, in a mouse-colored bathrobe, propped up in a Morris chair by the window. The portion of his face unobscured by white undergrowth was ruddy, as were the eyes behind their steel-rimmed spectacles. A drift of newspaper clippings overflowed his lap and swirled about the floor.

"How are you, son?" he said cordially. "Kick that Mannlicher off the chair there and sit down. You don't have to worry —it's loaded."

"Fine," I said, complying. "Well, Papa, you foxed 'em again, didn't you?"

"Yes," he said. "My luck, she is still running good. Look, what do you say we drop this patty-cake type of dialogue and talk like people?" I assented gratefully and asked him how he felt. "Touched and uplifted," he confessed. "The way Tom Sawyer did in the organ loft when he heard his own funeral sermon. I've just been reading my obits. They're superb—I'll never be able to live up to them."

"Where are they from mostly?"

"All over," he said. "The German papers are best. Here's one from Hamburg that's a bijou. According to them, I'd always been in love with death, so Mary and I chartered a flying swan boat and did a Wagnerian farewell dive into the crater of Kilimanjaro. It's real schmaltzy."

I was neglecting my professional duty and I hastened to discharge it. "Now, what's the medical picture?" I asked crisply. "Pulse and respiration O.K.? How's your appetite? Anything special troubling you?"

"No, I feel all right, considering," he replied. "I've got a double concussion and a ruptured kidney, and my liver has stopped functioning, but otherwise I seem to be in pretty fair shape."

"Don't be too sanguine," I warned. "You've probably sustained half a dozen lesions you wouldn't detect, the kind that show up gradually. We'd better auscultate your chest to be on the safe side." He refused flatly—still a bit agitated from his shakeup, no doubt—and I forbore. Overzealousness, my preceptors had taught me, ofttimes does more harm than good to a patient. "Eat plenty of greens," I instructed him before leaving. "I'll bring along some rhubarb and soda my next visit. That's good for your particular condition. It contains rhubarb."

"Right, and while you're at it, bring along some Campari," he said. "Drop in any time—the door's always there. We get a rather nice cocktail crowd."

I looked in frequently from then on, and, to be candid, I didn't at all like the way things were going. With a layman's obduracy, Hemingway consistently ignored my advice, followed his own regimen, and grew stronger day by day. He unquestionably would have recovered too soon—and thereby laid himself open to the relapse I feared—had it not been for a fortuitous encounter that weekend. I was settling down to my midday gimlet in the hotel lounge when Rootes-Muspratt of the tourist association descended on me. He was shepherding a hypertensed redhead in a bush jacket, with a passable figure and an equine smile, whom he introduced as a compatriot of mine, a Miss Birdie Wickwire of Milwaukee.

"Miss Wickwire's the young lady who was interviewed in yesterday's *Standard*," he said after they had ensconced themselves. "She's going to climb Kilimanjaro later this month."

"Yes, and bring back the leopard," she amplified. "You know, the one Ernest Hemingway wrote about."

"Ah?" I said. "Is that still up there?"

"Oh, yes," she said without hesitation. "Of course, it's been covered by snow through the years, but I know just where to dig. I got all that information back in New York." I asked from whom and was given a saga of research that outdid any of Schliemann's, involving a clerk at Brentano's, the Scribner publicity staff, and James Ramsay Ullman's doorman. "I expect to take photos up there for the magazines at home," she revealed. "Which one pays the best?"

"Well, it depends on what you wear, but I'd say your best bet is a picture periodical called *Frisson*," I said. "They specialize in daring—mostly indoor stuff, but it's worth a try. Are you going it alone?"

"No, I'm taking two porters," she said. "To help carry the leopard. Tell me, is it true Mr. Hemingway's right here in this hotel?"

It was idle to deny what everyone from Benghazi to Bloemfontein knew, so I didn't bother to. Nimbly seizing the cat's-paw that had fallen into her hand, Miss Wickwire at once fell to work on me. Would I present her to her dream prince, the inspiration of her project, the man on whose prose style her own had been molded, that Natty Bumppo incarnate, that sequoia of the literary forest—I halted her this side of tears and said I would cheerfully oblige if Hemingway approved. Leaving Rootes-Muspratt to sponge her down and pick up the tab, I retired into a booth and called the master.

"Um-m," he said pensively. "Is she pretty? . . . Don't give me that! How pretty? Is she as pretty as Justine Johnstone?"

"For God's sake, man," I protested. "This is Africa. What do you expect?"

"Well, Imogene Wilson, then," he countered. "What's her type? Amazon or one of those Betty Kane, boop-a-doop jobs?"

"Listen, I'm a medical man, not a talent scout."

"Oh, cut out the Pecksniffery," he snapped. "Just answer a simple question. How would you rate her with, say, Madeleine Carroll or Myrna Loy?"

"Go on with whatever you were doing," I said. "I thought you might want to give the kid your blessing, since you sired her expedition, in a way, but if you're busy—"

"O.K., O.K., bring her up," he said resignedly. "Mind you, I'm only agreeing to this because I'm concussed. I don't seem to fight back the way I used to."

Miss Wickwire—or Birdie, as she insisted I call her—was trembling visibly as I ushered her into the audience chamber. Within seconds, though, her tongue thawed out and began whirring like a dental drill. She knew as if it were the Koran everything Mr. Hemingway had written—better than he did himself, she hazarded archly. He had created a gallery of unforgettable characters, she asserted, apologizing for her inability to recall any at the moment. It was his style, however—so simple, compact of short, understandable words—that had enslaved her homage. No wonder he could write an entire novel in a fortnight, as she had been given to believe.

"Oh, you have, have you?" began Hemingway. "Let me—"

Birdie rode over him with thundering hoofs. Naturally, certain of his books weren't as successful as others; everybody had their ups and downs. For instance, the one on Spain. (She was devastated that she had forgotten its name, but she simply couldn't remember titles.) Now, in the movie version of that, Rock Hudson was not at all her conception of the hero, whereas, in the smuggling picture, Humphrey Bogart was altogether credible.

"Look, daughter, I don't pick the actors—" Hemingway managed to interject.

"It's too marvy meeting you here, just as I was organizing my climb!" interrupted Birdie exultantly. "I've got a million questions to ask you about the clothes I'll need, and the equipment, and tips, and all that. Do you think I ought to take a sleeping bag?" She giggled. "I guess if *anybody* should know about sleeping bags . . ."

From our host's expression, reminiscent of Bartholomew Sholto in "The Sign of Four" after his transfixion by the poisoned thorn, I judged our welcome was wearing thin. Admonishing Birdie that we must not overtire the invalid, I gracefully maneuvered her out. There was a soupçon of disappointment in her manner as we made for the lobby.

"He's not very talkative, is he?" she commented. "I visualized him as a more glamorous-type person—I mean, bubbling over. He hardly said boo."

"Well, he has a lot on his mind," I observed profoundly.

"And between you and me, I think his photographs flatter

him," she pursued. "I didn't see those muscles he's always bragging about. Still and all, he *was* wearing a bathrobe. That makes a difference." I agreed that in my experience, it generally did. By the time we parted, happily, her mood had brightened and she was fulsome in her thanks. "It's been a red-letter day," she assured me, and added, with what proved to be uncanny clairvoyance, "You wait and see. You haven't heard the last of this."

I didn't have to wait long. The instant I re-entered Hemingway's room, early that evening, he pounced. "You sneak," he said bitterly. "It's lucky for you I'm chairborne—I ought to skin you alive. As for your taste in girls, all I can say is you grew up on the wrong cigarette pictures. If that strident jade is your idea of beauty—"

"Well, you have to admit she was sincere," I hedged.

"So was Medusa," he said, glowering. "So was Messalina. Do you know what that harpy did after you two left here?" He retrieved a dog-eared manuscript from under his chair and waved it at me. "She sent this—this *schweinerei* over with a note asking for criticism and suggestions. What's more, she graciously offered to let me write a preface for it."

"Hasn't it any merit at all?"

"Yeah—nostalgia," he said. "It reminds you of those themes you used to write in high school called 'The Adventures of a Penny.' Where you described how a kindhearted pedestrian found you in a gutter and spent you in a brothel or someplace. The only difference is, she's coy. She refers to herself as a demi-virgin."

I of course suggested the obvious solution—that he decline with the usual regrets—but Hemingway was in a vindictive frame. As penance for exposing him to Birdie, he announced, I was to return her handiwork in person and squirm out of the imbroglio as best I could. Remonstrance was vain; the man was implacable, and, dispiritedly tucking the manuscript under my arm, I withdrew. Its author, luckily, was nearby, holding court in the bar to a boisterous group of R.A.F. types who implored me to accept a sundowner, but I sequestered her and outlined the position. Writers of Hemingway's eminence, I explained, were chary of reading other people's work lest they be sued for plagiarism. My friend was heartsick that fate should deny him the chance to sponsor a work he instinctively knew was a masterpiece. Nonetheless . . .

"Skip it," said Birdie magnanimously. "That's perfectly all right. I got all the material I needed for the story, anyhow."

"What story?" I asked, my extremities turning to jelly.

"Why, the one in my home-town paper," she returned blandly. "I mailed it off this afternoon. I shouldn't brag, but honestly, it's a whiz. You tell Mr. Hemingway I changed it around a little—I'm sure he won't mind."

"How—how do you mean?" I faltered.

"Oh, nothing really," she said with childlike candor. "I said I was the first white woman to reach his side after the crash, and told how cunning and sweet he was, and the compliments he paid me, and a few touches like that. I kept a carbon to show him."

"N-no," I said. "No, let's not do that right away. No, we mustn't do that . . . Look, would you call that whiskey over there and ask him for a glass of Senegambian? I—I feel a mite dizzy . . ."

It was a strange damn thing; there I was on the same floor as Hemingway the rest of that month, and yet somehow we never got together. I suppose I felt that, therapeutically, I'd done all I could for him and it was better to let Nature take its course. As for Birdie's ascent of Kilimanjaro, she must have struck a snag or two in her preparations—in fact, I know she did. One day, long after it was scheduled to begin, I ran into her at a wild-animal farm up at Rumuruti, beyond Thomson's Falls. She was trying to persuade the dealer, in the interests of publicity, to photograph her astride a cheetah, but it seemed he hadn't the proper insurance. Birdie was disconsolate.

"You can't make any headway with these British goops," she complained to me as we strolled about the grounds. "No imagination or initiative." It was inevitable, I concurred, that the Empire should be falling apart. "Oh, piffle," she said, tossing her head. "I should worry about them—I'm going back to Milwaukee next week. Listen, I don't have a single picture of you. Stand over by that ostrich pen a second."

Waiting bareheaded in the sun for her to adjust the lens— I never wore hats in Africa—I became somewhat dazed, and it was a full minute before I realized Birdie's peril. She was backing away, face down, toward a pit that had been dug for pythons or an artesian well or something of the sort. Before I could cry havoc, she did a reverse half gainer and disappeared in a swirl of Battenberg insertions and Leica equipment. And then I did a most appalling thing. Instead of rushing to the brink, or fainting, or behaving as any normal person would, I tiptoed back to my Land Rover and drove hell-bent for Thomson's Falls. On the way, it occurred to me that I really ought to update Hemingway on the thing sometime—perhaps in a simple high-school comp called "The Last of Birdie Wickwire" —but I never got around to it. He probably could tell *me* a few things. With a world-wide clipping bureau like his, he must have seen the Milwaukee papers.

Baby, I Will Enchant

Thine Ear—Maybe

CALL ME UXORIOUS, spoony, passion's plaything, but let a woman signify her whim by so much as a nod and, by George, I'll climb the highest mountain, swim the deepest ocean to gratify it. While the climbing and swimming this compulsion has entailed would stagger credulity, they're piffling compared to what I underwent recently in Europe to obtain a pair of earrings. Chronologically, the affair began last spring with a trivial observation of my wife's—one of those remarks that drop like a seed into the subconscious and germinate there over an entire summer. Halfway through a novel of David Garnett's she was reading, Madame looked up reflectively. "Remember that garnet brooch of mine?" she asked. "It's back in fashion again. Don't you think I ought to get a pair of earrings to match?" The only response she got was an indulgent chuckle from behind my newspaper, which was rather unaccountable, since I lay dozing a good ten feet away from it. At any rate, six months later I was in London after a protracted stay abroad, faced with the problem of a suitable homecoming gift. The usual pattern of perfume, sweaters, and Liberty squares seemed so deadly that I resolved to vary it, and betook myself to the Caledonian Market, that great repository of antiques, bric-a-brac, and pinchbeck in Bermondsey. For well over an hour, I rummaged through stalls laden with Victorian knickknacks, pewter, china, cutlery, glass, and miscellaneous rubbish of every description from passementerie to doorknobs, erotic nutcrackers to scrimshaw. Somewhere in this magpie's nest, I told myself with decreasing assurance, there must be a keepsake worthy of my spouse. A drophead sewing machine? The woman bought all her clothes from Dior. A sphygmometer? Her pulse never varied a hairbreadth. A wastebasket made from an elephant's foot? She doted on pachyderms, cried unashamedly at Babar. Homeward bound to the West End, I suddenly recollected her wistful reference to the earrings, and raced back to Bermondsey.

"Garnet eardrops, sir?" the dealers echoed as one man. "Shouldn't think you'd find a pair in England. Fearfully rare. Terribly *vieux jeu.* Nobody fancies them nowadays. Bad luck, they say. See them occasionally on a laundress or a skivvy, sir, but ladies won't have 'em. Sorry, old chap. Have you tried Torquay? Bournemouth? Blackpool? Ah, yes, for a costume party, no doubt. Haven't the foggiest, old man. Pawnshop near Ludgate Circus, but I wouldn't promise. For a *young* woman, you said, sir? Sorry, old boy."

Overwhelmed by futility, I was about to abandon the quest when a cherry-nosed beldam in a man's cap and rope-knit sweater came to my rescue. The only place that might conceivably handle such an item, she said, detaching an inch of Woodbine from her lip, was a shop near the British Museum whose stock of Edwardian jewelry was unrivaled. Be it a stomacher or a diamond garter, it could be found at Intaglio's; all the gentry, added my tarnished angel deferentially, traded there. In less time than it takes to leaf through *Burke's Peerage and Baronetage,* I sped to Bloomsbury, found the shop, and communicated my needs to the gentlewoman presiding over it. She gave me the weary smile one reserves for eccentrics, and produced half a dozen trays containing unimaginable splendors. Trinkets of sapphire, emerald, ruby, jade, fire opal, and every semiprecious stone except the garnet coruscated through her fingers, all mounted in settings antedating the Boer War. After doing her utmost to sell me a blue carbuncle choker, a sunburst studded with rose diamonds, and a pearl dog collar worn by the fifth Marchioness of Londonderry, my saleslady threw in the towel. "Personally, I think you're on a wild-goose chase," she declared. "Of course, you can always insert an advert in the agony column of the *Times*. I'm sure if you offered a couple of hundred quid—"

"Wait a minute," I said, realizing that I was in danger of succumbing to an expensive monomania. "Maybe garnets *are* a trifle démodé, at that. What do you have in a good, inexpensive scarab?"

With a click of dentures that graphically expressed her opinion of all tourists, and redskins in particular, she slid a trayful of scarabs toward me. I selected one I felt would blend nicely with any of my wife's blouses, especially those starched in Reckitt's Blue, and bore it away. Almost immediately, a couple of disturbing, seemingly unrelated incidents occurred that made me wonder whether I had unwittingly involved myself in one of Carol Reed's gaudier thrillers. Entering my hotel room about teatime the next day, I surprised a valet half submerged in the closet, ostensibly draping pants on a hanger. In response to my query, he gave me some curious, evasive answer to the effect that he had discovered them on the floor. As he withdrew, I was struck by his sphinxlike smile and the fact that his features had a distinctly Egyptian cast. Could his visit have had an ulterior motive, I asked myself, startled—my scarab, possibly? The tissue it was wrapped in appeared untouched, but I could have sworn the elastic had been tampered with. In the automatic elevator that very same evening, though, I had an encounter the significance of which was unmistakable. The car had hardly started upward when my nostrils detected the characteristic scent of some Oriental perfume like sandalwood. I turned and received a coup d'oeil from a pair of sloe eyes berimmed with kohl. The impact was so abrupt, their air of invitation so unabashed, that it was a moment before I had a chance to discreetly survey the owner. She was a ravishing Eurasian, her lissome figure swathed in sables and her sensuous lips curled in a mocking pout—Sax Rohmer's Kâramanèh to the life. In a trice, I saw through the whole design. Having failed to purloin my scarab, the ring in Cairo had detailed her to lure me to some unsavory grogshop in Wapping Old Stairs with a trapdoor opening conveniently into the Thames. A moment's irresolution and I would be done for, another unsolved file in Scotland Yard. I returned an equally mocking smile to the fair decoy and pressed the emergency button. "Queen's gambit declined, my gazelle," I said grimly, and descended. Her utter bafflement was comical in the extreme.

The precautions I now took to secrete the scarab, unfortunately, were so devious that I ended by losing it altogether, and with my departure imminent, the need for a present was crucial. The annual Kensington Antiques Fair, by a coincidence, was just concluding, and I determined to make a final search there for the earrings. To my immoderate joy, a handsome pair turned up in the second booth I visited—large, shapely garnets backed by silver filigree and a warranty from Mr. Plimsoll, the dealer, that they were at least a hundred years old. Mr. Plimsoll won my heart instantly—a gentle sexagenarian with silver hair and exquisite manners, the sort of elderly curate who populates English plays that fold in two nights. His scrupulousness especially endeared him to me; he insisted on retaining the earrings, even though I had paid for them, so that he could replace a somewhat flawed stone. "Nonsense, my dear fellow," he said, waving aside my protests. "I wouldn't dream of letting your good wife wear these unless they were letter-perfect. Take a day or two to pop in another garnet, but I'll fetch 'em around to your hotel in plenty of time before you leave. Here's my card, and may I say in passing that I consider your countrymen the salt of the earth?''

Well, I couldn't help choking up at that, and we had a pretty emotional parting, wringing each other's hand and so forth, but when four days went by and no Plimsoll, I began to get restive. Since the Kensington Fair had closed meanwhile, I tried phoning him at his place of business, and learned, with agitation, that no such number existed. After a nightmare bus journey involving three changes, I at length reached the address in Peckham Rye, the suburb of outer London where the shop was supposedly located. Nobody, needless to say, had ever heard of my antiquary. En route back to the hotel through endless mean streets, I consigned Plimsoll to the seventh ring of purgatory and, with a pinch or two of sophistry, effectively settled my gift problem. After all, it wasn't really the gift so much as the spirit, et cetera— and besides, my wife had probably forgotten the earrings long since. Ultimately, at my own convenience, I'd buy her an ounce of perfume, a sweater, and a Liberty square, and *Schluss*. If they were good enough for her grandmother, they were good enough for her. And anyhow, why were women so importunate nowadays? I became so worked up by the time we got to Marble Arch that I very nearly decided to bring her nothing at all.

I almost did, thanks to my precious Mr. Plimsoll. Late that afternoon, as I was strolling along Shaftesbury Avenue, I saw him jauntily cross the zebra swinging a dispatch case, sanctimonious as damn all with his silver locks fluttering in the wind. I shouted after him to stop. He threw me a frightened glance and took off in the direction of Great Windmill Street. For a man of his years, he showed amazing stamina, and I was well-nigh beat when he abruptly ducked into the Nosh Bar, a delicatessen close by. I pounded in after him, naturally, creating quite a tableau among the patrons munching their salt-beef sandwiches and drinking lemon tea, but do you know, he'd vanished without a trace. I was certain he must have slipped out the rear entrance, until the proprietor finally managed to satisfy me that he hadn't any. Maybe there was a trapdoor or something, like those in the grogshops at Wapping Old Stairs; I still can't figure out where the old bleeder went.

But that wasn't the last of him by a long chalk, and it fair makes me break into a muck sweat to think of what ensued. Two nights later, alighting from a cab in front of a music hall in Hammersmith, I spotted Plimsoll, bold as brass, lounging by the stage door with a cigar in his teeth. (At least, I think it was Plimsoll; if not, it was his twin brother.) Anyway, he caught sight of me simultaneously, and whipped like a rabbit into a passage alongside the theater. I gave chase, and, hot on his heels, found myself on a steep incline. It must have led into some sort of basement under the stage or thereabouts, because I glimpsed a costume rack and a lot of electrical gear in transit, but I was too distracted hunting for Plimsoll to pay much heed. Suddenly I heard a voice yell, "Hey, there, mate, don't tread on that!" and, glancing down, saw that I had stepped on a small wooden platform almost flush with the floor. Whatever took place in the next few seconds happened so swiftly that I can still hardly credit it. With a sickening lurch, the platform shot upward, carrying me with it, and as I cowered to protect my head I heard a deafening fanfare, climaxing in a crash of cymbals. For a moment, I was too dazzled by the flood of candlepower illuminating me to distinguish anything; then I made out a row of footlights dead ahead, and beyond it an infinity of grinning faces, tier on tier. Overcome at the realization that I had been elevated to stardom, I turned to flee, and felt a sinewy hand grip my arm. A tall, suave individual in evening clothes, his Mephistophelean eyebrows heightened by makeup, was bathing me in a smile not altogether devoid of menace. "Steady on, my beauty," he purred. "Just relax and let Scarpini the Great waft you into the Elysian fields."

"I don't want to be wafted," I squeaked, crimson with embarrassment. "Look, Mister, there's some mistake—I'm not in show biz—"

"Neither am I," he said glibly. "This is merely a little scientific experiment to demonstrate the power of mind over matter. Just stretch out on the table here and keep your eye on the shiny object in my hand."

"I won't, I tell you!" I panted, backing away.

"Oh, yes, you will," he said, with a catlike smile. "Now, down you go, you willful boy, and lie still. You're sleepy . . . you're getting sleepier . . ."

To retain your composure under stress is tough enough, but when you're forcibly levitated into the horizontal and a spiv in a rented dress suit starts passing hoops around you, you can't very well behave like Lord Louis Mountbatten. The orchestral din was such, furthermore, and the applause so shattering, that my pleas to Scarpini to lower me, to release the mechanism or whatever the hell was holding me, went unheard. Eventually—I wouldn't know how—I made my escape into the wings, and, limp as a rag, crept to the nearest cab rank. Speaking as a man who'd practically relived "The 39 Steps," the balance of my London sojourn was pretty humdrum. I spent the whole time in bed, except for a quick trip to the Burlington Arcade, where I bought Milady a nice woolen steamer shawl five feet long. It's the kind of fleece you won't get anywhere else in Britain—unless you run into Plimsoll, that is. If you do, tell him I'll catch up with him yet.

Oh, I Am a Cook

and a Houseboy Bland

In town for the Random House publication of her latest and finest thriller, *A Stranger in My Grave*, Margaret Millar (Mrs. Kenneth Millar) and mystery writer Ross MacDonald (Mr. Kenneth Millar) pondered the menu at the Four Seasons. . . . But you don't talk to this top-flight pair of mystery writers about food. How do they work—together or apart?

SHE: We live in a split level house, one part is his and the other part is mine.

HE: We occasionally meet on the stairs.

SHE: I'm a morning person, he's an afternoon person.

HE: Margaret starts at a quarter to nine, on a good day I start at 11, on a bad day about one. We each write for about three or four hours. I'm very fast, she is slow, but I rewrite more. . . . We both write about a book a year. If you try to do more than that you go over into hack writing.—*Martha MacGregor in the* Post.

MRS. YOUNGHUSBAND had told me to come back to her employment agency on Thursday, so that morning I got dressed up real nice in a dark suit and black tie and went around there. Santa

Barbara people are conservative—not like in L.A., where everybody wears rhinestones on their glasses to show they own an airplane factory. These retired old bankers with a face like an exploded eggplant you see up here standing around a supermart in knickers pinching grapefruit have so much money they can afford to look stingy, but they're plenty particular about their domestic help. One thing they won't tolerate is a jazz baby, a showoff with a loud mouth, and I knew that Mrs. Younghusband could place me if I made a good impression. She was very gracious.

"It's an excellent opportunity, Ngong," she said. She was a tall, skinny lady in two Scotch sweaters, one over the other, and a necklace of cultured pearls, and she must have been proud of her gums, because she smiled a lot. "Mr. and Mrs. Fingerhood were so thrilled at the prospect of getting an—ah—Annamite. Of course, they were a little vague about the geography, which is only natural, since yours is such a large country, isn't it? I mean, Asia and all that. Anyway, they'd just adore an Oriental houseman, and when I mentioned your three years at U.C.L.A. they were overjoyed. I gave them your whole background, that you'd been a messboy on freighters and cooked for several families in this area and Pasadena—"

"I forgot to include Mrs. Kluckholm, in Flintridge," I said. "I worked there two months last summer. She teaches one of the Indian religions—Bahai, I think—at Occidental College."

"Oh, your references were more than ample," she said. "Dr. Catchpole couldn't say enough for you, and the Patinas praised you to the skies. The only person I wasn't able to reach was this yachtsman of yours at Balboa—Mr. Angst. They suggested I call some sanitarium."

"That's his winter home," I said. "He claims a weevil is eating his liver."

"Well, we can forget about *him*, can't we?" she said, flashing her gums at me. I looked at a scar on my knuckle and kept quiet. "But getting back to the Fingerhoods. I made it quite clear the situation was merely temporary, to enable you to continue your schooling. They were perfectly agreeable—three months will be fine. Just what are you studying, Ngong?"

"Hotel management, Ma'am," I said. "There are numerous openings at home for trained personnel in that field. Eventually, I hope to secure a modest executive post at some crossroads like Bangkok or Rangoon."

"But how *splendid!*" she gushed. "Who knows? Maybe one day you'll be the Conrad Hilton of the Far East. You won't snub me when that time comes, will you, Ngong?"

I gave her a real suave smile, pure Charlie Chan. "Nobody ever could, Ma'am," I said. "May I ask what Mr. Fingerhood does?"

"Both he and his spouse are writers," she said. "Experts on the Civil War. They've each done a number of books about it. As a matter of fact"—she rummaged in her folder and brought out a page torn from a newspaper—"here's a note about him in the New York *Times Book Review.* 'Curtis Fingerhood, author of *Bright Magnolia* and *Mosby: Man or Centaur?*, is a frequent observer of the Southern literary scene. His wife, Grace, wrote *Bright Enigma,* the recent re-examination of Jeb Stuart.' "

I always welcome the chance to associate with well-read people, knowing the importance of good English in hotelkeeping, and I hustled right over to Bougainvillaea Drive for the interview. Once I got used to their accent, the Fingerhoods seemed to be nice, substantial folks. He was kind of a pale, fat man, a professor type, with a dry cough and a head shaped like a summer squash. She was older-looking—fifty-eight, I'd say—with quite short blue hair all frizzed up, and wearing these half glasses that you peer over. She did most of the talking, the way generally happens with a couple engaging help, and she laid everything on the line.

"Now, Ngong, you mustn't be surprised at our foibles," she said. "We're writers, and, unlike your previous employers, we're rather unconventional." I could have told her a few things about the peyotl candies Dr. Catchpole used to feed his lady patients, and a book in Mrs. Patina's dresser, but there was no percentage. "Mr. Fingerhood's a mole—he likes to work at night, and I create in the daytime. Since we occupy separate wings of the house, we see each other only at mealtime, and sometimes not even then."

"Do you have any special food preferences, Ma'am?"

"Decidedly," she said. "We both abhor Oriental cookery. We like pork chops with plenty of tomato sauce, salmon croquettes, macaroni timbales, and veal birds. Other than preparing these, and dusting, your only duty is to remain completely unobtrusive. Is that acceptable?"

I bowed.

"Very good. Then my husband will show you your quarters."

Well, the job certainly turned out to be a snap after I learned the ropes. The housework was easy, there was no company, and nobody ever came snooping around the kitchen to check the grocery accounts. They mostly ate from a tray in their rooms, and if they ran into each other at the table they'd prop up a paper or a book. As far as I was concerned, they were very considerate. I had the use of their car on my days off, and hardly a week passed without some present like ties, or a new wallet, or a pocket transistor radio. They also tried hard to fraternize, always pumping me about conditions in what they called my "homeland," though they couldn't decide if I was a Siamese, a Mongol, or a Filipino.

"Wouldn't you like some incense for your room?" Mrs. Fingerhood said to me one time. "Do tell me which kind—I never can distinguish between those strange religions you have out there."

To get rid of her, I said I was a follower of Mme. Blavatsky, which was a name I used to hear around Mrs. Kluckholm's, and she dropped the subject. The peculiar part about the two of them, though, was how they avoided speaking. A husband and wife under one roof, in the same profession—you'd think they'd have a lot in common. Well, pretty soon I found out that that was just the trouble. They were jealous. Not teasing or needling each other, like these Hollywood movie couples you see on "Person to Person," but burning up with hatred. He was a Civil War authority, and she was a Civil War authority, and they couldn't stand the idea that somebody might confuse them. Every Tuesday, when the mailman delivered the New York *Times,* he would rush down and hunt through the book section to see who was the more frequent observer of the Southern literary scene. If it was he, he'd clip out the item and leave it under the sugar bowl; if it was she, he stuffed the whole paper in the incinerator. She was more sneaky. Twice, while he was off at the barber's or getting diathermy, I caught her looking in his desk. She made believe she was hunting for carbon paper, but I knew from the way her eyes glittered that she was spying on him. The other thing I discovered about them was that they were secret lushes. The bottom of his filing cabinet was full of sweet cordials and liqueurs like Chartreuse and *crème de cacao* that he nipped away at all night long. She was a belter; she used to knock back straight shots of bourbon from two bottles, Old Busthead and Old Starlight, she kept hidden in a fake encyclopedia. So between them they were both half gassed twenty-four hours of the day.

Well, around six weeks from the time I went with them the fireworks started. Early one Wednesday afternoon, I was preparing some cold halibut squares with hard sauce from a recipe that Mrs. Fingerhood had found in *The Botulist's Cookbook* when the doorbell rang. A kind of owlish gentleman in glasses, with a pipe cemented into his face, was bouncing there on the patio. He looked like he was selling brooms, and we didn't need any.

"I'm Emmett Stagg, Mrs. Fingerhood's publisher," he said. He was so breezy that my nose began to tickle. "I'm on my semi-annual lecture tour of the West Coast, playing to packed houses everywhere, and thought I'd stop in."

"She's speaking at a women's club luncheon in Del Monte, sir," I said. "She's not expected back until six."

"Oh, drat," he said. "Well, I can't wait. Lenny Bruce and

eighteen of America's foremost sick comics are throwing me a—
ha, ha—Stagg dinner at Hillcrest. Just say that I—''

"Why, hello, Emmett!" I heard Mr. Fingerhood squeak. He
was standing right behind me in bathrobe and slippers, purring
like a cat. You could smell the Benedictine off him a mile away.
"Come to inquire about my new biography of Beauregard, have
you?"

"Er—no, not exactly," said Mr. Stagg, clearing his throat,
grinning, and puffing at the same time. "Of course, I knew you
and Grace were both working on one—"

"Ah, but hers is barely outlined!" my boss said quickly.
"Mine's practically complete, all but the index." He grabbed
hold of Mr. Stagg and pulled him inside. "This is next season's
Book of the Month, Emmett, old boy! I've had access to letters
Grace never saw. They'll revolutionize your whole thinking about
Beauregard!"

"Ye-es, it's about time his role in the Confederacy was re-
examined to conform with Otto Eisenschiml's theory," admitted
Mr. Stagg, following him. "I read something recently in the
Times Book Review—"

"I wrote that!" cried Mr. Fingerhood. "I'm the most frequent
observer of the Southern literary scene there is, Emmett, and
I tell you, my new synthesis'll stand Orville Prescott on his
head!"

"You think there may be a movie in it?" Mr. Stagg asked
eagerly, and then a door closed, so I couldn't catch the rest. By
the time I finished peeling the apricots for the salad, I figured
myself into the clear. If I told Mrs. Fingerhood her publisher had
been there, she might contact him and find that old Curtis had
sabotaged her. They wanted a good, impassive Oriental, did they?
O.K., from here in Angkor Wat would be noisy compared to me.
Pretty soon, the two came out in the hall, whooping and punching
each other. Mr. Stagg had a manuscript under his arm, and he
was going to phone his reaction from L.A. the minute he'd read
it. A little while later, Mr. Fingerhood showed up in the kitchen

with a check for fifty dollars—a small token, he said, of his gratitude for my loyalty and discretion. He didn't have to stick arrows on it. Anyone who's put into Hong Kong as often as I have knows the meaning of cumshaw.

It must have been three days afterward—a Saturday, because Mrs. Fingerhood had gone for a permanent—that Mr. Stagg called. He was terribly excited. His pipe kept knocking against the phone like a woodpecker, and he insisted I should wake up Mr. Fingerhood right away. I tried to, but he didn't budge; I could hear him snoring through the door, sleeping off the Curaçao.

"Never mind, never mind!" Mr. Stagg hollered when I returned. "Simply write down this message. First, I've just sold the screen rights of *Bright Scabbard: The Beauregard Enigma* to Jerry Lewis. Second, either *Ladies' Home Journal* or *McCall's* will serialize it next September, depending on whose circulation is larger that month. Finally, Pellagra & Wormser, the biggest chain store in Richmond, is absorbing two hundred thousand copies—or maybe two hundred copies; I don't have the figures with me—as a giveaway. Got all that? . . . Good—tell him I'll be in touch!"

It took me an extra few seconds, being in a hurry, to get the whole message straight and clear enough for Mr. Fingerhood to read, but I did. I was shoving it under his door when all of a sudden his wife's convertible rolled into the driveway. Oh-oh, I thought, that was a close shave—a good thing she hadn't come back five minutes sooner. And then, Brother, I froze in my tracks, remembering the notes I'd made on the phone pad while Mr. Stagg was talking. They were on the kitchen table, and she always came in the back way to pick up her calls.

The skipper of the *Steel Philanderer* gave me a piece of advice along with my first job in her galley. "Don't think big, Ngong," he said. "Think cool." I made up my mind not to panic, no matter what. I walked back to the pantry, rattled a couple of plates as if I was Mr. Clean himself, and took a swift look. There she was by the table, all right, with the pad in her hand. But she was foxy—I couldn't tell from her tone of voice how she felt.

"Who called Mr. Fingerhood this morning, Ngong?" she said, very sweet and quiet. "It wouldn't have been a Mr. Stagg, would it?"

I nodded. After all, why should I perjure myself for fifty bucks?

"And did he say where he was?"

"Yes, Ma'am. In Hollywood, I believe." That got me off the hook.

"So I thought from the context," she said dreamily. Boy, was I smart to skip any bobbery. "Well, well, fancy that. . . . By the way, you can have the rest of the day to yourself, if you like. We shan't be needing you."

"I haven't brought Mr. Fingerhood his tray yet—"

"Oh, pish-tush, I'll take care of that!" she said. Her eyes had got all sparkly and gay, like a little girl's. "It's so long since I served him breakfast that it'll be an adventure. Where do you keep the tea?"

I showed her, and after changing my clothes took the bus into town. I guess that's maybe the luckiest thing I ever did. If I'd driven back in her car that night, the cops and the coroner would have put me through the mangle. As it was, the whole thing was plenty rough: the questions, and the inquest, and the stuff in the papers about whether a Civil War bayonet could fall off a wall by itself. But, as Mr. Angst used to say when he was throwing those girls' sweaters overboard, all's well that ends wool. Mrs. Fingerhood not only got off but married Mr. Stagg, the movie won an Oscar, and here I am, assistant manager of the Santa Ponderosa, with a Ph.D. in Southern literature after my name. The Lord Buddha sure was cooking when he advised me to transcribe those notes of theirs on Beauregard.

Impresario

on the Lam

THE VOICE that came over the wire last Thursday was full of gravel and Hollywood subjunctives. It was a voice trained to cut through the din of night clubs and theater rehearsals, a flexible instrument that could shift from adulation to abuse in a syllable, ingratiating yet peremptory, a rich syrup of unction and specious authority. "Listen, Clyde, you don't know me from a hole in the ground," it began with deadly accuracy, "but I'm the agent for a friend of yours, Morris Flesh." Before I could disavow ever having heard of Flesh, his representative had washed his hands of him and was scuttling down the fairway. "I've got a client deeply interested in putting on a revue," he confided. "A smart, intimate show that kids the passing scene, the various fads and foibles like television and mah-jongg and psychoanalysis—dig me? Morris recommends you to pen the sketches, and while I personally would rather have a name, I'm willing to gamble on his opinion. Now, here's the score, Pops. My backer is strictly from Dixie, a peasant from the tall rhubarbs. I'm running the creative side and this is what I have in mind." I laid the receiver gently on the desk and went out to lunch. When I returned two hours later, the monologue was purling on as inexorably as the Blue Nile. "This girl composer has got Vassar in an uproar, baby," the voice was affirming. "She's the hottest thing that ever hit Poughkeepsie—another Cole Porter, only younger. Sophisticated but simple at the same time." I hung up, and dialing the business office, vanished into the limbo of unlisted telephone subscribers.

Though not constitutionally averse to the crackle of greenbacks, I learned many years ago—twenty-eight, in fact—that of all the roads to insolvency open to my profession, entanglement in a revue is the shortest. Every revue since *The Garrick Gaieties* has been hatched from the same larva, an impassioned declaration by some seer flushed with Martinis that what Broadway needs this season is a smart, intimate show like *The Garrick Gaieties*. In 1932, Poultney Kerr, a onetime yacht broker riding out the depression on a cask of brandy, said it with such persistence that a group of idealists gave him a hundred thousand dollars to demonstrate, and he did so with a *cauchemar* called *Sherry Flip*. Kerr's qualifications as a producer, apart from a honeyed tongue, were minimal. His executive ability was pitiful, his judgment paltry, and his equilibrium unstable in crisis. He did, nevertheless, look the big wheel—a corpulent, natty man given to Homburg hats and carnations in the buttonhole, with the classic empurpled nose of the *bon vivant* and a talent for imbibing oceans of Courvoisier without crumpling. I met him at a low ebb in my fortunes and left him at a lower. In between, I got so concentrated a dose of hysteria and wormwood that I still quail at the mention of sherry.

At a moment when my wallet was at its flabbiest, the project started in the classic tradition with an urgent phone call from Lytton Swazey, a lyric writer I had known casually around the doughnut shop in Times Square we both frequented. Could I, he asked, confer with him and his composer that afternoon at

Kerr's apartment about an upcoming revue patterned after *The Garrick Gaieties?* I blacked my shoes in a flash and pelted over. The portents seemed dazzling. Swazey, after years of grinding out special material for willowy chanteuses in cocktail bars, had recently teamed up with a Russian composer named Herman Earl. Together they had confected a valiseful of show tunes, and it was on these, plus the half-dozen sketches I would supply, that *Sherry Flip* was to be based.

It may have been wishful thinking that warped my perspective, or a greenhorn's superstitious awe of song writers as demigods, but Swazey had hardly bawled out a couple of ballads before I put down my glass and emotionally announced, "Gentlemen, count me in." Needless to say, our sponsor was not outraged by my quick assent. He plied me with flattery and cognac, hailed me as a theatrical sibyl rivaling Daniel Frohman. The few tentative ideas for sketches I broached evoked paroxysms of laughter. "I don't want to put a jinx on it, boys," exulted Kerr, wrenching the cork from a fresh bottle of Hennessey, "but I think we've got a hit." What with all the self-congratulation and the mirage of fat royalties he conjured up, I agreed to terms that even a Mexican migrant worker would have flouted, and bowled off straightaway to Bachrach to be photographed. I figured I might not have the leisure to sit for him later when I became the toast of Broadway.

Lodged in an airless cubicle in Kerr's offices, I spent the next five weeks chewing licorice fortified with Benzedrine and evolving skits, emerging only to replenish myself with corned-beef sandwiches. *Sherry Flip*, meanwhile, was subtly changing from a collection of grandiose phrases into a living organism. A director, scenic designer, and choreographer materialized; the anteroom boiled with singers and dancers, tumblers and ventriloquists, sister acts and precocious children. Kerr himself preserved a state of Olympian detachment for the most part, huddling with lawyers in his sanctum. There were disquieting whispers that our finances were shaky, but as rehearsal day neared, he secured additional pledges, sounds of wassail again rang through the corridors, and we began work on a note of the most buoyant optimism.

Rehearsals went swimmingly the first fortnight. Not a speck of artistic temperament marked the cast; everyone was bewitched by the vivacity of the score and the brilliance of the sketches. Manners were impeccable, the atmosphere as sunny as a Monet picnic. Then, abruptly, the lid blew off. Halfway through her big solo one afternoon, our prima donna developed an acute attack of paranoia. Derogating the number as an inept Russian plagiarism of "Rio Rita," she declared that she would never sully her reputation by singing it in public. The composer, justifiably stung to fury, flew into a storm of picturesque Muscovite cuss-words. He offered to punch her nose—which, he added parenthetically, was bobbed—and threatened to bring her up before Equity on charges. The director patched up a shaky truce, but the incident had abraded the company's nerves and opened the door to further insubordination. Mysterious excrescences began to appear on the material I had furnished the actors. A diplomatic travesty of mine suddenly blossomed out with a routine in which, using a wallet stuffed with toilet paper, our top banana flimflammed a Polish butcher from Scranton. When I complained, I was told that it had scored a triumph on every burlesque wheel in America. If it offended Percy Bysshe Shelley—as he jocosely referred to me—I could return to writing for the little magazines. The barometer, in short, was falling, there were mutterings in the fo'c'sl, and one didn't have to be Ziegfeld to prophesy that *Sherry Flip* was in for many a squall before it reached port.

By the week prior to the Boston tryout, stilettos were flashing in earnest and the company buzzed like a hive of bees. The comedians, made overweening by victory, had woven a crazy quilt of drolleries and *double-entendres* that made the brain reel. They impersonated androgynes and humorous tramps, thwacked the showgirls' bottoms with rolled-up newspapers, and squirted water from their boutonnieres. Their improvisations totally unnerved Wigmore, the director, an able man around an Ibsen

revival but a newcomer to the musical theater. The poor man
fluttered about in a continual wax, wringing his hands like ZaSu
Pitts and trying to assert his authority. In the dance department,
there was a similar lack of co-ordination. The production numbers, two portentous ballets in the style colloquially known as
"Fire in a Whorehouse," were being revised from day to day.
Muscle-bound youths stamped about bearing dryads who whin-
nied in ecstasy; shoals of coryphees fled helter-skelter across the
stage; and out on the apron, chin cupped in his hand, the
choreographer brooded, dreaming up new flights of symbolism.
To aggravate matters, a protegée of the composer's, a $55-dollar-
a-week soprano with whom he had dallied in good faith, was
loudly demanding a featured spot in the show, on pain of divulg-
ing the escapade to her husband. Whatever *Sherry Flip* lacked
in smartness, its intimacy was unquestionable.

The *estocada,* however, was yet to come. Six o'clock of the
evening before our departure for Boston, Murray Zweifel, the
company manager, called me aside to retail alarming news—our
producer had disappeared. Murray, a Broadway veteran, was on
the verge of prostration. "He's quit the show," he said brokenly.
"Walked out cold. We're done for." The particulars were simple
enough, readily comprehensible to any student of alcohol. Kerr,
unmanned by dissension with his backers and loath to open the
show on what he contemptuously termed a shoestring, had taken
refuge in the grape and abdicated. "The goddam fool is winging," Murray snuffled, grasping my lapels. "You've got to find
him and get him on that train, baby. You're the only one who can
do it—he won't listen to common sense."

The compliment was equivocal at best, and nine weeks of nightmare tension had taken their toll of me, but I realized that the
welfare of sixty-odd folk was at stake, my own among theirs, and
I knocked under. Pulling on a pair of waders, I set out to comb
the bars that Kerr frequented. About ten-thirty, after a fruitless
search of the West Side that extended to the clipjoints of
Columbus Avenue, I flushed my man in a blind pig on East 54th
Street. He was arm in arm with a prosperous Greek restaurateur

from Bellows Falls; they had just consummated a deal to open a chain of diners in Thessaly and were toasting the venture in boilermakers. For all his carousing, Kerr was clear-eyed and crisp as muslin. He embraced me affectionately and insisted we pour a libation on the altar of friendship. The moment I disclosed my purpose, however, he grew violent. He was done with tinsel and sawdust, he declaimed; he wanted no more of the theater and its cutthroat machinations. I tried guile, supplication, and saccharine, but to no avail. Toward midnight, I phoned Zweifel for counsel.

"For crisake don't lose him!" he pleaded. "Feed him a Mickey—anything! If he's not on the nine o'clock to Boston, we're dead!"

"He's an iron man, Murray," I wailed. "He's mixing Scotch, vodka, bourbon—"

"Listen," he broke in. "Dr. Proctor's his physician—he'll cool him out with a sleeping powder! I'll phone him to expect you."

The process of extricating Kerr from the Greek took a full hour and the cunning of serpents. Eventually, though, I prevailed and, a trifle jingled from the soda I had taken in the line of duty, got him to the doctor's flat. A party was in progress, celebrating, I believe, Jenner's epochal discovery of the principle of vaccine, but not all the guests were medical. Out of the haze, I recall a tête-à-tête on a davenport with a blonde in salmon-pink satin, who read my palm and forecast business reverses. The augury cast a chill on our friendship, and moving off, I fell into a long, senseless wrangle about George Antheil with a musician resembling a carp. At intervals, Dr. Proctor's bibulous face swam into my field of vision, giving me conspiratorial winks and assuring me, in tones from outer space, that Kerr was under control. "Chloral hydrate," I heard him intone. "Just a few drops in his glass. He'll cave any time now." Hours later, I remember clinging to some portieres to steady myself while the doctor thickly conceded defeat. "Can't understand it," he said, laboring to focus his eyes. "Enough there to foal an ox. Average person go down like a felled ax. Got to hand it to old Poultney. Hard as nails." I groped past him to a book-lined alcove where Kerr was waltzing cheek to cheek with a cadaverous, sloe-eyed beauty on the order of Jetta Goudal. Now that drugs and entreaty had failed, my only recourse was insult. Castigating him for a yellow-belly and a welsher, I challenged him to redeem himself.

"I dare you to fly up to Boston!" I cried. "I've never been on a plane, but I'll do it if you will. That is," I said witheringly, "if you've got the moxie."

His brow darkened and he discarded the bush-league Eurasian with an oath. "We'll see who's got more moxie," he snarled. "Come along, you little four-eyed shrimp!"

I had won the first round; speeding through deserted streets toward the Newark Airport, my impresario's choler abated and he sank into a light coma. Instinct told me that if I could only lure him aboard the milk plane, his egotism would make him stick till the curtain rose. But Fate was dealing from the bottom of the deck. A dense, pea-soup fog blanketed the field, and the solitary clerk at the terminal held out little promise of improvement. The entire coast was closed in from Hatteras to the Bay of Fundy, he reported, savoring the despair on my face; even the mails were grounded. Kerr, meanwhile, had seized the opportunity to vanish into the washroom, where I found him draining a fifth of gin he had somehow managed to secrete in his clothes. There was only one hope now, to shanghai him back to the morning train; but with no taxi in sight and a bankroll of forty cents, it would obviously take some fancy logistics. Day was breaking when I finally wheedled the driver of a towel-supply truck into dropping us at the nearest subway stop. The ensuing ride into Manhattan unraveled what remained of my ganglia. In his sheltered life, Kerr, it appeared, had never ridden on a subway. He was seized with repugnance for the overalled workmen about him, their unshaven faces and their surly glances, and promptly went pukka sahib.

"Look at these swine!" he barked into my ear. "That's who we beat our brains out to amuse! Do they appreciate what I've gone through, the aggravation, the sleepless nights I've spent over that show? Give 'em bread and circuses, hey? If I had my way, I'd give 'em something else!"

Heads turned the length of the car, and over the din I detected a subdued muttering like the sans-culottes in a Metro costume film. But Kerr, caught up in a crusading mood in which he identified himself with the Scarlet Pimpernel, was not to be diverted. He launched into a tirade on unions and the New Deal, concluding with a few generalizations that would have abashed even a Republican steering committee. I still marvel that we emerged intact from the Hudson Tubes. Up to the moment we did, I fully expected to expire in a blitzkrieg of lunch-pails.

Thanks to the headwaiter of the Biltmore, a paragon who refused to be intimidated by Kerr's hiccups and our crapulous exteriors, I got some breakfast into my charge, and at eight o'clock, Murray Zweifel appeared. His arrival was the signal for repeated fireworks. We were bracketed with Benedict Arnold and consigned to the devil, roundly notified by Kerr that hell would freeze over before he accompanied us to Boston. We argued and pleaded; at one point, under pretense of visiting the lav, Kerr slipped into a phone booth and was confiding all to Winchell when we extricated him by main force. In the quarter hour before train-time, the fracas degenerated into delirium. Just as the gates were closing, Murray and I bucked our way across Grand Central through a sea of astonished commuters, using Kerr as a battering ram. He was yelling vilification at us, a cataclysmic headache throbbed in my skull, and my reason hung by a thread, but nothing else mattered—the production was saved. From now on, I could relax, for the pathway ahead was strewn with roses. I was fated to learn something about botany, to say nothing of show business.

In the entertainment game, as Sir Arthur Wing Pinero was wont to observe in far loftier language, it don't pay to count your turkeys. At the Hub City premiere of *Sherry Flip*, the traveler curtain failed to open in the conventional fashion. Instead, it billowed out and sank down over the orchestra pit, perceptibly muffling the overture. The musicians fiddled manfully underneath, but Herman Earl's score was too fragile and lilting to overcome the handicap. The comedy, contrariwise, was all too robust—so much so that the police stepped in next day and excised four sketches. The reviews were unanimous. The show, it was agreed, was lavish enough to preclude spending another nickel on it; it should be closed as it stood. And then, on the very threshold of disaster, Kerr decided to rally. He fired the director and restaged the show himself, cut salaries to the bone, and sent a case of cognac to every critic in New York. His acumen bore fruit; we ran five nights there, and those who saw it grow garrulous even today at the memory of *Sherry Flip*. The last time I saw Poultney Kerr, he was a television nabob and beyond mortal ken, but he could not conceal his nostalgia for Broadway. He told me he was mulling an idea for a revue—a smart, intimate romp on the order of *The Garrick Gaieties*.

Rent Me and

I'll Come to You

I'M A STORY BOOK HOUSE. I Hate to Brag, but I Know You'll Love Me When You See Me! I'm an English farm house—artistic rustic, situated on a hillside in a lovely secluded spot in Sherman Oaks. Large living room antiqued, Gothic type beams; large picture window; floor to ceiling stone F.P.; artistic balcony. My floors are pegged planks, 2 bdrms. and den, adorable kitchen with brick recess for stove, canopy, plenty of tile. Floor furnaces. My doors have hand-made latches. Located on two lots, plenty of flowers and fruit trees. A peaceful, comfortable, inspirational hide-a-way—You'll want me! —*Adv. in the* Hollywood Reporter.

EVERYTHING was so new and exciting our first week in Hollywood that Hamish and I hardly slept a wink. I guess we were both pretty exhausted when we got there, after the strain of those last few days in New York—his agent dickering with Metro, and the farewell parties the cast gave him, and subletting the apartment, all the mad and glamorous stuff that happens when your husband lands a term contract. And goodness knows it all happened suddenly enough. One minute Hamish was just an obscure actor playing a wastrel in an off-Broadway production of Eugène

Brieux's *Damaged Goods,* the next he was Ranse Gantry, the new Western find, and we were rolling along La Cienega in the Carey Cadillac that had met us at the airport. "See all those, honey?" Hamish chuckled in his new deep-throated Western drawl, pointing toward the lights that sparkled on the hills. "I'm going to pull them down and make a coronet for your hair."

I saw the chauffeur up front cringe as if he had heard the words before, but I didn't care. "Silly," I said fondly. "There's only one thing I really want, Hamish. However big you become, you mustn't forget your first love—the theater."

"Don't worry," he assured me. "No matter what happens, I'll take time out to do at least two shows a year on Broadway." The glass panel between us and the driver slid up noiselessly. "Look, kitten, you *will* remember about my name, won't you? I mean, everyone at the studio'll be calling me Ranse—"

"Short for 'rancid'?" I teased, snuggling up to him.

He laughed, for, unlike most actors, he always saw the point of a joke. "I may be an actor," he said, and drew my face to his, "but this is one 'yoke' I understand." And so we rode into the golden future, two carefree children with quips on our lips.

Well, that was just the beginning. There was so much to do and see. Hollywood Boulevard, with its fabulous shops and eateries—quaint little nooks that served Fissionburgers and Sky-High Malteds Too Thick for a Straw, the footprints of all the greats at Grauman's Chinese, the scores of marvelous souvenir stores and booteries and saddleries that make it the most cosmopolitan street in the world. Then Beverly Hills, with row on row of aristocratic homes—stately Southern mansions and Renaissance palaces and Tudor deaneries—and Bel-Air, with its gracious country atmosphere, and the dreamy carillon in the bell tower of U.C.L.A., ten times the size of Harvard, summoning thousands of students to class with the strains of "Smoke Gets in Your Eyes." And that gray old Pacific at Malibu, stretching away endlessly to romantic places like Catalina and Pago Pago. And the Metro commissary, with the biggies democratically lunching alongside extras, and the Coconut Grove, and the oil derricks, and TV City—we lived in a perfect whirl. Riding around in our baby-blue Triumph, Ranse soon picked up a stunning tan, and though he always wore smoked glasses so people wouldn't recognize him, plenty did, even if he hadn't appeared in any pictures yet.

"I'm going to have lots of trouble with you, Alkali Ike," I used to kid him. "I dug that blonde at the intersection batting her lashes at you."

"Ease off, Smyrna," he'd murmur sheepishly. (He was practicing a sheepish murmur modeled on Gregory Peck's.) "Those switch-tailed heifers don't appeal to this cowpoke. I'm just a very lucky Joe starting a movie career."

And once he did, life wasn't so rosy for me, cooped up in one room at the Lespedeza Arms. I'd shop, have my nails done or return a bra, somehow fritter away the day till Ranse got back from the studio, but within a week or two the place began to give me claustrophobia. After all, as I explained to Ranse, this wasn't just a hit-and-run part; with his term deal, we could afford a home of our own, a little ranch house where I'd make him pizzas and he'd study his scripts or twang on his guitar. He bought the idea—it reminded him of those color photos of Hugh O'Brian in *TV Guide*—so we started looking. I didn't know there was as much real estate as I saw in the next three weeks, so many custom Regencies and split-level châteaux and smog-free Shangri-Las. Every single one, though, had some drawback, and nine-tenths were out of our price range. The one that came closest, a sweet Cape Cod rental on stilts in Laurel Canyon, fizzled out when Ranse told the owner his profession. "Vandals!" she screamed. "The last actor I had here baked a fish in my silver tea tray!" She caught up a broom and lunged at him. "Get out of here, you yahoo!"

Then, just as I was in despair, our dream house discovered *us*— in, of all places, the darlingest ad in the *Hollywood Reporter*. It was terribly clever, written in the first person, like a dog begging to be adopted—full of simply heavenly details, Old World yet functional, a combination of a Sussex cottage and Frank Lloyd Wright. We couldn't wait to see it, but there was some mystery about the exact owner and we had to go through a realtor, a kind of a fat man named Hitchcraft. "Never mind whose it is, dear," he told me, with a silky smile, as he drove us out to the valley. "This is the type property that speaks for itself. If you like it, we've got a deal." Well, it was one of those things—love at first sight. Ranse stood in the middle of the living room gloating like a big kid over the hand-hewn rafters, the crooked hinges.

"Is this sensational or is this sensational?" he crowed. "I tell you, Smyrna, it's not for real! Right out of Walt Disney."

"But very personal at the same time," I chimed in. "The place *says* something to me—do you know what I mean?"

"Yes, it does to everyone," Hitchcraft said in a hurry-up kind of way. "It—it grows on you. Er—why don't we step outside and discuss terms?" To our surprise, the price was a third of what we'd expected, and when he offered to rent for a spell with an option to buy, we jumped at it. As Ranse said later, if he weren't such a judge of character—actors have to size up people in a flash—he'd have suspected Mr. Hitchcraft was anxious to rent the house. But he was just being overanalytical—I suppose from the year he put in with the Actors' Studio.

We were a month getting settled, what with rugs and drapes and some occasional pieces that Harper Brothers lost in transit from the warehouse. I used a mixture of Spanish colonial and Chinese modern as my basic decorative scheme, and worked out a cozy dining area in rock maple under the balcony, from which I suspended driftwood lamps with glazed-chintz shades. Clumsy big bear that he was, Ranse was always lacerating his scalp on the driftwood, but he had to admit the effect was scrumptious. Except for my vanity, upholstered in a serape I found on Olvera Street, my bedroom was fluffy, while Ranse's was nautical in tone—a built-in bunk with a porthole painted above it, fish nets looped up on the walls, and all the accessories bound off in Manila rope. As for the den, we converted that into a Polynesian-style bar—oodles of rattan and chubby hogsheads to roost on as we quaffed the rum concoctions Ranse never tired of inventing. We both of us were dead with fatigue the night we tacked up the last bullfight poster, but we felt a sense of completion—the way Marlon must feel after a preview, or James Jones when he finishes a trilogy.

The first hint I got of anything uncanny was like a week later, one morning just before lunch. I was in the kitchen mixing a fig-and-avocado purée in the blender, humming away contentedly to myself, when all of a sudden this voice spoke up in a sneery, insinuating whisper. "Happy as a sandboy, aren't you?" it said with an oily little snicker. "Not a care in the world. Well, you're in for a surprise." My heart gave a great agonizing thump, and I was scared I was going to faint. The voice wasn't coming from any one direction; it was all around me, as if the house itself was talking. "You're awfully naïve about that husband of yours, my pet," it went on, in a hateful, fake-solicitous tone. "Do you really believe he was on location last night? That was pancake on his cheek, all right, but he didn't put it there. Stop deceiving yourself—you can depend on *him* to do that." There was a lot more, all about some Latin-American creature with jet propulsion, but I stuffed my fingers in my ears and ran out to the lanai. Once my panic subsided, I tried to rationalize the thing. It wasn't a hangover or a hallucination; I hadn't had a drink in days, and I never touch tranquilizers or bennies. The words had sounded as distinct, as clear, as a tape recording—a nasty, unctuous voice, neither a man's nor a woman's, with a pronounced English accent. That eliminated the only possibility I could think of—our Japanese gardener, who, in any case, was miles away at the incinerator, burning pecan hulls and talking to them in sign language. Unable to explain it, I finally decided the whole business was psychological and erased it from my mind, but I used every pretext to spend the rest of the day outdoors.

"Something troubling you, *querida?*" Ranse inquired lightly that evening as we sat over coffee in the patio—drinking it, that is—and listened to the traffic on the Freeway. Save for the occasional thud of a ripe grapefruit, no sound disturbed the velvety tropical night. Ranse's eyebrows, albeit his question was casual, were raised in concern.

"Why, of course not, *caro mio,*" I said, all froth and insouciance. "What ever could be, in this—this enchanted castle of ours?" Simultaneously, all the horrid jealousy implanted in me that morning boiled up, demanding to be placated. I adopted my most offhand manner. "Have you finished the hayride sequence yet?" I asked. "I'd love to watch the night shooting, if I'm not in the way."

Ranse hesitated in a fashion that immediately confirmed my worst fears. "Afraid that's out of the question, baby," he said. "You see, Chita Casaba and I do a pretty torrid scene there. She freezes when civilians are present, so the director's closed the set."

"How chummy for the two of you," I said gaily. "Heavens, I didn't mean to intrude. . . ."

"Now hold on a second," Ranse protested. "This isn't for kicks, sweetie—it's the way Daddy earns his bread. Can I help it if this Mexican spitfire is fantastically stacked and wears a flimsy blouse? I do what they tell me."

"And let the chaps fall where they may," I couldn't resist adding. Naturally, he flew into a passion at that—raked up the past and accused me of carrying a torch for Byron Wormser, my ex—and we both lost control. After I'd had a good cry, though, I realized how innocent the poor guy was and forgave him. A man of his talent was bound to encounter all sorts of reefs in his work, but thanks to my palship and wifely insight he could steer past them safely. I fell asleep that night supremely confident that be his name Phil Feldkamp, Hamish Trefoil, or Ranse Gantry—and they all were—he was mine.

My heartsease was doomed to short shrift. The following afternoon, I got home from the beauty parlor, made myself a cup of tea, and decided to take a quick tub before meeting Ranse at the Shrimp Basket, this cute spot where you lounge in baskets and the waiters bring you tiny, delectable shrimp. Just as I was pulling on my shower cap, that ghoulish voice began needling me again in its odious, caressing way. "Well, ducky, at last we're alone together," it purred. "So you thought a facial and a finger wave would help you hold him, eh? How delightfully artless you are! That crêpy neck and those middle-aged hips aren't much competition for the most luscious hellcat since Lupe Velez. How do you suppose *he* feels when he compares her creamy, satiny skin—"

"Stop it—stop it!" I screamed, beating away the noxious words that enveloped me. "Why are you telling me all this?"

"Because I'm yours," the voice exulted. "Every stuccoed inch of me, from the plaster pickaninny out front to the fireproof thatch on my roof. Because you acquired me in lawful money of the United States pursuant to the terms and covenants of the standard lease approved by the Los Angeles Real Estate Board. And because I'm watching over and under and all around you, which your husband isn't by a long shot. That lad's got other fish to fry, and take it from me, they're crackling. If you don't believe it, go over to the Casa Golondrina, on South Normandie Avenue, third floor rear. . . ."

I was sobbing on the divan when Ranse came in, and I was so hysterical I didn't even pretend to be subtle. I let him have it—told him that everything was over between us and that I had all the evidence I needed for a divorce. At first he was dumfounded, absolutely shattered. Then he began yelling denials and counter-accusations. He said that I'd been stepping out with five men I never heard of, one of them a chiropractor on Lankershim Boulevard, that he'd had daily reports on my didos from a source he wouldn't reveal. When I swore I'd drag him through the mire till he proved it, he collapsed like a pup tent, started whimpering about his career and his mom.

"Honey, I don't know how to say this," he faltered. "M-my report didn't come from a private eye or anything. It—it was a voice." He paled with alarm at the expression on my face. "Smyrna—what's the matter?"

"Oh, darling!" I cried, taking shelter in his arms. "My precious sweet, can't you see what's happened? We've both got the same horrible delusion!" Breathless and yet strangely relieved, I poured out the story of my visitations. It tallied with his in the main, except that the voice had wounded Ranse professionally, calling him an adenoidal oaf and advising him to grease cars for a livelihood.

"It's senseless to fight this obsession by ourselves, dearest," I pleaded. "Maybe we ought to consult—well, a doctor who knows about such things."

"Gee, get involved with a shrinker?" He hesitated, clouding over. "We can't afford— Wait a minute, though, I've got a hunch! Do you remember Morris Carnarvon, who plays those psychiatrist roles in pictures? He could give us some advice. I'll phone him—"

"No, we mustn't lose our heads," I broke in. "First, let's call the rental agent, that fat man—what's his name? Hitchcraft, that's it. Here, you talk to him—I'll get on the extension. And be cagey—don't say too much."

My warning was unnecessary. The moment the agent heard Ranse's voice, I could tell that he knew what was up, that there'd been trouble before. He didn't admit anything, of course—gave out with a lot of double talk about the rhythm of the house, and not everybody adjusting to its special appeal, and so forth. When Ranse insisted he come over, however, he got slippery and said he was involved in a big deal he couldn't abandon. "Your landlord?" he said, obviously stalling. "Why—er—yes, understandably. Well, the fact is, Mr. Gantry, we're not quite sure who it is. . . . My dear sir, I'd be only too happy to if I did. . . . No, I never have, and neither has anyone else in this office.'' His tone had become definitely snappish. ''Your checks? Well, I merely obey instructions. I deposit them in the trunk of that English walnut at the rear of your garden.''

That was all we needed to know. Half an hour later, Ranse and I crammed the last of what clothes we cared about into the boot of the Triumph and backed it out of the driveway. As he fumbled on his smoked glasses, I turned for a final look at the house. Under the trellis near the laundry area stood a character like out of a novel by Thomas Hardy, only a little more ectoplasmic— a gnarled old man in a rustic-type smock, leaning on a staff. He was waving farewell and grinning from ear to ear. I kept mum till we hit the Freeway, but then— Oh boy, Flipsville.

Front and Center,

Kiddies!

I KNOW it sounds incredible, but up to yesterday there was not the slightest indication from the New England Council of Hotel and Resort Proprietors regarding its slogan for the summer. As June faded slowly into July, thoughtful people began biting their nails and wondering what was amiss. "What slogan will govern more than a few New England resort hotels this summer?" everybody kept asking himself fretfully, lying down in a hammock and shading his face with a white drill hat. Then, just as the tension had become well-nigh unbearable, the Council broke silence in an electrifying release to the Boston *Globe:*

"Keep the guests tired out and happy" is the slogan that will govern more than a few New England resort hotels this summer, according to a survey recently completed by the New England Council. . . . One particularly inspired New Hampshire hotel man outlined his plan for the current season so well that his program will be adopted by many another hotel in New England this summer.

"There'll be no rocking chair brigade here, if we can prevent it," he said. . . . "This year everyone in our establishment will double in brass. We're eliminating the doorman and stationing a bellhop outside. He'll also deliver cars (if any) to our garage. Everybody, including the manager, doubles in something. All help will be well paid and well fed. Two or three times during the season, we plan to give the employees a dinner and have the guests wait on them. . . . Our main job is to keep everything moving at such a fast pace the guests will forget to complain about anything," he said.

For the benefit of any shut-in forced to forego his annual visit to Franconia, Truro, or Bar Harbor by his bank balance, I submit a reasonable facsimile of what he might have encountered. To properly establish the mood, one should rub the ankles lightly with poison ivy and swallow a bad clam.

(*Scene: The porch of Eagle's Mere, at Durfee's Notch in the Berkshires. As the curtain rises, Pudovkin, the manager, is discovered lounging on the steps. He wears a bellhop's jacket much too small for him and chews on a half-dead cigar. The Bessemers, a stout, middle-aged couple, totter slowly up the driveway, laden with baggage. They collapse on the gravel, their faces streaming.*)

PUDOVKIN: Kind of pooped, eh? You'll lose that bay window before we're through with you.

BESSEMER (*panting*): Say, bud, bring me a glass of water, will you?

MRS. BESSEMER: I'll take some plain ginger ale.

PUDOVKIN: Wouldn't you rather have a tall, cool rum collins with mint and lots of ice?

MRS. BESSEMER: Why, that sounds delicious.

PUDOVKIN (*comfortably*): Doesn't it? I'll hop down the mountain and get one. It's only four miles—the exercise'll do me good.

BESSEMER: Look, if it's any trouble, I'd just as soon—

PUDOVKIN: Nonsense, that's what I'm paid for, to run down every time some lush wants a snort. Or if you prefer, I can carry you down on my back.

MRS. BESSEMER (*nervously*) : Maybe we ought to register first, Roy. Is the manager around?

PUDOVKIN : You're looking at him.

BESSEMER : That's right—of *course!* You've heard me speak of Mr. Pudovkin, lovekin—I mean, love.

MRS. BESSEMER : Many times.

BESSEMER : Well, this is Mr. Pudovkin. (*A pause*) You remember me—Roy Bessemer. I've been coming here for years.

PUDOVKIN (*shortly*) : I've seen the face. It isn't the kind you recall.

MRS. BESSEMER : We'll just slip up to the room, if it's ready.

PUDOVKIN : It will be, when you change the linen. Did you bring a broom?

BESSEMER : Yes, right here in the golf bag. Rhoda's got the oil mop and the Dutch Cleanser in her suitcase.

PUDOVKIN : Wait a minute, you. What's that niblick doing there?

BESSEMER (*guiltily*) : Er—I—I figured I'd play a few holes—you know, after my chores were done and like that—

PUDOVKIN (*savagely*) : And get out of mowing the lawn, eh, you little sneak? I've got half a mind to bundle you back to town. If I didn't need waiters for the employees' banquet tonight—

BESSEMER : Honest, Mr. Pudovkin, I don't have to use the greens. I'll practice in my room; it's more fun anyway.

PUDOVKIN : Well, we'll let it ride this once, but watch your step, Bosco. All right, go up and dress; you'll never get those napkins folded.

MRS. BESSEMER : Hurry, Roy, we'll have time for a quick bath.

PUDOVKIN : You don't think we turn the water on just for guests, do you?

MRS. BESSEMER : I'm not particular. An old rain barrel's plenty good enough for me.

PUDOVKIN : I know your kind. First it's a bit of soap, then ice water, and the next thing I know, you want the same food as the help. Now beat it. I don't like a lot of riffraff lousing up the front of the house.

BESSEMER: Yes, sir. Did you wish to see our references, Mr. Pudovkin?

PUDOVKIN (*wearily*): No, they're probably forged anyway.

(*As the Bessemers exit, the curtain is lowered to denote the lapse of an hour. It rises on the dining room. Pudovkin, Nick, the busboy, and Hedwig, the maid, are seated amid rows of empty tables receding into the gloom. They wear paper hats marked "Savannah Line" and languidly sip their consommé, Pudovkin without removing his cigar. The Bessemers, in decent black, fuss over the second course at the sideboard.*)

PUDOVKIN (*cackling*): Wait, you haven't heard the payoff. So we break down the door, and there's Mrs. Poultney in the Senator's pajamas!

NICK: Ha, ha, that's a pip! (*Snapping his fingers at Bessemer*) Hey, droopy, you forgot the butter chips.

BESSEMER: Coming right up, Mr. Eumenides.

HEDWIG (*indignantly*): Say, is this supposed to be chicken consommé?

PUDOVKIN: Boy, what a swindle. Waitress!

MRS. BESSEMER: Yes, sir?

PUDOVKIN: If this is chicken consommé, so is Lake Louise. And you can tell the manager I said so.

MRS. BESSEMER: But you're the manager, Mr. Pudovkin.

PUDOVKIN (*to the others*): Well, I've heard all the excuses, but that's a new one.

NICK (*pinching Mrs. Bessemer*): Hello, sweetie pie, how's about a little loving?

MRS. BESSEMER (*giggling*): Now you stop. I've got my work to do.

NICK: She's a red-hot mamma. I'll date her up yet.

HEDWIG (*taking out some crocheting*): Skirt-crazy, if you ask me. A regular wolf.

PUDOVKIN: Hell, you're only young once. What are you making, Miss Swenson?

HEDWIG: It's an all-purpose accessory. This way it's a purse, but when you put it on your head, it becomes a beanie.

PUDOVKIN: Very flattering. Listen, that reminds me. (*Lowering his voice*) How much do you give these people?

HEDWIG: I generally leave a dime. That's all the service is worth.

NICK: Or the grub either. Jeez, it's brutal. We should have gone to Siegel's Mere.

PUDOVKIN: Up there you get free samba lessons by the pool.

NICK (*voluptuously*): You said it. Beautiful, shapely maidens with nothing on.

HEDWIG: Don't you ever think of anything but sex?

NICK: No, it's kind of a hobby with me. Like woodworking.

BESSEMER: Are you ready for the roast, folks?

NICK: What is it—lamb?

PUDOVKIN: It's always lamb. (*He starts uncontrollably as he sees his portion.*)

BESSEMER (*anxiously*): Anything wrong, sir?

PUDOVKIN: Somebody swiped one of the nubbins. (*Slowly*) And I've got a *pretty* . . . *good* . . . notion who it was. (*He collars Bessemer, plucks from his pocket a napkin containing the missing morsel.*)

BESSEMER (*falling to his knees*): It was midsummer madness, Mr. Pudovkin. Don't turn me in!

PUDOVKIN: There's an ugly name for that sort of thing, Bessemer.

BESSEMER: I know—nubbin swiping. (*Moaning*) The shock will kill my mother.

MRS. BESSEMER: Oh, Roy, for shame! The first night, too—before I even had a chance to steal a towel.

PUDOVKIN (*relenting*): Well, you've had your lesson. The Cannonball passes the junction in twenty minutes. If you're smart, you'll be on it.

MRS. BESSEMER (*fervently*) : I'll never forget you, Mr. Pudovkin. I'll save my money and repay—

PUDOVKIN: No. Turn down my bed before you go.

(*They slink out.*)

HEDWIG (*softly*): You're a very gallant gentleman, Mihail Mihailovitch.

PUDOVKIN: No—just a sentimental Slav. (*He clears his throat roughly and lights a fresh cigar.*)

CURTAIN

Open Letter to

a Cold-Slough Mob

DEAR SIRS:

LET ME BEGIN by clearing up any possible misconception in your minds, wherever you are. The collective by which I address you in the title above is neither patronizing nor jocose but an exact industrial term in use among professional thieves. It is, I am reliably given to understand, the technical argot for those who engage in your particular branch of the boost; i.e., burglars who rob while the tenants are absent, in contrast to hot-slough prowlers, those who work while the occupants are home. Since the latter obviously require an audacity you do not possess, you may perhaps suppose that I am taunting you as socially inferior. Far from it; I merely draw an etymological distinction, hoping that specialists and busy people like you will welcome such precision in a layman. Above all, disabuse yourselves of any thought that I propose to vent moral indignation at your rifling my residence, to whimper over the loss of a few objets d'art, or to shame you into rectitude. My object, rather, is to alert you to an aspect or two of the affair that could have the gravest implications for you, far beyond the legal sanctions society might inflict. You have unwittingly set in motion forces so malign, so vindictive, that it would be downright inhumane of me not to warn you about them. Quite candidly, fellows, I wouldn't be in your shoes for all the rice in China.

As you've doubtless forgotten the circumstances in the press of more recent depredations, permit me to recapitulate them briefly. Sometime on Saturday evening, August 22nd, while my family and I were dining at the Hostaria dell' Orso, in Rome, you jimmied a window of our home in Bucks County, Pennsylvania, and let yourselves into the premises. Hastening to the attic, the temperature of which was easily hotter than the Gold Coast, you proceeded to mask the windows with a fancy wool coverlet, some khaki pants, and the like, and to ransack the innumerable boxes and barrels stored there. What you were looking for (unless you make a hobby of collecting old tennis rackets and fly screens) eludes me, but to judge from phonograph records scattered about a fumed-oak Victrola, you danced two tangos and a *paso doble*, which must have been fairly enervating in that milieu. You then descended one story, glommed a television set from the music room—the only constructive feature of your visit, by the way—and, returning to the ground floor, entered the master bedroom. From the curio cabinet on its south wall and the bureaus beneath, you abstracted seventeen ivory, metal, wood, and stone sculptures of Oriental and African origin, two snuffboxes, and a jade-handled magnifying glass. Rummaging through a stack of drawers nearby, you unearthed an antique French chess set in ivory and sandalwood, which, along with two box Kodaks, you added to your haul. Then, having wrapped the lot in an afghan my dog customarily slept on, you lammed out the front door, considerately leaving it open for neighbors to discover.

So much for the tiresome facts, as familiar to you, I'm sure, as to the constables and state troopers who followed in your wake. The foregoing, aided by several clues I'll withhold to keep you on your toes, will pursue you with a tenacity worthy of Inspector Javert, but before they close in, gird yourselves, I repeat, for a vengeance infinitely more pitiless. Fourteen of the sculptures you took possess properties of a most curious and terrifying nature, as you will observe when your limbs begin to wither and your hair falls out in patches. In time, these minor manifestations will multiply and effloresce, riddling you with frambesia, the king's evil, sheep rot, and clonic spasm, until your very existence becomes a burden and you cry out for release. All this, though, is simply a prelude, a curtain-raiser, for what ensues, and I doubt whether any Occidental could accurately forecast it. If, however, it would help to intensify your anguish, I can delimit the powers of a few of the divinities you've affronted and describe the punishment they meted out in one analogous instance. Hold on tight.

First of all, the six figures of the Buddha you heisted—four Siamese heads, a black obsidian statuette in the earth-touching position, and a large brass figure of the Dying Buddha on a teakwood base. Now, you probably share the widespread Western belief that the Lord Buddha is the most compassionate of the gods, much more so than Jehovah and Allah and the rest. 'Fess up —don't you? Well, ordinarily he is, *except* (as the Wheel of the Law specifies) toward impious folk who steal, disturb, or maltreat the Presence. Very peculiar retribution indeed seems to overtake such jokers. Eight or ten years ago, a couple of French hoods stole a priceless Khmer head from the Musée Guimet, in Paris, and a week later crawled into the Salpêtrière with unmistakable symptoms of leprosy. Hell's own amount of chaulmoogra oil did nothing to alleviate their torment; they expired amid indescribable fantods, imploring the Blessed One to forgive their desecration. Any reputable French interne can supply you with a dozen similar instances, and I'll presently recount a case out of my own personal experience, but, for the moment, let's resume our catalogue.

Whether the pair of Sudanese ivory carvings you lifted really possess the juju to turn your livers to lead, as a dealer in Khartoum assured me, I am not competent to say. Likewise the ivory Chinese female figure known as a "doctor lady" (provenance Honan); a friend of mine removing her from the curio cabinet for inspection was felled as if by a hammer, but he had previously drunk a quantity of applejack. The three Indian brass deities, though—Ganesa, Siva, and Krishna—are an altogether different cup of tea. They hail from Travancore, a state in the subcontinent where Kali, the goddess of death, is worshiped. Have you ever heard of thuggee? Nuf sed. . . . But it is the wooden sculpture from Bali, the one representing two men with their heads bent backward and their bodies interlaced by a fish, that I particularly call to your attention. Oddly enough, this is an amulet against housebreakers, presented to the *mem* and me by a local rajah in 1949. Inscribed around its base is a charm in Balinese, a dialect I take it you don't comprehend. Neither do I, but the Tjokorda Agoeng was good enough to translate, and I'll do as much for you. Whosoever violates our rooftree, the legend states, can expect maximal sorrow. The teeth will rain from his mouth like pebbles, his wife will make him *cocu* with fishmongers, and a trolley car will grow in his stomach. Furthermore—and this, to me, strikes an especially warming note—it shall avail the vandals naught to throw away or dispose of their loot. The cycle of disaster starts the moment they touch any belonging of ours, and dogs them unto the forty-fifth generation. Sort of remorseless, isn't it? Still, there it is.

Now, you no doubt regard the preceding as pap; you're tooling around full of gage in your hot rods, gorging yourselves on pizza and playing pinball in the taverns and generally behaving like *Übermenschen*. In that case, listen to what befell another wisenheimer who tangled with our joss. A couple of years back, I occupied a Village apartment whose outer staircase contained the type of niche called a "coffin turn." In it was a stone Tibetan Buddha I had picked up in Bombay, and occasionally, to make merit, my wife and I garlanded it with flowers or laid a few

pennies in its lap. After a while, we became aware that the
money was disappearing as fast as we replenished it. Our suspi-
cions eventually centered, by the process of elimination, on a
grocer's boy, a thoroughly bad hat, who delivered cartons to the
people overhead. The more I probed into this young man's
activities and character, the less savory I found him. I learned,
for example, that he made a practice of yapping at dogs he
encountered and, in winter, of sprinkling salt on the icy pavement
to scarify their feet. His energy was prodigious; sometimes he
would be up before dawn, clad as a garbage collector and hurling
pails into areaways to exasperate us, and thereafter would hurry
to the Bronx Zoo to grimace at the lions and press cigar butts
against their paws. Evenings, he was frequently to be seen at
restaurants like Enrico & Paglieri's or Peter's Backyard drunk-
enly donning ladies' hats and singing "O Sole Mio." In short,
and to borrow an arboreal phrase, slash timber. Well, the odious
little toad went along chivying animals and humans who couldn't
retaliate, and in due course, as was inevitable, overreached himself. One morning, we discovered not only that the pennies were
missing from the idol but that a cigarette had been stubbed out in
its lap. "Now he's bought it," said my wife contentedly. "No
divinity will hold still for that. He's really asking for it." And
how right she was. The next time we saw him, he was a changed
person; he had aged thirty years, and his face, the color of
tallow, was crisscrossed with wrinkles, as though it had been
wrapped in chicken wire. Some sort of nemesis was haunting his
footsteps, he told us in a quavering voice—either an ape specter
or Abe Spector, a process-server, we couldn't determine which.
His eyes had the same dreadful rigid stare as Dr. Grimesby
Roylott's when he was found before his open safe wearing the
speckled band. The grocery the youth worked for soon tired of
his depressing effect on customers, most of whom were sufficiently
neurotic without the threat of incubi, and let him go. The beautiful, the satisfying part of his disintegration, however, was the
masterly way the Buddha polished him off. Reduced to beggary,

he at last got a job as office boy to a television producer. His *hubris*, deficiency of taste, and sadism carried him straightaway to the top. He evolved programs that plumbed new depths of bathos and besmirched whole networks, and quickly superseded his boss. Not long ago, I rode down with him in an elevator in Radio City; he was talking to himself thirteen to the dozen and smoking two cigars at once, clearly a man *in extremis*. "See that guy?" the operator asked pityingly. "I wouldn't be in his shoes for all the rice in China. There's some kind of a nemesis haunting his footsteps."

However one looks at it, therefore, I'd say that your horoscope for this autumn is the reverse of rosy. The inventory you acquired from me isn't going to be easy to move; you can't very well sidle up to people on the street and ask if they want to buy a hot Bodhisattva. Additionally, since you're going to be *hors de combat* pretty soon with sprue, yaws, Delhi boil, the Granville wilt, liver fluke, bilharziasis, and a host of other complications of the hex you've aroused, you mustn't expect to be lionized socially. My advice, if you live long enough to continue your vocation, is that the next time you're attracted by the exotic, pass it up—it's nothing but a headache. And you can count on me to do the same.

Compassionately yours,
S. J. PERELMAN

Revulsion

in the Desert

THE DOORS of the D train slid shut, and as I dropped into a seat and, exhaling, looked up across the aisle, the whole aviary in my head burst into song. She was a living doll and no mistake—the blue-black bang, the wide cheekbones, olive-flushed, that betrayed the Cherokee strain in her Midwestern lineage, and the mouth whose only fault, in the novelist's carping phrase, was that the lower lip was a trifle too voluptuous. From what I was able to gauge in a swift, greedy glance, the figure inside the coral-colored bouclé dress was stupefying. All the accessories, obviously, had come from Hermès or Gucci, and you knew that some latter-day Cellini, some wizard of the pliers like Mario Buccellati, must have fashioned the gold accents at her throat and wrists. She was absorbed in a paperback, the nature of which I guessed instinctively; it was either Rilke or Baudelaire, or even, to judge by the withdrawn and meditative expression on her lovely face, Pascal. Suddenly a pair of lynx eyes, gray and exquisitely slanting, lifted from the page and fixed on me a long, intent scrutiny that set my knees trembling like jellied consommé. Could she have divined my adoration in her telepathic feminine way? Ought I spring forward, commandeer the book, and read out to her the one passage that would make us kinsprits forever? Before I could act, the issue had decided itself. The train ground to a stop at the Thirty-fourth Street station, and as she arose and stowed the book in her handbag, I saw that it was Ovid's *Art of Love*.

A lump of anguish welled up in my throat at the opportunity I had let slip, the encounter that might have altered my whole destiny; I sought surcease in the advertising placards overhead, but they were as bitter aloes. How could a craven like me dare aspire to Miss Subways, whose measurements were 37-24-33, whose hair was auburn, and who was an enthusiastic kegler? Vic Tanny, urging me to discard adipose tissue at his health club, was at best a cruel reminder that I was no longer the arrowy Don Juan I supposed, and Breakstone's injunction to diet on its cottage cheese merely compounded the affront. I was preparing to debark at Forty-second Street, lacerated by self-pity, when I beheld a poster that mercifully set me off on quite another tangent. "Win a fantabulous week for two at the Cloudburst in Las Vegas plus $3500 in cash!" it trumpeted. "Play Falcon Pencil Company's Super-Duper Guessing Game!" I never ascertained whether I was to watch for some magic serial number or to hawk the pencils from door to door. In the next breath, I was ejected to the platform, and there superimposed itself on my mind a memory of this selfsame Cloudburst, fantabulous indeed, as I saw it during a brief enforced visit to Las Vegas just a year ago.

My trip to the gambling mecca was no casual stopover between planes; I flew there from Rome, a matter of seven thousand-odd miles, to honeyfogle an actor, and I undertook the journey with the direst misgivings. The circumstances were somewhat as follows. Several months before, an Italian film producer had engaged me to devise a vehicle for a meteoric American tenor, whom it might be prudent to call Larry Fauntleroy. The latter, through his records and personal appearances, had scored a phenomenal success in the United States and Europe; his presence in a picture, it was universally felt, would make it a bonanza; and Signor Bombasti, from the moment I began work in Rome, announced himself ready to go to any lengths to win Fauntleroy's approval of our story. I soon found out what he meant. Shortly after completing the treatment, which is to say the narrative outline of the scenario, I was summoned to my employer, hailed as a composite of Congreve, Pirandello, and Norman Krasna, and urged to convey the manuscript in person to Fauntleroy. Nobody else, affirmed Bombasti, could adequately interpret its gusto and sparkle, its rippling mirth and delicious nuances. (And nobody else in the organization, he might well have added, spoke even rudimentary English.) My expostulations, my protests that I was anathema to performers, went for naught; in a supplication that would have reduced even Louis B. Mayer to tears, Bombasti entreated me, for the sake of the team, if not my own future, to comply. Seven hours later, I weighed in at Ciampino West airdrome.

The Milky Way, the hotel where I was scheduled to stay in Las Vegas and whose floor show Fauntleroy was currently headlining, was the town's newest—a vast, foolish beehive of plate glass rearing fifteen stories above the sagebrush, so ruthlessly air-conditioned that I was wheezing like an accordion by the time I unpacked. My quarters could only be described as a harlot's dream. The dominant colors of the sleeping chamber, a thirty-five-foot-long parallelogram, were jonquil and azure. A bed large enough to accommodate a *ménage à trois,* flanked by modernique gooseneck lamps with purple shades, occupied one wall; along the other, three abstract chairs in yellow plastic confronted a lacquer-red television set. To facilitate any makeup I might require, there was a theatrical vanity bordered with hundred-watt bulbs in the adjacent dressing room. Beyond it lay a ghastly black-tiled bathroom from which one momentarily expected Lionel Atwill to emerge in the guise of a mad surgeon, flourishing a cleaver.

Within a few minutes, my reason was sufficiently unsettled to regard the décor as normal, and, having erased the ravages of travel, I went in search of Fauntleroy. He was breakfasting at a table near the pool, encircled by the usual retinue of the popular entertainer—agents, managers, song pluggers, masseurs, and touts —all of them vying with each other to inflate his ego. I was introduced boisterously, if inaccurately, to the rest of the levée; Bombasti's cable heralding my arrival, it seemed, had miscarried, and for a while the troubadour was under the impression that I was a disc jockey from Cleveland. Rather than launch into tedious explanations, I accepted the role and ordered a steak and a cigar to render myself inconspicuous. Sprinkled around us on the greensward, half a hundred of the Milky Way's guests dozed in the fierce sunlight, leaching away their cares to the strains of Nelson Riddle. When the voice of Frankie Stentorian started booming forth "Ciaou Ciaou Bambina," I chose the auspicious moment to properly identify myself as the emissary from Italy.

"Man, that story you wrote for me is a gasser!" Fauntleroy chortled, wringing my hand. "I haven't had a chance to read it yet, on account of I just opened here, but I'll get to it tonight between shows. Then you and I can spend the whole day tomorrow tearing it apart, analyzing and tightening so the plot practically writes itself. How does that suit you?"

I assured him I could hardly wait to eviscerate my handiwork, and, amid ecstatic predictions from his claque that the picture would outgross *The King of Kings,* withdrew. Inside the Milky Way casino, though it was only noon, several dozen patrons were already gathered at the faro and crap tables. They all moved with the languor of somnambulists—woebegone creatures condemned to spend eternity hopelessly defying the laws of chance. I watched a couple of blue-haired clubwomen pump silver dollars into the slot machines until their *cafard* communicated itself to me, and then progressed into a coffee shop that might have been lifted, along with its clientele, from a Southern bus terminal. Just as I was struggling to master a sandwich composed largely of lettuce and toothpicks, a music arranger out of my Hollywood past, named Dave Jessup, accosted me. Our salutations could not have been more joyful had we met on a sheep station in Queensland.

"Listen," said Jessup, after we had exhumed the age of fable and interred it again. "Everybody here flips about this new spectacle at the Cloudburst—the French revue called 'Oo La La!' What say we catch it tonight?"

To be candid, I was planning to retire early with the copy of Ruskin's *Stones of Venice* I had begun on the plane, as I wanted to see how it came out, but, sensing Jessup's desperate need of companionship, I good-naturedly yielded. Shortly before six, the fashionable dinner hour in Las Vegas, a cab deposited the pair of us under the neon volcano that skyrocketed from the block-long façade of the Cloudburst. In a ballroom the size of the Cirque Médrano, five hundred hysteroids in play togs were gorging themselves to a medley of jump tunes, magnified tenfold by microphones, issuing from a boxful of musicians on one wall. The din was catastrophic; we were shoved pell-mell into a booth, barricaded behind a cheval-de-frise of celery, and supplied with vases of whiskey that drenched our shirt fronts. A distracted waiter, hovering on the verge of collapse, unhesitatingly recommended snails as our main course, only to reappear in the blink of an eye with two filets that drooped over the sides of the plate. What with the uproar and the kaleidoscope flickering upon us, it was not easy to find my dish in the murk, and but for a sudden agonizing stab as Jessup tried to sever my knuckles, I never would have known I had eaten half his steak. Then our dinner vanished altogether, and as the orchestra sounded a fanfare, a deafening Gallic voice ushered in the pageant.

Whoever the creators of "Oo La La!" were, they were admirers of the undraped female form, for after establishing the locale as Montmartre with an apache dance and a chorus of gendarmes, they got down to brass tacks. A procession of sinuous long-stemmed beauties wound its way to the footlights attired in peasant costumes, large sections of which evidently had been lost in shipment from France. The mishap seemed to occasion the ladies small concern, however; they bore themselves proudly and endured the gaze of the audience without flinching. Their fortitude was rewarded by hearty applause intermingled with whistles, and as the last of them undulated offstage the scene inexplicably shifted to Naples. A *festa* was in progress, and a number of masked revelers of all sexes were holding carnival, dancing the tarantella and beating tambourines fit to wake the dead. Suddenly the clamor subsided, and another procession of coryphées, whose clothes had arrived piecemeal from Italy, wove downstage. They exhibited as much aplomb in the face of adversity as their French cousins had, and the audience paid them equal tribute. In both Turkey and Polynesia, to which we were then whisked in quick succession, the same regrettable shortages prevailed, but the houris and wahines were similarly undaunted. Having demonstrated to everyone's satisfaction that human nature under duress is constant the world over, the production soared to a climax. Four embossed trapdoors in the ceiling, hitherto masquerading as ventilators, vibrated shakily downward in time to the "Skaters' Waltz," disclosing a quartet of robust and untrammeled vestals clad in wisps of stockinet. They were lit from below, an angle calculated to maximize their charms, and the effect was hauntingly reminiscent of that greatest of all equine masterpieces Rosa Bonheur's "The Horse Fair."

I had become so preoccupied with the entertainment that I was ready to watch it a second, or even a third, time to familiarize myself with its catchy tunes and stage business, but Jessup demurred. He had arranged with two shapely girl violinists at the Golden Drugget, which from his description appeared to be a branch of the Juilliard School, to help them with their solfeggio, and invited me to accompany him. Mindful of the commitment I had made to disembowel my script the next day, however, I begged off and turned in at eight-thirty. About four, a phone call from Fauntleroy aroused me. He apologized for the intrusion, but he was terribly upset by the few pages of the treatment he had read. The background, the characters, the entire orientation were wrong. Nevertheless, he added quickly, I was not to agitate myself; I must get a good sound sleep, and in due course he would assess all the shortcomings. I rolled over and slept like a log.

It was midafternoon before I finally managed to awaken Fauntleroy, and another hour before he tottered into the coffee shop, unshaven and numb with seconal. When dexamyl had loosened his tongue, his whole mood changed. All the apprehensions he had voiced earlier on the phone, he told me, were groundless. Somewhere between sleep and waking he had evolved an idea for a series of production numbers that would make ours the most talked-of film of the century. "This is a whole fresh approach to the story, mind you," he began. "So for crisake be flexible in your thinking. Instead of a happy-go-lucky archeologist, the way you wrote me, I figure I'm a happy-go-lucky talent scout or an agent—sort of a singing Irving Lazar. I'm always going around to various exotic places, like France, Naples, Turkey, and Tahiti, rounding up these gorgeous contest winners for a floor show at the Copa or the Rainbow Room. So far so good. Now, here comes your drama. These girls arrive in plenty of time for the opening, all right, but the different parts of their native wardrobes are always confiscated at the last minute by the customs or lost in a typhoon or something. Do you get it? It's a race against overwhelming odds—a suspenseful strip tease that grows out of a real human situation. . . ."

Seventy-two hours afterward, in the Eternal City, Signor Bombasti beamed at me across the managerial mahogany and rubbed his hands in satisfaction. Not only was I the wiliest diplomat since Prince Metternich, he declared, but, as Fauntleroy's cable in front of him attested, I was a grand human being. "And let us remember something else in our hour of triumph, my dear fellow," he reminded me. "It was I, Ettore Bombasti, who had the vision and the genius to marry your two outstanding talents."

"I'll remember it till the day I die," I said fervently. "I thought of it every minute I was in Las Vegas."

"Good," he said. "So long as you and our Larry saw eye to eye, so long as there was a meeting of minds, I ask for nothing more. This will be the biggest box-office attraction since *The King of Kings*. Now go back to your study and write as you have never written before."

I did. In fact, I wrote as *nobody* had ever written before.

I Declare, Under

Penalty of Milkshake

I WAS drifting around the periphery of the Village the other morning, luxuriating in the sunshine and mingling freely with the indigenes—the Method actors with stormy faces and fat ankles, the models as angular as the Afghans who drew them along, the leather craftsmen nursing dreams of sandals too abstract to contemplate—when a placard in a drugstore suddenly beckoned. The window was one whose anatomical displays had long endeared it to me; many's the time I had browsed over its variegated charts of the human interior, full of conduits and stairways, in which Lilliputians played badminton in the cranium and stoked furnaces in the belly to demonstrate the efficacy of some gland preparation. Latterly, the principal exhibit had been a full-size wax replica of a man's head, the left side of it bald as Henri Landru's and the right sprouting wiry black bristles. This miraculous rebirth, the work of a tonic displayed nearby, appeared to have unhinged the user to a degree, for his eyeballs were rolling wildly and his tongue protruded in anguish. Whether conducive to hair or dementia, however, the lotion was now nowhere in evidence. Instead, the forefront of the window was occupied by a boldly lettered sign reading, "Income Tax Returns Prepared Here by Expert."

Ordinarily, I leave such grubby matters to a worthy whom I'd pit against any comprador in Hong Kong, but, as it happened, he was cruising in the Norfolk Broads—or so I had interpreted his last message—and the chance to dispense with his services excited my cupidity. Why not avail myself of this windfall and save a considerable fee? After all, there was nothing so recondite about executing a tax form; I had read a goodish bit of Sylvia Porter and J. K. Lasser in my day, and without vainglory felt I had an instinctive flair for elucidating the mumbo-jumbo of revenue. I pushed open the door and strode in forcefully. At once I went into a Chaplinesque stagger to circumvent half a dozen tables, littered with breakfast debris, that consumed most of the floor space. At the fountain, and plainly impervious to the clutter, a swarthy attendant in a green surgical smock was draped over a scratch sheet. I squirmed through the forest of libidinous paperbacks obscuring the rear of the store and sought out the prescription desk. It was so burdened with toiletries, greeting cards, candy, analgesics, and assorted medical lumber that it took some reconnaissance to find the druggist, who, it developed, was merely a pharmacy major spelling the proprietor.

"I don't handle the tax work," the youth told me feverishly. "I'm busy on a rush order—digitalis for a heart case. Talk to the guy over there."

"The soda clerk?" I asked, taken aback. "Does he make up the declarations?"

"I think so," he said, "but I'm new here. I took over while my uncle's away. He went to Peru for some ipecac."

He flew back to his pestle, and as I stood irresolute, the party behind the fountain hailed me. "What type return you want to file, bud?" he called out genially. "Individual or corporation?"

"Well, I haven't quite made up my mind," I began, chilled by a premonition of disaster. "I was just scouting around—"

"Probably the head of a household—right?" he said encouragingly. "Okey-doke. Sit down by the table and I'll bring a 1040 blank." Before I could collect my faculties, he had circled the counter, cutting off the only avenue of retreat, and plumped himself down. "Now, give me the whole picture, remember," he warned, spreading out his documents fanwise. "No chiseling—you dig? We don't want to do anything that smacks of fraud."

"Good gracious, no," I protested in a high, girlish voice that seemed altogether alien. For some inexplicable reason, there arose before me an image of the two of us in a railroad coach, manacled to a federal marshal. The muscles in my calves started to flutter.

"After all," he pursued, "why should I perjure myself for some measle who gives me a lousy three bucks to fill out his form?"

"You'd be a fool," I agreed.

"In spades," he said. "All right, let's get going. To the best of your knowledge and belief, is everything you are about to disclose a true, correct, and complete statement?"

"Well—er—truth's pretty much of an abstraction, isn't it?" I asked, suddenly conscious of how warm it was in the store. "I mean, the ancients held, philosophically speaking—"

"Look, save that schmalz for the review agent later on," he interrupted. "I'm just trying to extract the info they want on this blank. During the taxable year, did you derive any income out of dividends, interest, rents, pensions, and like that?"

I shook my head.

"How about wages, salaries, bonuses, commissions, tips, or other compensation?"

"I think so," I replied, after a moment's reflection, "but I haven't any figures on me. I'd have to look in my checkbook at home."

"Ach, nobody's twisting your arm for the exact amount," he said carelessly. "The main thing is, was it under or over a hundred dollars? That is, after payroll deductions."

"Let me see," I pondered. "Do you want the gross or the net?"

"I don't understand what those words mean," he said, with

an irritable gesture. "You made a hundred dollars more or less—that's close enough. Now, then, what source did you get this income from?"

"Well, a movie outfit in Europe, mainly," I said. "I did a picture for this Italian studio in Rome last summer."

My counselor beamed and smote the table resoundingly. "How do you like that!" he exclaimed. "The minute you came in, I spotted you for an actor. There was something flashy about you."

"I—er—I'm not actually a performer," I pointed out. "I wrote the screenplay, as they call it." He blinked at me. "You know, the plot and the lines the different characters say."

"What are you trying to do, con me?" he demanded, with manifest cynicism. "The actors make up all that junk as they go along."

"Yes, but somebody has to take the blame for it in case of a lawsuit," I explained.

"Like a scapegoat, you mean," he said thoughtfully. "Say, that wouldn't be a bad racket to break into. Do they really pay off for that kind of a rap?"

"Well, it brings me in walking-around money," I admitted. "But listen, getting back to my return—"

"Excuse me a minute while I wait on these heads," he broke in, jumping to his feet. Two young ladies, in toreador pants and mohair sweaters, whose swirling coiffures looked as though they had been squeezed from an icing gun, had ranged themselves at the fountain. They studied the menu posted over the coffee urn with languid contempt.

"Tuna-fish and cream-cheese sandwiches," one of them sighed, wrinkling her nose in distaste. "Holy cat, Dominic, don't you ever have any hot dishes?"

"You two are the hottest on the lower West Side," the soda clerk returned gallantly. "It's fracturing the fire laws just to let you in here. What'll it be, girls?"

After extended thought, the pair chose some dire amalgam of apple butter, sausage, and raisins called a Driftwood Special, and, plunging straws into their malteds, lapsed into an intent discussion of hair lacquer. I studied the section of the document before me pertaining to medical and dental deductions, but soon floundered into a bog of technicalities about the excess of Line 3 over Line 4 that brought back all my youthful reading reversals. Just as I was mulling the advisability of paying Dominic his three-dollar ransom and decamping, he rejoined me, energetically rubbing his hands.

"Now, one or two questions and you're all through," he said, with the brisk benevolence of a doctor in a TV commercial. "First, we fill in this space here." He laboriously printed the word "scapegoat" in the block designating my occupation, and then, turning to the instructions overleaf, scanned them narrowly. "In connection with that job in Italy, you had certain travel expenses, like transportation and hotels, did you not?"

"Reimbursed," I said.

"Sure, but you must have laid out dough for *something*," he insisted. "What about starlets from the production that you had to take out and coach them in their roles?"

"There was—ahem—a minimum of coaching," I said. "My wife accompanied me on the trip."

"Listen, Clyde, get the rocks out of your head," he sighed. "You need that moo more than the government. Try and think."

"Well . . ." I hesitated. "Come to think of it, I did ship my dog overseas in the middle of the summer."

"There you are!" said Dominic, his face lighting up. "In your view, was the animal necessary to your peace of mind while you were working?"

"*Necessary?*" I repeated. "They gave him equal billing with me on the screen credits—that's how necessary he was."

"Then it's deductible—every Goddam cent," he replied firmly, "and we'll carry it right up to the Supreme Court if we have to. How much did it cost to send over your pet?"

"Hmm, let's see," I ruminated. "A hundred and thirty-eight dollars for plane fare, nine for the cab to Idlewild, and eighteen for the crate they made me buy there. Then he broke out of the box in Amsterdam while they were transshipping him—"

"And you had to hire a lawyer to trace him," Dominic prompted.

"I did?" I asked in surprise. "What sort of a lawyer?"

"Why, a Dutch one," he said blandly. "The most expensive kind in the world. Yes siree, I figure we can knock off about seven hundred bucks on that item alone."

"It seems a trifle high," I said. "Do you think we can make it stick?"

He shrugged impatiently. "All *right*, so they'll disallow half," he said. "My motto is give a little, take a little—we don't want to be a hog. Now, there's still one more point to cover—Line 9 here. Did you make any profit or loss from farming in the taxable year?"

"Well—ah—a little of each," I said cautiously. "We had a nice stand of grain down at my place in Pennsylvania. I don't remember what they call it—it's something like Wheatena, only more crunchy."

"How much did the seeds cost?" Dominic inquired. "If it's more than you got for the crop, then you finished in the red. You see why, don't you?"

"Not exactly," I said. "To be frank, I concentrate mostly on our other crops, such as honeysuckle and woodbine. My work's largely managerial—you know, watching them through the windows, seeing that the different roots are in place, that sort of thing."

"Good," he approved. "Then you're entitled to charge for your services at, say, fifty bucks a week against any profit you made from the Wheatena, which means you write off another twenty-six hundred smackers." He made a rapid calculation and emitted a whistle. "Man!" he said. "With those expenses and your wife's exemption, you're going to get a hell of a rebate from the Treasury Department."

"I'm certainly glad I saw your sign in the window," I said,

reaching for my billfold. "Is there a notary public around who could witness my signature?"

"Yep, at the delicatessen in the next block," he replied. He stowed the fee in his smock and shook my hand warmly. "Much obliged, Jack, and good luck. Say, I forgot to ask—what's that picture you did in Italy about?"

"A kraut named Baron Munchausen," I said. "An eccentric who used to make up fibs."

"Not for Baby," said Dominic emphatically. "I get enough screwballs here in the daytime. When I go to the movies, I want to see a story based on real life."

As if on cue, the door shot open to admit a paper-thin individual no taller than a Watusi and no more bizarre, except that his face was a distinct turquoise blue. He hurried to the fountain and, mounting a stool, began to drum a nervous tattoo on the Bromo-Seltzer tap. With a wink in my direction that rattled the fixtures, Dominic departed to serve him.

A few seconds later, loungers in the vicinity of Sheridan Square might have observed another individual, paper-fat and ashen-faced, emerge from a local drugstore. He deposited the paper in an adjacent trash can, entered a coin booth, and dialed the long-distance operator. "I want to speak to this tax consultant in Norfolk, Virginia, Miss," he said urgently, "but I don't know precisely where. I think he's cruising with some broads."

La Plume de Mon Ami

Est dans le Flapdoodle

CREATIVE WRITER THRIVES ON COMMERCIAL COPY. Today's question: Does the commercialism of advertising destroy the creative writer? Rot, says Sherman E. Rogers, copy chief of Anderson & Cairns, who has long had the best of two worlds. "One thing feeds the other," the craggily-handsome Rogers told us in an interview. "Advertising teaches you to say a thing in a tight way—to write volumes in a paragraph. And creative writing restores and freshens you for the daily job of writing copy." Rogers has written five movie scripts, hundreds of articles and short stories, radio scripts, and is now finishing his first novel, *And the Evening, And the Morning*. He props himself in bed at 10:30 P.M.; works on his novel until 12:30 A.M., long-hand. Other Anderson & Cairns copy writers are equally creative after hours. One translates movie scripts into fiction; another does TV dramas; a third publishes verse. Among Rogers' most successful headlines for ads are "Done—in two shakes of a Waring" . . . "The Scotch with the Secret you can Taste—Peter Dawson" . . . and "The calculating female figures on Facit" . . . Conclusion: If you want to write good ad copy, write novels too.
—*Doris Willens in the* Journal-American.

You and I go back a long time, brother, I thought as Crunch Budlong leaned across our table in the Oak Room and clinked his Martini against mine. A devil of a while; it was thirty-five blessed years since, as underclassmen at Brown, we had worshipfully studied rhetoric under Percy Marks, the author of *The Plastic Age*, jointly dissected the nervous system of simple invertebrates (including our parents'), and toddled to the rhythm of Al Mitchell and his Arcadians. Over the intervening decades, I had heard little of him apart from an occasional fatuous puff in the alumni bulletin. He had left one advertising agency to affiliate with another, resigned in due course to mismanage a third. I'd gathered that on the whole he was prospering, but it was not until we collided on Fifth Avenue a half hour before, and agreed to solemnize our meeting with lunch, that my wraithlike memory of him had taken on substance. Looking at him now, I saw he was still personable, handsome in the way that female interviewers love to describe as craggy.

"Man, you should have come up for the thirtieth reunion," Crunch was observing with a reminiscent sigh. "What a toot that was! We threw a clambake out at the Squantum Inn and everybody got sloughed—absolutely blotto. Charlie Rust—remember him? He's head of Rust & Korozian down in Philly, plumbing supplies—stuck a plate of fruit on his head and gave an imitation of Eleanor Roosevelt. You'd have died."

"I bet," I said. "I tried to get there, but—well, to be candid, I didn't have the fare."

"To Providence?" he said in pained surprise. "Hell, it's only eight dollars."

"Not from Northern Rhodesia," I corrected. "Frankly, I thought it'd be self-indulgence to come all that way for a mess of clams."

"Yeah, guess you're right," he said uncertainly, and nursed his glass a moment. "Er—what were you doing in that neck of the woods?"

I looked around to make sure nobody was eavesdropping. "Remember King Solomon's Mines?" I asked. "Well, I . . . sort of picked up a lead on their whereabouts."

"I could have saved you the trouble, bub," he said with a lofty smile. "They're fictitious."

"Perhaps so," I concurred, inspecting my nails like Lou Tellegen, "but wouldn't you like to see the contents of a certain safe-deposit box at the Irving Trust?"

Crunch studied my profile, as dissimilar as possible to Tellegen's. "Mmm," he ruminated. Suddenly his manner changed. "Say, pardon me a sec, will you?" He sprang up to proffer fulsome greetings to an elderly, cigar-colored pirate nearby, and returned a trifle breathless. "That's Luther Fluther," he confided. "Big wheel in Allied Confectionery, one of our accounts." It was obvious that he was thirsting for me to prime him on his present status, so I primed him. As copy chief of Prinzmetal & Sludge for the past eight years, he informed me, he had devised some of the most dynamic slogans in advertising—among others, a classic for Lox Pops. He seemed incredulous that I hadn't heard of the sweetmeat. " 'Lox Pops, the Only Lollipop with the Built-In Smoked-Salmon Flavor,' " he quoted with manifest pride. " 'They're Tops on Your Chops. Send in Your Pop's Box Tops for a Trial Phial of Lox Pops.' Kind of great, isn't it?"

"A whiz," I said. "But tell me—whatever became of those youthful ambitions of yours? Back at school, you always dreamed of writing a trilogy, novellas, plays . . ."

"Why, I did write 'em," he returned blandly. "Yes, sir, I've penned five novels since joining Prinzmetal & Sludge, not to mention four plays, a shelf full of whodunits, and essays galore. Mind you," he went on quickly, "none of 'em was ever published or produced, but that wasn't the object. I wrote them merely to sharpen my faculties for the agency job."

"Where on earth do you get the energy? It's all I can do to answer my mail."

"I suppose I'm just a little better organized than most people," admitted Crunch. "My brain's kind of a beehive, you might say. I create every minute of my spare time—in the shower, while I'm commuting, on the golf course, all over. You see, the beauty of the thing is that my copy and my outside prose cross-fertilize each other.''

"I'm afraid I don't follow," I confessed. "How does it work exactly?"

"Well, give you an example," he offered. "We were handling a campaign for Victor Hugo Frozen Soups—you know, they get out a line of madrilène, vichyssoise, and so on for household consumption. To be candid with you, I was stumped for an approach, completely stymied, and the longer I simmered over it, the more barren I became. Somehow, all the old superlatives like 'appe-teasing' and 'goodylicious' sounded hollow. I wanted a real block-buster, a slogan that would capsulize the lip-smacking flavor of the soups, their authentic French *goodness*. You grasp the problem?"

"Insofar as any layman can," I said. "Naturally, I'm not too well oriented on soup merchandising."

"Naturally," he agreed. "Anyhow, I kept stewing over it, and then, out of the blue and seemingly unrelated to my dilemma, came a hunch for a play. I wrote the first scene at white heat that night, and it immediately sparked the solution. Like to hear it?" I nodded fatalistically, and Crunch, wrapping himself in the mantle of Sardou, emitted a premonitory cough. "As the curtain rises," he explained, "we see the living room of a small villa in the South of France. The time's about dawn, and through a set of French doors at rear we glimpse the sun just peering over the Mediterranean. Seated in a rocker at mid-stage is this elderly woman with a workbasket in her lap. She's obviously awaiting someone, because as she knits she keeps glancing expectantly toward a door at left. At last it opens, and in comes this impressive figure in a frock coat, carrying a physician's satchel. From his bent shoulders, the weary way he takes off his old-fashioned derby, we sense that he's been through some critical ordeal. 'Oh, hello, Pierre,' says the old lady anxiously. 'Tell me, was it a difficult *accouchement?*' 'Very, very,' he replies gravely, and then his face brightens. 'But . . . it was worth it.' 'Why so?'

she asks. 'Because,' he says with an exalted look, 'that little baby's name was—Victor Hugo.' ''

I tried my utmost, but the relevance of the vignette to frozen soup eluded me. "And that triggered the inspiration for a slogan?"

"A humdinger," said Crunch, aglow with self-satisfaction. " 'Victor Hugo—the Soup That Babies Your Palate. Appeteasing—Goodylicious.' Within three months after we started using it, their sales skyrocketed two and a half per cent, which shows what a simple little phrase can do."

"Excuse me, gentlemen," a voice apologized. We looked up to behold Fluther, the confectionery tycoon, standing over us, accompanied by a portly, well-tailored individual with magnetic eyes. Mr. Dudley Nightshade, his luncheon guest and a distinguished publisher, had expressed an urgent desire to meet Crunch, and, once seated, he lost no time in trivialities.

"Fluther's just been telling me about your Lox Pop slogan," he told my friend. "You know, at our firm—I guess you're familiar with my imprint of the Running Faucet—we're always on the *qui vive* for new literary talent. If you don't mind my saying so, yours is a very remarkable gift." He stilled Crunch's disavowal with a wave. "Don't be modest, Mr. Budlong," he enjoined. "The point is, how'd you like to do a novel for us?"

"I've written several—" Crunch began.

"I could tell you have." Nightshade cut him short. "But the one I have in mind could create a whole new genre overnight—an ingenious union of belles-lettres and salesmanship never attempted before. Now, the plot I'm about to suggest isn't gospel, you realize," he warned, disabusing us of the fear that it might be gospel. "It's a wholesome, pastoral-type story of the kind Robert Nathan excels at, but with a hidden consumer angle. As I see it, the central character—let's call him Max Farintosh—is a wealthy middle-aged broker, a man who commands the respect of his associates and is intensely attractive to women. He's got a magnificent estate on Long Island, his own yacht, and a penthouse apartment in town, but underneath he's discontented, unfulfilled. I mean, he has the feeling he's lost something.''

"What?" I asked.

Mr. Nightshade withered me with a glance. "His innocence," he snapped. "The thing all of us have lost in our worship of the bitch goddess Success, as William James put it."

"He put it very well," approved Fluther. "I like that. Go on."

"Well," the publisher resumed, "one evening, while strolling in Central Park, Farintosh runs into a strange old mystic—a saintly, ascetic sort of hermit who lives in a cave there. Maybe he's got a small band of disciples that he expounds his philosophy to—a retired postman, a little Negro boy, a beautiful but slightly fey young girl who's run away from her rich, conventional family. Anyway, as a result of these contacts Farintosh gradually acquires a whole new perspective. He communes with the animals and birds, gets to know the names of the various wild flowers—in short, for the first time, he savors the sweetness of existence."

"Don't you think he and the girl would tend to fall in love?" asked Crunch, with the novelist's inherent flair for braiding the elements of a situation.

"An excellent twist," said Nightshade. "Speaking out of forty years' experience as a distinguished publisher, a good romantic complication never yet hurt the sale of a book. However, to cleave to our central thread for the nonce: Realizing how tawdry his life is, Farintosh renounces his business, his de-luxe yacht—"

"Hold on there, Dudley," objected Fluther. "I won't buy that. I'm an average reader, and it doesn't ring true to me."

"O.K.," Nightshade rejoined. "He doesn't renounce the yacht. Perhaps he only puts it in storage—"

"You don't store a yacht," Fluther contradicted, with the executive's inherent flair for detail. "You haul it up on the ways."

"Yes, yes." Nightshade curbed his annoyance with an effort. "That doesn't affect the story. What I'm driving at is Farintosh's conversion. The hermit convinces him that if people could only communicate simply and sincerely—say, by means of sharing and enjoying some universal delight like candy—most of their neuroses would vanish. You see where this train of thought takes us?''

"Goddam right I do, Mr. Nightshade!" Crunch chortled. "Recover the innocence of childhood with lollipops—in fact, with the Lox Pop!"

"Precisely," said Nightshade, his eyes sparkling. "The minute Farintosh sets out to translate the philosophy into action, he's a man inspired. As a starter, he distributes a few thousand lollipops, urging the recipients to buy and give away more, like a chain letter. Then, as the idea captures the popular imagination, a veritable frenzy of benefaction overtakes everyone. Millions of lollipops change hands—"

"Great Scott, Dudley!" said Fluther, awe-stricken. "If a thing like that ever caught on, we'd have to retool to supply the demand!"

"Wait a minute," Nightshade expatiated. "Go beyond the commercial implications. Out of this upsurge of altruism, Farintosh forges a potent political weapon, a brotherhood of good citizens with the motto 'Lox Pop Means Vox Pop'—dedicated to stamping out ignorance and graft. In turn he's elected mayor, governor, even President. All mankind hails him as a savior—everybody, that is, but one person."

"The fey young girl in Central Park," said Crunch intuitively.

"Correct," said Nightshade. "In saving the world, he's lost the one thing he really loves—and you end on a lovely, bittersweet note of renunciation."

"But he's still got the yacht," Fluther appealed.

"Yes, *yes,* he's had it all the time," the publisher quieted him, and turned back to Crunch. "Well, Mr. Budlong, how does that strike you as a theme for a novel?"

"It's a heller," said Crunch exultantly. "Of course, I won't be able to devote much time to it at the office, but I can knock it out in a couple of evenings."

"I guarantee it'll write itself," predicted Nightshade. "And it could earn us all a very tidy pfennig. A first edition of fifty thousand (exclusive of the book clubs, that is), the movie sale, paperbacks, a tie-in campaign with Allied Confectionery—yes, this may have been a most providential encounter. Look here," he proposed energetically. "Why don't the three of us step over to my office while we're hot, and draw up a contract?"

Crunch rose to his points like Eglevsky. "Yowzer!" he assented. "I *was* going to lunch with my friend here, but I know he'll understand—won't you?" I managed a self-sacrificial nod. "Look me up soon and we'll really tie one on, eh?"

"Yes, or you look me up in Rhodesia," I wanted to say, but it was already too late. The trio was halfway out the door, framing a capital-gains evasion and cackling over dividends. I relapsed into my chair, waved away the menu, and ordered another Martini. Somehow I wasn't a bit hungry. Indeed, I could have sworn I felt a touch of dyspepsia.

I

Birth of a

Conquistador

Up into the cerulean vault of heaven, a titanic Nabisco with a thousand windows aflame in the waning sun of a winter afternoon, rose the RCA Building, proud diadem of New York's fabled Radio City. In the lengthening shadows at its base, the Rockefeller Plaza rink glowed like a pearl as skaters revolved sedately around it to muted waltz rhythm. It was a tranquil scene, a lacy Currier & Ives ballet posed against the backdrop of the age of electronics, and, one would have thought, an unlikely setting for drama. And yet so unpredictable is life that within a few moments, skater and spectator alike were destined to witness here a deed of signal heroism, an act whose momentous consequences none could have foretold. Who could have divined what journeying into far places, what desperate stratagems and high derring-do—but let us lay aside our dusty Victorian carpetbeater, dear reader, and chronicle the facts in the case.

It all began, as have so many other breakneck enterprises, with a woman's taunt. I had been lunching that day with an old schoolfellow, a tall, flamboyant divorcee with Titian hair and an hourglass figure whom I had met at an obedience school where our dogs had struck up a flirtation. Knowing my wife's curious aversion to tall, flamboyant divorcees with hourglass figures, I had taken Velveeta, the person in question, to a small, dark chophouse well out of the turbulent shopping district. To my surprise (for I expected a shallow coquette), I found her a deeply thoughtful person who had read widely in Elbert Hubbard and Robert W. Service, a student of numerology, palmistry, and other occult arts, and possessed of an amazing range of scientific knowledge. She could, for example, distinguish real diamonds from paste at a glance, and had your true biologist's ability to differentiate between small mammals like sables, chinchillas, and platina minks.

"It's a strange thing, doll," she mused over our fifth Martini, smoothing my palm with her cool fingertips and studying the lines. "Most people born under Aquarius are tightwads, but you're generous to the point of folly. I mean, like if you were to befriend someone, why you would try to lavish your last dollar on imported perfumes and little crepe-de-Chine knickknacks to make them happy. Am I warm?" she asked, with an appealing upward smile that revealed what I could have sworn was more than two rows of teeth. I assured her that nobody had ever divined my character so cannily and waved away the maître d'hôtel with instructions not to interrupt us unless the liquor license was revoked.

Approximately three hours later, I came to in Cartier's, a jewelry store plumb in the middle of the turbulent shopping district. Due to some steam on my glasses, I was unable to see with my usual acuity, but a salesman was pressing me to make a choice between a cabochon emerald choker and a star sapphire the size of a Brazil nut.

"I—er—there's been some mistake," I stammered. "I'm in the wrong section—I was supposed to meet my wife at the kitchenwares in the basement—"

"Just a second, brother," Velveeta snapped, blocking my exit.

"The last john that welshed on me wound up with his feet in a barrel of cement. Did you ever hear of Tony Cobra of the Purple Gang?" I saw how fatuous was palaver, and thrusting her aside, made for the street. She scurried a few paces behind me down the avenue, filing brief sidelights on my morals and antecedents in a whiskey tenor that drowned out the roar of the traffic. We passed several people I dimly recognized—our family dentist, a gossipy second cousin, and my wife's corsetiere—but I did not acknowledge their salutations. As I dodged down Rockefeller Plaza toward the rink, Velveeta overtook me and redoubled her objurgations. With all the dignity at my command, I informed her I was late for a skating appointment. She emitted a howl of derisive laughter. "Why, you pathetic old dodo," she cackled. "You couldn't stand up on a pair of skates if they were set in concrete!"

The references to cement were beginning to abrade my nerves. I scanned her witheringly from tip to toe and produced my watch fob. "If you examine the reverse of that medallion, my good woman," I said coldly, "you will discover that I was substitute goalie of the Pawtucket Wolverines in 1919. Good afternoon." Before she could recover from her chagrin, I had descended to the arena, donned a set of tubular blades, and was skimming away over the ice. In all modesty, Mercury himself seemed to have lent wings to my heels. Round and round I spun, gliding effortlessly through figure eights and arabesques, now balancing on one leg, now swooping backward in lightning reversals, until the tyros about me cowered open-mouthed against the barriers. The spectators above craned down in silent awe, shielding their eyes and shuddering convulsively as I defied every law of gravity. And then the unpredictable, the fluke in a million, happened.

Out on the ice, square in my path and blissfully unaware of my dizzying momentum, strayed a tiny golden-haired tot. She could not have been a day more than nineteen, though her proportions were already as opulent as a ripe gooseberry. In a second's flash, I foresaw the peril, took the only course open, and swerved aside. As I ricocheted into the outdoor café and struck a buffet wagon laden with glassware and pastry, a resounding roar of homage to my gallantry welled from the onlookers and wafted me into oblivion.

Mile after mile of Florida scrub flowed past the bus windows, interspersed with marshy inlets and billboards proclaiming the world's largest alligator farm, the world's largest hamburger, and the world's largest saturation of odious billboards. The fifteen-odd tourists who had embarked with me at Jacksonville that morning for St. Augustine slumbered fitfully in their chairs, yawning and fanning themselves with comic books. Chin cupped in my hand, I stared out at the landscape and reviewed the relentless, almost inevitable steps that had led me to my present situation. The doctor attending me after the mishap in Radio City had become seriously concerned at my condition and given me an exhaustive checkup. The prognosis was sustained; I was on the edge of the abyss.

"I'd like to see him get away for a while," he told my wife, taking the words out of her mouth. "He's too good a sport to complain, of course, but the man's been carrying a heavy load."

"You mean those compacts I find in his pockets?" she asked. "Funny how he always comes back from conferences with lipsticks and bobby pins—"

"Now, now, dear," I broke in. "I don't think Dr. Peritonides is interested in our domestic trivia. What do you recommend, Doctor?"

"A complete change," he said unhesitatingly. "New environment, new faces. Go to Florida, California, anywhere—get out of your rut, so to speak. Mix with young people; find out what makes them young, and follow suit."

"Sort of a self-evaluation and rejuvenescence, eh?" I reflected aloud. "I *could* do with a spot of sunshine, now that you mention it. I've felt rather seedy of late—how shall I say?—long in the tooth.'' Between ourselves, I had noticed a somewhat villainous customer, whose description coincided with that of Tony Cobra of the Purple Gang, skulking outside our brownstone and balefully eying the windows, and the idea of a short interlude of travel seemed felicitous. Pondering the doctor's words, it suddenly occurred to me to take his admonition at face value: to first reconstitute my energies with a visit to the Fountain of Youth in Florida as a symbolic gesture, and then, refreshed by its life-giving ichor, laze away a few sun-drenched weeks in Hollywood. The major obstacle confronting me, I realized, would be my wife's welfare during my absence, but luckily, an unforeseen solution arose. Through the intercession of friends, I was able to obtain her a sinecure tidying up the Fisk Terminal Building at night. The mop and wringer I contributed to launch her new assignment did much to dispel the woman's fancied grievances, and by the time I stepped aboard the Florida-bound plane, I knew that if her lot might seem a bit arduous at times, she was prepared to sacrifice anything to restore my emotional equilibrium.

''Five-minute stop, folks!'' The bus driver's voice booming over the amplifier dissipated my reverie, and an instant later, we lurched to a standstill at a weedy crossroads depot in the scrub. Straggling inside, my fellow voyagers and I were presented with the world's most dubious hamburgers and the fiat that prior to St. Augustine, we would pause at Marineland, the renowned oceanarium a few miles down the coast. Since neither the meat nor the prospect of enforced sight-seeing aroused any visible dismay in the company, I decided mutiny would be quixotic and sullenly re-entered the bus. Within half an hour, we drew up before the portals of the celebrated tank.

As it developed, it was a pleasing experience to eavesdrop on the sharks and porpoises, turtles, squid, and rays in their habitat, although one slight contretemps intervened to mar it. I had mounted a ladder to better observe the undersea activity through a porthole when a six-year-old boy scrambled up beside me. He prattled so incessantly that I laid a gentle finger on his lips to enjoin silence. To my stupefaction, he hurtled from our perch and cracked his immature noggin on the promenade below. Forthwith, there was a hullabaloo and a caterwauling fit to wake the dead. From the behavior of his parents, one would have thought he was the Dauphin on his deathbed, whereas any objective person could see that the fillip had quickened the child's circulation and stimulated his tissue tone. To show his gratitude, the little ingrate willfully and deliberately placed me in jeopardy. "He pushed me!" he screamed, empurpling like Tony Cobra. "He threw a bag over my head and tried to kidnap me!" Fortunately, I am not one to show the white feather in a crisis. I quietly took the parents aside, made them a small peace offering ample enough to reshingle their home and send the boy through Groton, and dismissed them. If they cherished any thought of blackmailing *me*, they had sadly misjudged their man.

Midway through our junket around the historic site of St. Augustine that afternoon, I threw in the sponge and seceded from the organized tour. What with the oldest wooden schoolhouse in America, the oldest outdoor kitchen, the oldest wax museum, and the oldest burial crypt, I was trembling with palsy and buttonholing strangers to quaver out reminiscences about Pickett's Charge. Fearful that I might dwindle into a mound of sodium potash if I tarried, I hailed a surrey driven by a worthy in a plug hat and directed him to convey me to the Fountain of Youth. He whipped up his nag and we set off briskly through a maze of alleys. Half an hour later, after passing the same storefront three times, we plodded into a dismal backyard littered with scrap metal. With a flourish, he helped me dismount and indicated a rusty pipe topped by a spigot under an ailanthus tree.

"You sure this is the right place?" I queried doubtfully.

"Look, boss," he said earnestly. "You ain't no ordinary tourist—right? You got to have the real McCoy or nothing—right?" I modestly admitted I had seen too much of the world to be hoodwinked. "It sticks out all over you," he said. "Just taste this here spring and if it ain't the one Ponce drank out of, the attendant will refund your money."

"Where *is* the attendant?" I asked, unpinning a bill from my shirt.

"He's laid up with yellow jack," he replied. "I'm taking custody of the scratch till he gets back." The water had a sweet, flavorsome tang and I drank several dipperfuls. By the time the evening plane put me down in Miami, its rejuvenative properties had demonstrated themselves beyond cavil. My wrists and ankles were swollen to chubby little barrels and I was chewing on my toes as lustily as an infant. The hotel clerk who registered me flinched when I burst into a plaintive wail, but he needn't have. I was merely teething.

Coruscating like a string of jewels along the moonlit sweep of Miami Beach, Collins Avenue's ninety-seven blocks of skyscraper hotels outshone the solar spectrum. As far as the eye could see, a serried row of floodlit edifices, resembling gigantic bureaus with their drawers pulled out, trumpeted to the newcomer that he was in the nobbiest winter playground ever devised by the mind of man. Cheek by jowl they stood with chrome canopies ablaze and plate-glass doors twenty-five feet high, their names a subtle tribute to the vocation of their guests: the Saxony, the Cheviot, the Worsted, the Mohair, the Seersucker and the Buckram. Some, doubtless catering to the peerage, bore names of unbearable elegance—the Lord Corduroy, the Chambray-Plaza, the El Shantung, the Broadloom. But the labels were arbitrary, for their lobbies all had the same décor, the same tufted leather walls and mirrored pillars, the aggressively modernique sofas upholstered in bile-green, the schizophrenic drapes. The surroundings, apparently, had exerted a powerful influence on the plumage of the customers, which was as resplendent as that of the Lesser Superb Bird of Paradise. Clad in Dubonnet-colored slacks and playtime jackets of woven jute piped in suede, in visored West Indian caps on which bobbled weird excrescences of straw, the males milled about the foyers forcing cigars on each other and bemoaning the state of business. Their wives, stoutly refusing to hide their lights under a bushel, sported cabana blouses whose necklines plunged to the navel, sarongs that automatically made every bystander a Peeping Tom. The vacation they were undergoing seemingly caused them only woe, for they lay about with an air of heavy discontent. The food was too fattening and the prices exorbitant, they complained; their hotel was outmoded, a social leprosarium. This year everyone was stopping at the Sherry-Nylon, where the *kreplach* were rumored to be fabulous.

It was my second evening in this Shangri-lollapaloosa that I was seated on the porch of my own hostelry, the Gabardine, feeling rather bushed. I had just finished mailing quantities of citrus fruits, dates, cocoanut patties, and pecan rolls to anyone I could think of who abhorred them, and I was looking forward to a quiet session in the kip with Motley's *Rise of the Dutch Republic*.

"Have a cigar, young man," a voice on my left ordered me abruptly. Turning, I beheld a mahogany-faced ruin in a phosphorescent pullover and a tropical helmet fashioned of red cardboard. I explained that I rarely indulged. He nodded sagely. "Hyperacidity," he said. "Only one thing for it—sauerkraut juice and cold baths. I had the exact same thing; all the biggest professors in the Mayo, the Massachusetts General, they all gave me up. But I'm a fighter. I said to them, 'I'll be walking around when you're pushing up the daisies.' And look at me today. How old a man would you say I was?"

"Er—eighty-five?" I hazarded.

"Forty-six," he said triumphantly. "Florida—that's the answer. Down here they know the secret of eternal youth. That's why I finally sold out my various interests and located here. Now I go to my stomach specialist every day, he takes my metabolism, and I know where I'm at."

"How about the doctors you saw at the Mayo?" I asked. "Dead long ago, I presume?"

"Those leeches," he said contemptuously. "I wouldn't soil my brains thinking about them. Excuse me," he said, rising, "I have to talk to a party over there." I was sorry to see him go, as there is nothing so refreshing when one is weary as the maunderings of a health faddist; but the eiderdown was calling, and I was afraid I might oversleep a sartorial treat scheduled for the morning, a fashion show of masculine resort wear beside the Balbriggan pool.

It exceeded my most sanguine expectations. Before a critical audience of retailers, style scouts, and assorted loafers of both sexes, a quartet of male models paraded about displaying finery undreamt of outside the hallucinations of Little Nemo. They wore peekaboo dinner coats made of hopsacking, slacks and singlets of burlap, hemp, rush, raffia, oakum, and sisal, and headgear ranging from Confederate kepis to imitation coonskin caps of terry cloth. Men's underthings during the coming season, it appeared, would stress aqua, peach, greige, and other pastel colors, and one magnificently muscled Adonis, in platinum-tinted swim trunks, led around a Kerry Blue in shorts that were an exact replica of his master's. I was fairly modish myself, having dressed for the occasion in fire-engine red hobby jeans with a magnetized waistband that dispensed with belts, a taupe sports shirt with liquor signs on the bosom, a railway fireman's denim cap outlined in neon, and white kid scuffies. While I made every attempt to efface myself, it was obvious from the outset that my togs had captured the spotlight. Barely had the preview terminated before I was encircled by retailers begging me for representation rights in their territories. The thought of commercializing my taste filled me with aversion, and I hastily fled the scene. The artificiality, the pretense of Miami, suddenly enveloped me like a pall. I longed for mangrove-covered keys and the boundless blue of the Gulf Stream, for a rolling deck beneath my feet and the music of the reel as some lordly sailfish fought to pit his strength against mine. When the sun sank over the yardarm, I was ninety miles south in Key West and bedded down at the Barracuda, the jauntiest motel that ever begrudged a guest a towel.

Mrs. Yancey, the widow lady who owned it and acted as concierge, was a sugary Southern gentlewoman with marcelled blue hair, false choppers, and the profile of an iguana. Her Dixie-fresh, cornpone labials had a way of embedding themselves in one's skin and festering there like spicules of steel wool. Simpering ghoulishly, she allotted me a pistachio-colored oubliette full of furniture upholstered in pink tufted plastic. My immediate neighbors, the first night, were a red-faced hooligan couple who staged an epic binge and beat each other into insensibility, and a recluse who, to judge from the grinding sounds that filtered through the wall, had perfected a perpetual motion machine. The next morning, however, the entire clientele cleared out at dawn with a roar of exhausts like the Indianapolis Speedway, the bottles were carted off, and a new contingent of Yahoos swept in, uttering a wild rebel yell.

Among the arrivals were two not unattractive girls who drove up in a white Cadillac convertible—student teachers, Mrs. Yancey implied, from a nearby normal school. They were comely lassies, clearly in very moderate circumstances, since their linsey-woolsey halters were threadbare and just barely adequate to contain their charms. I took no notice of the pair until one chanced to drop her handkerchief on the patio a scant thirty yards from my door. Overhearing the crash, I strolled over and retrieved it. By a fantastic coincidence, it turned out that Billie and Yvette belonged to the very same hospital plan I did.

"Look here," I suggested, after a bottle of Apollonaris had sealed our friendship. "Why not let's go deep-sea fishing together? I'm—harumph—pretty well heeled, and I'd welcome a bit of feminine company."

They clapped their hands in joyous assent. The arrangements were soon complete: they were to foot the cost of the boat and provide lunch and a case of beer, and I pledged myself to furnish sunburn lotion without stint. That evening they appeared at my cubicle in a chopfallen mood, accompanied by a swart individual whom they introduced as Gomez, a charter-boat captain.

His sleeve garters, flashy tie, and diamond stickpin seemed rather urban for a simple fisherman, but I decided not to cavil.

"He wants four hundred clams a day for the *Spindrift,*" said Yvette, employing a term infrequently used by schoolteachers. "We thought it was too expensive, so he has another idea."

"That's right," said Gomez. "Tell you what I'll do, Mac. I'm a sport and I can see you're one too. I'll roll you for it. You win, you get the boat, all my tackle, the whole shebang. You lose, pay me four C's." I made guarded inquiries that satisfied me the craft was worth close to nineteen thousand dollars, and decided the odds were favorable. Gomez plucked a pair of dice from his vest, the girls spread out a blanket without any prompting, and the contest was on.

About ten o'clock the following morning, I finished poring through a batch of photographs in the station house. Between the mounting humidity and lack of sleep, I was not at concert pitch, and a peculiar buzzing in the ears did nothing constructive for my condition. I listened to it attentively for a while, and finally identified it as *Vox frustrata,* the characteristic call of a Key West sheriff dusting off a chump.

"Not a prayer, mister," he was saying tonelessly. "They're in Jamaica or Nassau by now. We'll keep an eye on the hockshops for your watch and chain."

"B-but they looked so sweet and—and well brought up," I snuffled. "One of them had a puppy with her—and then that big white convertible—"

"They glommed it from a guy in Tarpon Springs," the sheriff said, filing his nails. "He's flying down tonight to reclaim it." I sponged the moisture from my eaves, and picking up my bindle, started for the door. "If you want the bus station," he called after me, "it's on the northwest corner of Southard and Bahama."

"Never mind," I mumbled. "I'll just get a hitch up the Overseas Highway."

"You do that," he said encouragingly, "and keep on going. It's open season on pigeons."

I came out into the broiling sunlight, removed a bit of marl from my shoe, and trudged numbly toward the outskirts. By and large, my initial attempt to restore the bright luster of youth had foundered, but it was infantile to repine. All the way back to Faust, mortals bent on the same errand had taken a drubbing. Chin up, steady on, and *nil desperandum*, I counseled myself, stepping aside to avoid an open manhole. I promptly wrenched my ankle, fainted, and had to be carried into a supermart. But at that, I was luckier than Ponce de Leon. He didn't even have ammonia.

II

In Pixie Land

I'll Take My Stand

BLUE AS AN AUCTIONEER'S JOWL, the pool of the Hotel Belshazzar in Bel Air, Southern California's most opulent suburb, lay shimmering in the noonday heat. Around it, barbecuing themselves an expensive cordovan, a dozen guests drowsed and gossiped languidly, narcotized by the remorseless sun. No breeze stirred the jacarandas and eucalyptus trees overarching the tile-roofed bungalows; an immense, weedy lethargy, reminiscent of a bankrupt miniature golf course, shrouded the premises. Suddenly, without warning, the loungers by the pool were galvanized into attention. A man of imposing mien, who wore his white terry robe with the dignity of a toga and whose profile might have graced some early Roman post office, had approached the diving board. As he slipped from his robe, there stood revealed a body as flawless as a banana: the shoulders small and exquisitely formed, a chest that would have shamed Tom Thumb's, a magnificent melon-shaped paunch that quivered like junket at its owner's slightest command. With the ease of the born gymnast, he dropped on all fours, crept out warily to the very end of the diving board, crept back, and sides heaving painfully, collapsed on a beach mattress. To execute so perilous a feat without histrionics—nay, without even collecting a small fee—would have elicited a tribute from the most blasé, and it was not slow in coming. As cheer after cheer rang out for my spunk—the observant reader, needless to say, has long since penetrated my disguise—I waved smiling acknowledgment, and stretching out, re-examined the feverish events of the preceding evening.

Some twelve hours earlier, I had deplaned at the Los Angeles International Airport, my nose bloated by sunburn and my bankroll decimated. My resolve, nonetheless, was unshaken. Wherever the magic elixir of youth might be, I was determined to quaff it; wherever the bee sucked, in the words of the Bard, there would suck I. What more natural *point d'appui* than the Belshazzar, haunt of the movie elite and the affluent vacationer? Instinct guided me true. Hardly were my keisters unpacked before I was snowed under by phone calls begging to assist me. Wilshire Boulevard's most exclusive lubritorium offered slashing discounts on its weekly carwash; rival massage parlors vied for my favor, volunteering to send at any hour of day or night courteous, sympathetic operatives who could minister to my every need; promising me twenty months to pay, a firm of cut-rate morticians in Hermosa Beach sought to entomb me; voices that wheedled and entreated and bullied beat on the eardrum, proffering laxatives, psychiatric guidance, custom-built strudel. At length the barrage subsided, and leaden with fatigue, I sank into bed. I had just opened Motley's *Rise of the Dutch Republic,* drained a soothing cup of bouillon, and immersed myself in a photo-magazine survey of lady wrestlers when a discreet knock sounded at the door. A sultry brunette in a flame-colored negligee, with a figure conforming to the most advanced zoning laws, glided in sinuously.

"I'm Ruby, the night watchman," she said. "I saw a suspicious thread of light under your door whilst making my rounds, and thought I'd check." I asked whether she had credentials to support her assertion. "And how, big boy," she returned serenely. The bottle tucked under her arm, she disclosed, was primarily a weapon to fend off prowlers, though it also contained a specific called corn squeezin's which was effective against pleurisy. I assured her my bronchi were in apple-pie order, and vowing to summon her without hesitation at the first twinge, bade her good night. As she paused on the threshold to adjust a garter, she looked back in obvious concern. "Sure you wouldn't like me to wrap an afghan around you?" she asked. "The nights get pretty nippy out here." I was touched by her solicitude, but a deep-seated antipathy to dogs against my skin made it tabu. With a tiny shrug and some inaudible remark about quirks (I may have mistaken the actual word), she sailed out. No doubt she was nettled at my reluctance to share my bouillon with her, but after all, bouillon does not grow on trees.

What with the heat of midday plus that of my speculations, I had fallen into so complete a torpor by the Belshazzar pool that I did not realize a soft voice was impatiently reiterating my name. I sat up and found myself blinking into the face of an enchanting Nereid. Her azure eyes exactly matched the size of her swim suit, each tooth revealed in her impish grin was a cultured pearl, and the spray dappling her flanks gave her the succulence of a chlorinated herring.

"Why, Bitsy von Auchincloss!" I burst out, the seven syllables tumbling over each other. "Whatever in the world are you doing here?"

"Darling, it's too fabulously divoon—I'm making a screen test!" she cooed, twining her arms around my neck in an embrace that drowned me in Fabergé's Woodhue. I could not believe she was real, and insisted on pinching her to see if she were real.

"But, Bitsy!" I protested, when I had finished pinching her to see if she were real. "This is positively uncanny! I was just laying here in a brown study, wondering where I could grub up a girl to take to the world premiere of *Show Boat* tomorrow night at Grauman's Egyptian and little dreaming that I was like a stone's throw from my erstwhile playmate of the Stork Club, Gotham's most gifted young Thespian and *Life* cover girl! Are you honestly flesh and blood or some radiant mirage?" I asked, taking her between thumb and forefinger.

"Now, stop it, contumacious boy," Bitsy rebuked, withdrawing the goodies from my reach. "Look at all those goons rubbernecking at us." Her nose wrinkled in a pretty frown. "Of course I should dearly adore to have you squire me to the preem, but let's be practical. What color should I wear to match your toupee?" Sensing she might feel awkward if she were too conspicuous, I advised a neutral, mouse-colored shade. I also suggested she wear flowers of the same hue, and extracting a pledge that she would pay the C.O.D. when they arrived, sent her packing. A whirlwind program loomed before me; I must hire a dinner coat, reserve a table at the Cocoanut Grove, have my teeth capped and my briefies monogrammed—in short, demonstrate that I was as suave a coxcomb as Greg Bautzer or Gene Markey. Compressing my lips into a grim line at the outlay of no more than one inlay, I resolved to show these Hollywood tinhorns some pyrotechnics they would never forget.

"Ah—er—aren't these trousers a trifle baggy?" I asked, backing off from the mirror of the El Poltroon Tux Rental Shop and peering in dismay at my extremities. Two vast and trunkless legs, like those of Ozymandias, confronted me, encased in ballooning midnight blue and sporting innumerable pleats. The salesman, a remote, disdainful type who was merely marking time in trade until some movie scout detected his resemblance to John Carradine, surveyed me down his cheeseparing nose.

"Well, I haven't heard any beefs out of Dean Martin," he said frigidly. "Of course, he's got the physique to carry it, which you—ahem. Still, for a high-school dance such as you contemplate—"

"My dear young man," I said with murderous calm. "It may interest you to learn that these are for the premiere tomorrow night at the Egyptian."

"Oh, you're an *usher*," he said. "Why didn't you say so?" I saw the futility of trying to civilize a bumpkin and slipped into the jacket. As if by sorcery, my reflection changed. Leering out of the glass was a Raymond Chandler torpedo, the squat, foreshortened trigger-man of a second-rate gambling casino. From my brachycephalic forehead to my splay feet, I was a Windy City gunsel on the take. Ere I could repulse him, the salesman whipped open the coat.

"I—I don't need a shoulder holster," I began feebly.

"Hold still," he grunted, strapping a maroon cummerbund around my middle. The extra touch of gigolo made the illusion complete. From afar I heard the tinkle of platinum cuff links and the rhythm of maracas. The salesman cocked his head approvingly. "There," he said. "That's the real English drape. You're as sharp as a tack." Ten minutes later, thoroughly browbeaten, I emerged into Melrose Boulevard lugging an envelope the size of a kite, emblazoned with the name of the shop. My evil star clearly must have been in the ascendant. As I stood on the curb awaiting a taxi, a Jaguar convertible in salmon pink slid up alongside and buzzed me. Behind the wheel was a producer out of my Hollywood past, his toad's face suffused with pity.

"I heard things were tough with you," he commiserated. "Criminal, a man of your age delivering suits for a dry-cleaner. Look," he silenced me before I could explain, "you don't have to grovel. Any time I can't spare a deuce for a poor *schlemiehl* which he's on Skid Row, I know I've gone Hollywood." With a deep-throated purr, the car nosed out into the traffic, leaving me agape at the bill in my hand. I have the pride of a Spanish hidalgo, and had I but had another Jaguar, I would have overtaken him then and there and flung the alms in his face. Well, I reflected darkly, some day our paths would cross again and I would wipe out the affront with the vichyssoise in his veins. Pocketing the moola with a philosophical shrug, I went my way.

No Hollywood sport worth his weight in vicuña would permit his hair to be trimmed elsewhere than at Zworkin's, a sleek haberdashery-cum-barbershop on Asphyxia Drive in Beverly Hills, and it was there that I now betook myself. A cathedral hush enveloped the store proper; several acolytes who hoped to be mistaken for Morgan Farley were kneeling reverently before the Scotch brogues, and a floorwalker, whose shot-silk vest testified that he had made the pilgrimage to Finchley's, was blessing a pile of cashmere sweaters. Inside the tonsorial section, a sloe-eyed receptionist at an escritoire abandoned her copy of *This Is My Beloved* and addressed me graciously. Under cross-examination, I admitted that I had no appointment.

"But you must have one," she objected in Pasadena pidgin. "They'd not have let you in the door otherwise." She unfurled an elaborate chart divided into classifications of various colors. "Which studio did you say you were at?"

"Why—uh—none at the moment," I faltered. "I dropped out—that is—I did a rewrite on *She Cooked His Goose* at Columbia in '42, but they shelved it."

"You mean you want a Zworkinalysis and you're not even in *pictures?*" Her mouth fell open. "Mr. Hornbostel! Mario! Come quick!" Wheeling in panic, I found two barbers with drawn razors barring my escape. A babble of voices rose up on the air, sliced by the high, shuddering scream of a manicurist. "Look out, he's a hophead! . . . It's Muriel's husband, he tried to stab her! . . . Shoot at his legs!" Luckily, in the hurly-burly a fuse blew; I scrambled out a rear window, crawled through an adjacent funeral home, and soon was safe in a vegetarian bar in Westwood, fortifying myself with a parsnip cocktail. The good offices of the barman finally netted me a haircut at a petshop down the street. Since its proprietor had concentrated chiefly on poodles theretofore, I looked more or less like Int. Ch. Nunsoe Duc de la Terrasse, Best of Breed at Westminster, when he finished, but what the hell. A man can't have everything.

Fireflies twinkled in the lush subtropical boscage screening the Belshazzar; peccably groomed and savoring an excellent

cheroot, I loitered by the entrance awaiting Bitsy. It pained me
that she could not have shared my solitary meal of filet mignon
and crêpes Suzette, but anticipating the strain of the premiere,
I had limited her to a sandwich in her room. The precaution
proved well-founded. As she swept toward me in a strapless creation of peacock blue, superstructure foamier than a charlotte
russe, I saw she was delirious with excitement.

"Tab Hunter's going to be there, and Rory Calhoun, and Tony
Curtis!" she burbled. "I know I'll absolutely faint away—"

"There, there, child," I soothed her. "Must preserve our poise,
you know." I bent down to retrieve the evening bag she had
dropped in her nervousness, and simultaneously a most perplex-
ing thing happened. Whether it was a loose pebble underfoot or
the fact that I had not stooped over for several years, I described
a slow somersault and landed on the gravel with my neck out of
joint. Young people reared in café society have an extremely
primitive sense of humor. Bitsy dissolved in wild shrieks of
laughter.

"Oh, Lawdy!" she guffawed, clapping her hands. "That's the
funniest pratfall I ever did see! Do it again!" Needless to say,
the agony I experienced was well-nigh unendurable, although my
stoic mask betrayed no hint of it. In a few clipped phrases, I
directed her to fetch attendants from the parking lot, who
portaged me into the lobby. Instantly a hubbub arose; people
began loosening my clothing and shouting advice, and Bitsy,
overcome by the dramatic potentialities of the situation, took full
stage. "It's a stroke," she sobbed, disordering her hair like the
Divine Sarah. "He's had two already. No, his other wives and
mistresses are back in New York. Oh, the publicity, the shame of
it. It's the end of my career." Just as the cigarette girl from the
Marsupial Room was preparing to take a flashlight photo of
Bitsy weeping on my chest, one of the guests, a chiropractor, was
hurried in. He pressed a nerve in the vicinity of my billfold, and
in a trice my anguish was forgotten. Within fifteen minutes, my
companion and I were bowling down Sunset Boulevard in the

smart 1926 Chalmers coupe I had engaged specially for the occasion. A moment of tension ensued when Bitsy demanded an overhead light so that her fans could recognize her.

"You're cheapening yourself," I objected. "Take a leaf out of Garbo's book—be remote, unattainable."

"But you said in New York I was the pagan type, a creature of fire and ice," Bitsy accused. I retorted that on the same occasion I had also eaten a goldfish for no logical reason. "I don't care," she pouted. "Tonight I want to be mad, a wanton thing, a bacchante who recks not of the morrow." A prickly suspicion that spectacular events were in the brewing dawned on me, but it was too late to draw back. Already the car was sucked into the Niagara of traffic descending on the premiere; bumper to bumper, we inched toward the arc lights clustered about the Egyptian. The laity, in triple rows that overflowed sidewalk and gutters, hailed our arrival with awestricken murmurs.

"Boy, look at that cupcake in blue," a bystander exclaimed. "She brought a real live chimp! What'll those actresses think up next?" Bitsy, by now in a state of exaltation dangerously close to that of a mullah, grabbed my arm and dove under the marquee. Lit up more brightly than a Polack wedding, the forecourt was jammed with notables, all radiating the distinction of an advertisement for expensive toilet water. Through their midst bubbled an official greeter with a microphone, belaboring every chick and child of them with a monstrous conviviality. Before I could expostulate, Bitsy had dragged me forward and was braying into the mike.

"So happee!" she bellowed. "And I hope you'll all come to see me in *Robin Hoodlum*, starring Jackie Biesemeyer and Qvetch, the Wonder Duck!"

"Thank you, Bitsy von Auchincloss!" boomed the announcer. "And now a few words from her escort, that well-known sportsman and man-about-town—" He leaned over to me. "What did you say your name was?"

"F-Fenwick," I said desperately. "Boy Fenwick . . . Howdy,

folks. Well—er—it seems there were two Irishmen, Pat and Mike—''

"*Muchas gracias,* Pfennig," he cut in, spinning me into the discard. "Coming up now, that sensational wizard of the puck, Hugger Muggins!" I slunk quickly after Bitsy as she ebbed forward into the theater, inclining her head like a dowager to the canaille. Of the succeeding interval, I retain only the most confused memory. I recall my vis-à-vis rising and haughtily appraising the audience through a lorgnette, somewhat in the manner of Corinne Griffith in *Black Oxen*. She also delivered a scathing critique of the coiffures in our vicinity, couched in a voice that blistered the varnish off the seats. When darkness mercifully veiled us and we floated at last on the bosom of the Mississippi with Cap'n Andy, I was reduced to the consistency of farina and the breath whistled in my lungs. To this day I shudder uncontrollably at the first four bars of "Make Believe."

It was shortly after midnight, and the dance floor of the Cocoanut Grove crackled with electricity. To the ecstatic beat of the King Porter Stomp, youths whose bodies were apparently boneless scaled their partners out into space, whisked them back, contorted them into improbable shapes. At the center of the vortex, close-packed couples locked in a cataleptic trance swayed like corn under a summer storm. Seated at our ringside table, I fidgeted with a spoon and waited for Bitsy to return with the young popinjay who had cut in on me. At long last they whirled into sight, giggling over some inane jest. The interloper's crew haircut and white buckskin shoes were definitely juvenile, and without prejudice, he struck me as a bit of a bosthoon.

"Sweetie, do you mind if I circle around just once more with Teddy?" coaxed Bitsy. "He's going back to Choate School tomorrow and we may never see each other again." The thought of such a tragic contingency naturally sent a chill through me, and reclaiming my property, I swung her off. If I say so myself, my dancing that night was inspired; gyrating and oscillating, every muscle of my loose-knit frame working in harmony with its neighbor, I symbolized the very spirit of ragtime. Bitsy, left dazed and breathless, was hard pressed to keep up with me. She had just laughingly begged me for a respite when a neolithic blackguard in a madras jacket cut in. One could see from the court plaster on his fuzzy, adolescent chin that the beggar had only recently begun to shave.

"I got your signal, gorgeous," he told Bitsy, treading on my corns. "Put your head on my shoulder, our dream boat is drifting away."

"Hold on there, bub," I said, and in my tone there was a metallic ring that had oft spelled disaster to the unwary. Before he could marshal his wits, I had uncorked a right, a left, a right, and a left. They all connected, but, regrettably, not with him. With singular devotion, Bitsy had thrown herself between us to shield me, and, poor innocent lamb, crumpled under the sledge-hammer impact. Simultaneously, a variegated pinwheel exploded inside my skull, my knees turned to calf's-foot jelly, and I knew no more.

The stewardess of the eastbound plane reached into the rack over my head, and producing a pillow, fluffed it out. She leaned down solicitously over me.

"Aren't you roasting to death, bundled up in that huge polo coat?" she inquired. "Let me put down your collar and make you comfy." I warded her off, and enunciating with some difficulty due to a fat lip, assured her I was perfectly fine. Actually, the hatbrim slanted over my smoked glasses, and the beefsteak concealed in my handkerchief, did not make for ideal breathing, but they gave me the illusion of privacy I needed. I drew a labored sigh and succumbed to the drone of the engines. A moment later, the stewardess was back again. "Here's the L. A. evening paper, if you'd like to read it."

"Doh, thax," I said, averting my head in distaste. After all, I knew the sort of thing that fills the average Los Angeles newspaper—the torso murders, the garish movie premieres, the distorted accounts of brawls in night clubs. Surely life held more significance than febrile gossip and the dingy amours of a lot of half-baked whippersnappers. Perhaps in Manhattan's towering canyons, in the stimulating camaraderie of the poets, artists, and musicians I knew—to say nothing of those tall, flamboyant divorcees one meets at canine obedience schools—I could again purge the dross from my spirit and truly revivify it. I opened my well-thumbed copy of Motley's *Rise of the Dutch Republic,* and extracting the bookmark, gently closed my eyes.

Love Sends a

Little Gift of Noses

AROUND ELEVEN-THIRTY yesterday morning, at the confluence of
the Old York and Easton roads outside Philadelphia, a huge
Diesel trailer bearing the inscription "Mother Taciturn's Shoo-
Fly Pies" had paused for the light when an MG tourer of elderly
vintage slid up alongside. In the front seat were a strikingly
middle-aged couple (if I may so characterize my wife and
myself), and in the rear a massive, box-shaped object swathed in
a blanket. Just as the truckman was examining us with heavy-
lidded amusement, an abrasive noise like a child's ratchet amplified a hundredfold burst from our vehicle.

"Hey, sport, your transmission is shot," he informed me
genially. "Better put that thing in a pail of water before it
explodes."

"We know all about it, thanks," my wife returned. "It isn't
the car. We've a bird back there."

"What kind?" he asked, ogling her. "A vulture?"

"No, a toucan," I said shortly. "A bird with a long beak who
likes to pry into other people's affairs."

"O-ho, a smart aleck!" he exclaimed with relish, starting to open the door of his cab. Luckily, as I turned green, the light followed suit, and within seconds, we were in a maze of side streets he could never penetrate. The encounter cost me a homily from Madame and a half-hour delay in reaching our destination, but I eventually gained it and got shut of one *Ramphastes sulfurata*, and beside that, nothing else mattered.

I got into my ornithological pickle quite inadvertently, through a visit last fall to the aviary of the Regent's Park Zoo in London. I had spent a most enriching hour there, rubbering at the hornbills, cockatoos, whydahs, and birds of Paradise; sharply admonished a coster for sniggering at them and nearly was knocked down for my pains; and held an extended parley with a cageful of mynahs, in which I intimated, as tactfully as I could, that my own specimen in the States was far more articulate. As I was leaving, I spotted the toucan who indirectly led to my imbroglio, and despite myself, I was bowled over. Why so flamboyant a creature, all blue-green, lemon, turquoise, scarlet, and orange, with a bill disproportionate to his body and a look of utter malevolence, should have aroused anyone's desire, I can't explain, but he did. I certainly hadn't awakened an equivalent feeling in him; he just studied me balefully, as though he knew my clothes hadn't been cut by a smart West End tailor and my hotel bill was overdue. A brass plaque on his cage identified him as a bequest of Guinness—the brewers rather than the actor, I judged, dimly remembering that I had seen such a bird in their advertising. The attendant I questioned about his disposition was unencouraging.

"Sly brute, guv'nor, between you and me," he said. "Sna your arm off as soon as not. I never saw one yet you could trust.'

Inasmuch as he himself had a pretty shifty look around the gills—not to mention a cube of unmelted butter in his mouth—I thought him hardly qualified to criticize, but I let it pass, finished my tour, and dismissed the matter. Three or four months later, at a soiree in New York, I shared a Lawson couch with a not unattractive person in black *mousseline de soie,* who exhibited a surprising knowledge of tropical birds for a youngster. As the evening wore on and my tongue loosened under the influence of the cordial, I mentioned several varieties I yearned to possess some day, among them a sulphur-breasted toucan like the one in Regent's Park. Had I suspected that my vis-à-vis, the wife of an oil geologist, was bound for Nicaragua, where the breed is as thick as mosquitoes, I might have been more circumspect, but it never occurred to me anybody would take me literally. I mean, now that I look back, Mrs. Hinchingbrooke, while voluptuous in a coarse way, had kind of a sneaky expression around the chops. My wife, in reviewing the party, commented on it; women are quick to notice that sort of thing.

Well, less than a month ago, a letter arrived from the lady postmarked New Orleans—how she obtained my address Heaven alone knows—with an ecstatic blurb for Central America and some electrifying news. It appeared she was en route to Iraq to join her husband and was bringing me a little feathered souvenir from Managua, to wit, a short-keeled toucan. Since she barely had time to change planes in New York, though, I was to meet her two days thence at Idlewild to receive the bird and instructions for its care.

"How exciting, dear," said my wife, when I casually introduced the subject. "But look here—why not send the bird on to Iraq and bring Mrs. Hinchingbrooke home? Isn't that what you've had in mind from the beginning?"

Though her tone was one of affectionate raillery, it was plain she was less than radiant at the prospect of a fourth pet in a household that already contained a poodle, a cat, and a mynah. My rhapsodies about its beauty, however, and my fervent promises to feed and groom it personally, won her around, and at the designated hour, I was on hand to salute Mrs. Hinchingbrooke at Idlewild. Hysteria was the keynote of our rendezvous; her plane was delayed, her baggage was incomplete, and we finally met in a maelstrom of porters and officials speeding her takeoff.

A round paper hatbox, precariously secured by twine, was thrust on me, along with a typewritten sheet, and calling out some breathless injunction to avoid drafts and parasites (or parakeets, I didn't exactly gather which), my benefactress vanished toward the Middle East with her bonnet askew and her seams twisted.

By the time we boarded our train for eastern Pennsylvania, the toucan evidently had a snootful of travel, and following a series of exploratory bumps, worked it through the top of the carrier. It was a handsome affair some eight inches long, with serrated edges and colored in pastel shades of green, blue, vermilion, and orange, but the conductor, a Philistine only concerned with interstate livestock laws, made me finish the trip in the baggage car. To cajole Cyrano, as we provisionally named him, into the Victorian wire chalet I had prepared was our initial problem. My wife solved it in short order; while she beat on a tin pie-plate to distract his attention, I clawed open the hatbox, smothered him in a bungalow apron, and stuffed him through the gate. When we all regained a measure of tranquillity, I had to admit he exceeded my expectations. His over-all plumage was iridescent blue-black, relieved by a golden bib fringed in crimson. He had lavender-tinted legs, a scarlet tail, and apple-green patches around the eyes blending into his polychromatic beak. Not a whit discomposed by his whereabouts, he devoured the mixture of tomatoes, grapes, peaches, and melon I compounded, tossing each piece into the air so that it would land in his gullet. Once his hunger abated, unfortunately, he grew temperamental and flicked half his pablum out of the cage, with the result that the kitchen floor was more treacherous than the Jungfrau. To alleviate the peril, as well as give Cyrano room to stretch his wings, I transferred him to a chicken coop rehabilitated for the purpose. At once, of course, I ran into typical feminine squeamishness; my wife began ululating that her domain had become a henhouse and banished him to the screened porch. Providentially, it contained so many insects that I was able to cut down on his rations and effect a substantial saving.

Except for one getaway when he had to be wooed back into

captivity with avocadoes skewered on a curtain rod, Cyrano was quite tractable, if you took the precaution of donning a catcher's mask, and altogether silent for about a week. Then, one morning at dawn, he found his voice—a dry, rasping croak suggestive of a giant cricket, audible in the farthest recess of cellar and attic, that annihilated sleep, dominated the whine of the utilities, and threatened to unhinge the reason. Infrequent at first and lasting only a few seconds, it became sustained and more importunate daily until it sounded like New Year's Eve at Small's Paradise. Concentration, phone calls, even family squabbles were impossible while Cyrano was vocal; faces gray and strained, everybody catfooted around—all but the cat himself, who disappeared for keeps—cringing in anticipation of the next salvo. What zoological advice I could glean, and I dropped everything to glean it, indicated that his behavior was characteristic of the genus, and falling back on Flents and some Buddhist fatalism left over from a trip to Siam, we numbly tried to re-establish our usual routine. It was lonely work, for people exposed to Cyrano could never be enticed to dinner again. They bound their arms in slings to escape our hospitality, simulated nervous breakdowns, summoned themselves abroad to engage in fictitious balloon ascensions. The only weekend guest we were able to lure down, a chap recently divorced, sequestered himself in a patch of sumacs until Saturday noon, when he left with the hurried announcement that he and his wife were reuniting. There must have been a phone booth in the sumacs we were unaware of, or perhaps even a domestic relations counselor.

I was fatuously hoping that the situation would somehow resolve itself, that the fate of Lot's wife would overtake Cyrano so we could feed him to the cows, when the annual community lawn festival popped up. Lacking any artifacts like jelly or needlework, my wife apprised the committee that I might be persuaded to display our new acquisition. Their enthusiasm was unrestrained; a booth was decorated with plants to simulate a tropical habitat, descriptive signs and literature were struck off, and my arrival at the fete evoked such a turbulent welcome that I was sure I could run for selectman any time I saw fit on an avian ticket. Cyrano, docile and oyster-quiet, was a model of deportment throughout his installation. He posed for photographs with the aplomb of a beauty contestant and bestowed gracious nods on the multitude, visibly flattered by its homage. I whizzed home and began clearing space on the whatnot for the ribbons he undoubtedly would garner. Inside an hour, a palpitation of ladies was on the phone, wailing like muezzins. What with Cyrano's screech in the background, they were a trifle hard to comprehend, but the essence was that I had better hasten over before necks were wrung. The indignation that greeted me was so intense that it almost ignited the bunting. Patrons were deserting the grounds in droves, and there were dark insinuations that somebody would pay through the nose for disrupting the fair. Our exit was partially slowed by the refusal of my car to start, and I had to recruit bystanders to rock it back and forth to overcome the air-lock, with Cyrano urging us on vociferously the while. At home, the mysterious telepathy that obtains between the long married had already roused my wife to action. Representing herself on the phone as a Swedish baroness who had been recalled to Stockholm to liquidate the family estate, she had cunningly induced the Philadelphia Zoo to receive our songster, implying that a donation of several thousand *thalers* might result. The idea, she modestly admitted, was inspired by something Garbo had once said.

There was a card from Iraq in the mail this morning—from some silly young thing I used to know, full of double talk about the local bird life—and coincidentally, a notice from the quarantine people in Hoboken. Seems they're holding a couple of African crested cranes consigned to me by a chap out in Tanganyika. I recall telling him out there, in a moment of exaltation, that I'd love to own a pair, but I never dreamed he'd take me literally. Oh, well, let the authorities cope. From now on, the only exotica I collect are stamps. They're as quiet as a mouse, and moreover, you can handle them without gauntlets.

A Brush

with the Quality

EARLY one Friday morning in London last fall, midway through a dream sequence of the type I thought had gone out with rarebit fiends, I was awakened by a resonant voice on the phone identifying itself as Lady Hester Traphagen. The abrupt juxtaposition of two fantasies dazed me, naturally, and I was unable to make any courtly response. None was needed, it appeared, for my caller came straight to the point. Six days before, she had extended to our mutual friend Godfrey Roach and myself an invitation to weekend with her and Sir Aubrey at this house in Kent. Had dear Godfrey (whom she knew I adored as much as she did) relayed the message? I guardedly allowed, short of adoration, that Godfrey was a lovely person but he had mentioned not a word to me. Quite, said the lady, with a hint of impatience. Nevertheless, her invitation still held; the two of us were expected at Mealmouth Hall the next day, and I was to arrange with Godfrey to drive me down in his car. With a couple of grace notes to indicate how radiant she and her husband were at the prospect of entertaining us, Lady Traphagen rang off.

"Good old Hester," grunted Roach when I finally managed to reach him at his office, an hour later. "Typical of her. She always dragoons one like this at the eleventh hour. Still, I think we might go, if you've nothing better to do. Magnificent Elizabethan house, decent beds, and the food isn't too filthy. Definitely the sort of thing you ought to see."

"Done and done," I agreed, and then a worrisome thought stuck me. "The only hitch is, I'll need a dinner jacket. I didn't bring one with me."

"No problem whatever," he said. "Pop around to Foss Brothers, in Covent Garden, and hire one—everybody does. Here, my secretary'll give you their address. And I'll pick you up at your hotel at eleven tomorrow."

As he had predicted, renting dress clothes in London was simple enough, but, I discovered, rather abrasive to the ego. Though it took the outfitters only fifteen minutes to process me, it was done *coram populo*, before a jury of four other clients awaiting their turn. Nobody, unless his name is Mickey Hargitay, likes to have his waist and chest measurements bawled out in public, and although utter courtesy prevailed, I intercepted plenty of Cheshire grins. I also felt that the garment selected for me hardly lived up to the lofty pretensions of British tailoring. Its Neanderthal shoulders and spiky lapels seemed more suitable for a rock-'n'-roll soirée than for a Kentish house party. However, I paid the requisite charge, as well as a stiff deposit, and left with the assurance that the suit would be delivered by evening. The promise was duly fulfilled. When I re-entered the hotel at five, the hall porter ran toward me waving a fiber laundry box that displayed the legend "Foss Bros.—Hire Dept." in large white letters. To say his voice was audible at John o' Groat's would be exaggeration, but among the guests in the lobby there was certainly no doubt where I got my threads.

As we traversed the green belt of outermost London at noontime on Saturday, Godfrey filled me in about our hosts-to-be, whose lineage and beneficence, according to him, were legendary.

A Brush with the Quality

Sir Aubrey's manifold tastes embraced politics, blood sports, and farming; his wife, a *salonnière*, was musical and a tireless committeewoman. Furthermore, confided my friend, with characteristic British candor, the Traphagens were used to scruffy bohemians like myself. Conformity was unknown at Mealmouth Hall. I could stay in bed all day if I wished to or, alternately, lose myself in the woods without exciting comment. Both extremes, I decided on reflection, were inadvisable. I would sleep a standard eight hours and keep away from copses—in other words, behave in normal, bourgeois fashion and avoid the limelight without being mousy.

What with Godfrey's insistence on sampling the pink gin at various historic pubs en route, it was midafternoon when we got to our destination. The manor itself, a mossy structure the size of a fireproof warehouse, crenellated and mullioned beyond belief, surmounted a ridge overlooking ten miles of countryside. Before I could quite encompass its dimensions, Sir Aubrey, a florid, effervescent party in tweeds, burst through the front door to welcome us.

"You chaps must be fagged out from your drive, what?" he inquired hospitably. "I'll wager you'd like a liedown and a nice cup of tea in your room, wouldn't you?"

Grateful for his quick understanding, I started inside.

"Well, there'll be plenty of time for that later," he said, pinioning my arm. "First we're going on a short tour of our hop fields. Kent supplies one-sixth of all the hops used in Britain's breweries, you know. We've compiled some fascinating statistics I'll show you presently. Right now, though, let's start with the growing process, step by step."

I cast an anguished glance at Godfrey, but he was too intent on saving his own skin; mumbling some lame apology, he twisted out of Sir Aubrey's grasp and vanished into the house. In a trice, I was bundled into an old truck and my guide was jolting me through endless acres of the vine, explaining each minute phase of its culture with painstaking care. By the time we completed our circuit of the barns, the drying ovens, and the sacking machinery, dusk had settled over Mealmouth, to say nothing of my morale. A glum conviction seized me, as I followed our host through the dim-lit, cavernous rooms of the Hall, that I had deliberately put my neck in a noose. In a downstairs sitting room, Godfrey, thoroughly refreshed from his nap, was having tea with Lady Hester, a vinegary, equine-faced woman, and a pudgy couple named the Savitts. The awkward hush attending my introduction made me suspect that they had just been discussing me.

"I say," said Lady Hester, staring at me as though I were a bacteriological smear. "It *is* the most extraordinary resemblance, isn't it?"

Mrs. Savitt exhaled sharply. "Uncanny," she said. "The same undershot jaw, the way his nostrils curve—"

"Er—whose nostrils?" I put in.

"Hawley Harvey Crippen's," said Godfrey blandly. "We were chatting about Lombroso's theory of criminal types, and I observed to our hostess that you look very much like him."

"Well, better keep the hyoscine locked up!" I chuckled, draining my teacup with the nonchalance of one who often found himself mistaken for the noted uxoricide. Unfortunately, some of the liquid trickled into my windpipe and I went into a coughing spasm so violent that I had to excuse myself.

A footman chancing by as I clung weakly to the balustrade, I asked him to guide me to my room and was conducted to a commodious chamber in the east wing. From its pargeted walls, the ducal canopy over the great double bed, and the profusion of oriflammes, I judged it to be one reserved for persons of consequence. Whoever had unpacked my overnight bag, though, could have had no such illusions about me; my skimpy little store of socks and lingerie was ranged in a neat row on the bureau and my dinner coat folded over a chair to plainly expose the Foss Bros. label. Whether it was the subarctic temperature or a delayed reaction to the scent of too many hops, my teeth suddenly began chattering as with the ague. Thinking to restore myself with a hot tub, I turned on the tap in the adjacent bathroom. It had yielded barely three inches of tepid brown fluid when I heard a discreet knock and the footman reappeared. "Beg pardon, sir," he said, with a servile smile. "Sir Aubrey presents his compliments, and would you mind not using any more hot water, as it strains the facilities of the geyser?"

The flush of resentment his words provoked, added to the sitz bath, effectively dissipated my chill, and as I prepared to descend to dinner, arrayed in my rented finery, I felt, if not relaxed, at least less alien to the background. My self-confidence, it turned out, was premature. Congregated in the library were a dozen or so of the local landed gentry and their wives. All of them, without exception, had been reared in the saddle, and though they made every effort to be civil, it was instantly apparent to them that I could not distinguish a surcingle from a snaffle bit. One leathery old harridan finally could contain herself no longer.

"Damn it all, sir, you people *must* ride in America!" she expostulated. "We've seen your cowboys on the telly!"

"Yes, yes, Aunt Agatha," a young woman temporized, "but it seems that this boffin doesn't."

"Why not?" snapped the elder. "What's wrong with him? Is he a Bolshie or something?"

The entrance of Lady Hester in full fig, blazing like a Forty-seventh Street jeweler's window, luckily diverted attention from me, and, after proper lubrication, we proceeded to the table. For the greater part of the meal, my ignorance of horseflesh condemned me to sit wrapped in frozen silence. Then the conversation veered around to the theater, a milieu with which I was relatively familiar, and I essayed a couple of anecdotes that established me as a raconteur, or would have had I been able to recollect their point. Lady Hester's passion for music, as Godfrey had described it on our journey down, I discovered to be utterly without foundation. The woman had never even heard of Earl Hines, Ziggy Elman, and Pee Wee Russell, let alone such artists

as Peanuts Hucko and Muggsy Spanier, and when she began
rhapsodizing about Frank Chacksfield and Ray Noble, I realized
I was dealing with a Hottentot and cut her adrift. Perhaps it was
pique at my unmasking her pretensions, or again merely pro-
vincialism, that prompted her next question. Turning to me a few
seconds afterward, she asked whether Godfrey had misinformed
her—did I really own a farm in Transylvania? Contrary to what
she might suppose, I replied, with an acid smile, I was *not* Count
Dracula—any more, I added pointedly, than I was Dr. Crippen—
and the farm, at last reports, was in *Penn*sylvania. Discerning
in me an adversary to be reckoned with, as well as without, Lady
Hester took excellent care not to cross swords with me again, and
I was allowed to finish my dinner undisturbed.

I had innocently imagined that once our savories were disposed
of, the gentlemen would retire to the billiard room to exchange
ribaldries while the ladies devoted themselves to crochet. Nothing
so prosy was in store. At a sudden signal from Lady Hester, the
entire company was herded back into the library, equipped with
pencils and paper, and marshaled into two teams. A sickening
premonition smote me that we were about to play The Game, and
I groaned aloud. To no avail. Within a quarter of an hour, the
remnants of my dignity stripped from me, I found myself
asquirm on the floor, flippers waving feverishly, miming the Wal-
rus in *Through the Looking Glass.* It was a doubly painful experience, because, in spite of a graphic performance, my team
was too stupid to guess what I was enacting, and we were roundly
trounced. To compound the humiliation, Godfrey drew me aside
when the guests had gone, and, exhibiting more of his confounded
British candor, took me to task on several counts.

"Bad show, old man," he said bleakly. "Never thought you'd
let down the side this way. Lady Hester's in a dreadful wax about
you. I daresay it'll be years before I'm asked back to Mealmouth."

"What's all the uproar about?" I protested. "I can't see that
I've done anything to get so excited about."

"Well, since you force me to say it, I quite understand Hester's agitation," Godfrey retorted. "A man walks in here looking exactly like Hawley Harvey Crippen, runs the bath water all afternoon, and then turns up in a dinner jacket a coster wouldn't put on his back. Great Scott, where on earth did you ever find such a costume?"

"At Foss Brothers—the place you sent me to," I said.

"Well, if you'd had an ounce of initiative, you wouldn't have gone there," he countered. "I didn't realize you were such a sheep. At any rate, the situation isn't altogether hopeless. I've interceded in your behalf with Sir Aubrey." The latter, he went on to explain, had consented to let me remain another day on condition that I refrain from bathing and wear a dress suit borrowed from one of his grooms. The main thing, Godfrey emphasized, was that I must try to make a better showing when we played The Game the next evening.

"You mean we have to go through that *again?*" I faltered.

"Of course," he said. "They hold the big test match here every Sunday. The whole neighborhood's coming in." My hands began to twitch uncontrollably, and I asked how one usually spent the Sabbath at Mealmouth. "I believe Sir Aubrey's taking you under his wing," he replied. "The old boy's dead keen on hops, you know, and he wants to show you all the intricacies of raising 'em. Worthwhile experience, I'm told. Shouldn't miss it if I were you."

Twenty minutes later, I finished changing into mufti in my room, opened a window, and leaned out gingerly to explore the ivy twining up the wall. The vines, to my touch, seemed as sturdy as cables; they could sustain a weight twice my own. I swung over the sill, and, clambering down noiselessly, dropped into a graveled path below. Between the darkness and the unfamiliar terrain, it was an eternity before I crept out of the grounds onto a paved road bordered by cottages. Thanks to a kindhearted publican, a lorry driver, and several other Samaritans, I stumbled into my hotel in London just as day was breaking. At two-thirty that afternoon, I was awakened by a resonant voice on the phone I had no trouble identifying.

"Look here, old man," it said anxiously. "This is Godfrey Roach calling from Mealmouth, in Kent. We've been frightfully concerned about you. Whatever happened?"

"Well," I began. "I'll tell you . . ."

I trust I've told him.

The Slicker the Vet,

the Sicker the Pet

The demeanor of the veterinarian should be serious, though friendly; somewhat aloof, though with an air of sincerity; firm, though gentle and definite in his course of action. The client should be repeatedly reminded of every single thing that is being done for his pet until it sinks in. Charges should be clearly and distinctly specified; and because neurotics are unpredictable, total payment or at least a substantial payment should be made in advance. The payment will have a further salutary effect in instilling the client with the confidence that not only is everything possible being done, but in paying for it he feels that he has done the best for his pet's benefit.

Some neurotic clients will often abuse the telephone service. It is therefore both disarming and pleasing to the client to be telephoned by the veterinarian. This is dramatically satisfying especially if the news is good. When the news is not good, the veterinarian should express deep personal concern—as if the possible loss of the pet is as poignant to him as to the owner.—*From "The Neurotic Pet Owner," a paper by A. Barton, D.V.M., reprinted in* Philadelphia Medicine.

THE BLACKTOP ROAD out of Churl's Point, where they confirmed my directions, was fringed by stock farms, great barbered estates full of pedigreed Angus and Guernseys eating their heads off on the rolling clover slopes. A warm glow enveloped me as I thought of their harassed owners, advertising men toiling away over media and research in some Manhattan honeycomb to meet the feed bills. It would have been sweet to pause and gloat over their predicament, but Buddy, tethered in the rear of the station wagon, was yelping so dolorously that I decided to press on. Less than a mile beyond, I came abreast of a squat oblong of redwood with a row of exercise pens in back which answered the description of the vet's establishment. The glass-brick portico sheltered a geometrical pair of ilexes and a sign reading, "Burning Bush Animal Hospital—Walk In."

"Well, here we are, good boy," I said, with forced heartiness, untying Buddy's leash. He sniffed suspiciously, then flattened his ears and bared his fangs in a half snarl. "Come on, now," I urged, tugging him down. "Nobody's going to hurt you. Be nice." He wanted to be nothing of the sort, and, for an undersized Shetland sheepdog, managed to simulate twice his weight as I dragged him inside. The only occupant of the claustrophobic anteroom was a hard-featured blonde in slacks, holding a Pekinese. Selecting the chair opposite, I sank into contemplation of the knotty-pine wall, graced with a flyblown diploma and Senator Vest's tribute to his dog, behind her head. Within a few seconds, Buddy finished his inspection of the area around us and started edging toward our neighbor.

"Pardon me, Miss," I said as she leaned forward to pat him. "I'd be careful, if those slacks you're wearing are flannel."

She withdrew her hand, eying me with hauteur. "What's that got to do with it?"

"I was only trying to warn you—"

"I don't see it's any of your business what my slacks are made of," she said, her nostrils distending dangerously.

"Please don't misunderstand," I apologized. "I'll tell you why I brought it up."

"Tell your diary," she snapped, and arose. "I've heard that

ploy before, Mister, and it creaks. Lucky for you my husband's in the Navy.''

Lucky for my aplomb as well, a door at the rear simultaneously flew open and Dr. Myron Vulpein emerged. His smock and his sallow, concave face, bisected by a hairline mustache, gave him the rather anomalous look of a barber, but a duly portentous frown betokened the medical man. With a crisp injunction to follow the treatment he had outlined within, he extended a phial to the blonde. She was to further remember, he continued sternly, that every scientific resource was being expended on her pet, all the knowledge gleaned from decades of painstaking research. "Do you understand that? Has that sunk in?" he demanded. "O.K., then, forget about your pooch. He's in the lap of the gods—your conscience is clear. . . . This way, sir.''

With a grimace indicative of her deep distaste for me, the lady swept out, and Buddy and I straggled into the consulting room. After a grueling interrogation on why I had sought him out, as though I were a junkie, Vulpein bade me relate my story. I explained that my wife and I were boarding the animal temporarily for his master, an actor friend currently on tour, and that his deportment had been unexceptionable up to the previous weekend. Then, for no apparent reason, he had begun to evince a disturbing penchant for the nether garments of our guests, furtively gnawing and perforating their trouser legs under the dinner table.

"Let me get that straight,'' said Vulpein. A faintly sardonic smile revealed that he had already classified me psychologically. "Did—er—anyone else besides you notice this phenomenon?''

"What do you mean?'' I said, bristling. "The people whose clothes he ate, my wife— You couldn't *help* but notice. Their pants were full of holes.''

"Of course, of course,'' he said soothingly. "And was that the only occasion on which he molested your friends?''

"No, the same thing happened the next night, with a whole different group,'' I said. "The worst of it is, you're not conscious of what he's doing. He just nibbles at the cloth, soft little bites, like fish stealing bait off a hook.''

''I see,'' said Vulpein, joining his fingertips in Baker Street fashion. ''Now, were there any other factors you consider pertinent or relevant?''

''Well—'' I hesitated. ''Maybe it was coincidence, but he seemed to concentrate mainly on woolen slacks and flannels. He didn't bother the people who were wearing cabardines or gorduroy.''

His eyes, narrowed in absorption, opened to betray a sudden gleam. ''Mmm, highly significant,'' he said. ''For your information, it's *gab*ardines, and *cor*duroy. Excuse me a moment—I must call one of my clients.'' He dialed a number, and as a reedy voice echoed from the receiver assumed a rabbinical, almost seraphic expression. ''Mrs. Horniman?'' he inquired. ''Dr. Vulpein. I have very encouraging news for you about your parakeet. He took a little spin on his Ferris wheel this morning after breakfast. . . . Well, I wouldn't be too optimistic, but I think we're over the hump. . . . You're welcome. Goodbye.'' When he turned back to me, however, all geniality had flown. ''From the symptoms you describe,'' he announced, ''I'd say the animal was suffering from a serious nutritional deficiency. In layman's terms, he's not getting some vital ingredient.''

''I never knew dogs needed wool in their diet,'' I said, puzzled. ''We feed him round ground, table scraps—''

''It might be one of a hundred things,'' he broke in. ''Some obscure oil or vitamin in the cloth that he seeks out instinctively— we won't know till I analyze the material. I presume you brought along a swatch for that purpose?''

''How could I?'' I objected. ''I can't very well ask my friends to hack up their trousers. I mean, they're pretty browned off as it is.''

''Well, it's not really essential,'' said Vulpein. ''In any case, we'll have to keep him under observation here a few days to watch his behavior. That'll be sixty dollars—in advance.'' I opened my mouth to protest, but he quickly forestalled me. However excessive I deemed the fee, it was puny; the heartsease it purchased, the assurance that I was doing my utmost for Buddy, was incomputable. At last, in view of my limited responsibility to the beast, he grudgingly agreed to accept half the amount, and with a caveat to refrain from introspection and unnecessary phone calls, dismissed me. "He'll be on his feet in no time," he declared (a somewhat loose interpretation of the problem, I felt). "I'll ring you as soon as we have any developments to report, if not sooner."

He was as good as his word; three days later, I received a bulletin that Buddy had been allowed free access to Vulpein's table at mealtime but had caused no visible depredations. Knowing the dog's sly nature, I hazarded the opinion that he was aware he was being watched. "He's too foxy to tip his mitt to a stranger," I insisted. "Couldn't you lock him up in your bedroom, say, with an old pair of flannels?"

"Force his hand, eh?" mused Vulpein. "By jingo, I'll do better than that! You know those dummies they have in haberdashery stores? I think I'll borrow one from Guzik's, in Allentown, and duplicate the exact conditions under which he ate the material."

Whether he meant to reconstruct our dining room in its entirety—a job that would have necessitated more cobwebs than he possessed—he failed to specify, but, on deliberation, I detected a flaw in his scheme. Whatever Buddy's shortcomings, he was much too crafty to be deluded by a wax mannequin mutely posed at a table; some form of sound or dialogue was obligatory to give the scene the illusion of reality. Unluckily, the only record I had on hand at the moment was a poetry reading of Mr. Eliot's, and the thought of Buddy nuzzling the dummy to the lugubrious cadences of "The Waste Land" was inadmissible. Extensive search of the attic, though, yielded up a fair copy of "Cohen on the Telephone," which I forthwith sent along, with a chit outlining how it was to be used. When, after a lapse of several days with no contact between us, I phoned Vulpein, there was a distinct note of wariness in his manner.

"How are you feeling?" he asked.

"Tiptop," I said, taken aback a bit. "Why shouldn't I?"

"Oh, nothing," he replied casually. "You—er—you haven't heard any unusual noises, or voices in your head?"

"Look here," I barked. "What the deuce are you implying? I call up to inquire about a dog—"

"Now, don't get hot under the collar," he placated me. "In my profession these days, we strive for the over-all picture. If your emotional barometer's stormy, your pet may be wacky, too." Such was far from the case with Buddy, he hastened to add; despite prolonged exposure to the dummy and three changes of trouser, the animal had not ravaged a single thread. "Probably just a passing aberration," concluded Vulpein, "but I'd advise making one last check to set your mind at rest. Invite some person to dinner that he originally pestered, if possible wearing the exact same clothes. I'll bring the dog over during the meal so we can study his reactions together."

The project, as I foresaw at once, was going to be no chocolate soda; solicited to break bread again with us, most of Buddy's victims refused point-blank. Finally, Joyce and Waldo Muscatine, a couple enslaved by six poodles and hence past-experts on canine behavior, consented to attend, but I decided it would be crowding my luck to designate their attire, and I was relieved when Waldo showed up in suntans. The cocktail interlude and soup passed off uneventfully, except that I caught Waldo stealing repeated glances under the table.

"Where's that crummy sheepdog you had around here?" he queried at length.

"The Shetland pup?" I said lightly. "Oh, he's over at the vet's having a checkup—at Dr. Vulpein's."

"Vulpein?" Joyce repeated. "*Myron* Vulpein?" I nodded, and her eyes protruded in horror. "That—that monster!" she exploded. "I took one of our dogs to him for a simple flea bath, and he told me I was a masochist!"

"Well, he's right," asserted her husband. "Anybody who has six dogs—"

"I don't care!" she declaimed, propelled on by Martinis. "He's a nasty, insulting creep, and if I ever meet him again, I'll tell him so!"

"Joyce, there's something you ought to know," I began, but the doorbell cut me short. I skillfully avoided looking at my wife, having seen a stone wife before, and went to answer it. Dr. Vulpein in mufti seemed even less the healer than he had during our colloquy; in his raglan topcoat and sporty porkpie, he could have been an insurance adjuster or a tout. "Er—come in, won't you, Doctor?" I said, and peered around him. "Where's the dog?"

He blinked at me, obviously reluctant to answer. "I'm afraid I'm the bearer of bad tidings," he said, advancing into the room. "He's vanished—disappeared into thin air." His voice took on a tremulous, grief-stricken quality. "I can't account for it," he said hoarsely. "We'd just left the turnpike at Cross Keys when he suddenly leaped from the car and ran into the fields. I searched and searched—"

"Well, that doesn't surprise *me!*" I heard Joyce announce triumphantly behind me. "He's got more sense than some people I've met!"

As Vulpein, perplexed, wheeled to confront her, I uttered a sound intended as a conciliatory chuckle. "Excuse me," I said. "I believe you know each other. Mrs. Muscatine, Dr. Vulpein."

"Oh, yes indeedy I know him," Joyce grated. "He's the kid who's assumed the mantle of Sigmund Freud. Haven't you, Doctor?"

Vulpein subjected her to a Himalayan stare. "I'm merely a licensed veterinarian, Madam," he rejoined glacially, "but I can recognize a hysteroid when I meet one."

"Hey, wait a minute, you!" Waldo called out, springing up. "What did you call my wife?"

Well, that was it in a nutshell, so to speak. The next thing I knew, the air was full of curt Anglo-Saxon words and women's shrieks, and two gladiators were slugging it out, toe to toe, on the Axminster. Waldo, whose myopia had not been measurably improved by four gimlets, got a swollen nose for his gallantry, and Vulpein got a summons the next day for assault, which I doubt will stand up in court. I fully expect to do so, though, when our actor friend returns from the road. He'll never believe my explanations about Buddy. He's an absolute neurotic on the subject of pets.

All Out! Change Cars

for the Living Room

THE OTHER EVENING I was flashing like a tiny jewel through the columns of the Hollywood *Citizen-News*, a minute drop of information in my beak and a ringing headache in the offing. (Never mind *why* I was doing it; every man has a right to torture himself in his own way.) I had sucked the venom from the last snarling paragraph of the editorials and was about to tuck my head under my wing when my eye startled into focus at the following:

"FRONT ROOM NOT CARBARN," WOMAN CHARGES IN SUIT. A lady whose sleep was disrupted rudely when a Los Angeles Railway Corporation streetcar left its track and plowed through her house last August today filed suit against the company for $15,000 damages.

Plaintiff Procapia Portugal charges negligence of the operator of the Gage Ave. shuttle line inasmuch, she contends, as the front room of her house at 463 N. Gage Ave. is a private home and not a carhouse for wandering streetcars. She charges that the car jumped the tracks at Hammil St. and Gage Ave. last August 4 late at night and struck her home with "great speed and violence," destroying part of the place and shaking the rest of the house and her. She suffered serious injuries, including nervous and heart shock, she said.

I do not propose to try the case in these pages, though it needs no Solomon to decide where the verdict lies. The fair plaintiff's pique is pardonable; a trolley in one's lap is a deliberate and flagrant invasion of privacy. My sympathy extends rather to someone whose name does not appear in the dispatch—her attorney. To be forced to live in Los Angeles and practice law is punishment enough; to be asked to plead a cause like the foregoing demands that a man keep a tight rein on his reason. Using several odds and ends, like bits of string, old spools, and goose fat, I have constructed a masque around a vaguely parallel situation which occurred to me. The characters, of course, are completely fictitious, and any eccentricity in their behavior is rooted in my own ganglia. If you will slip on an opera cloak lined in flame-colored satin, I think we may dispense with the overture:

Scene: The law chambers of George Essick and Hosmer Figg. A sparsely furnished room containing several sectional bookcases in golden oak, two battered desks, and a steel engraving of the late Chief Justice Marshall, with a balloon issuing from his mouth, reading "In orthodontia est pecunia" ("In dentistry there is money"). As the curtain rises, Noel Prosse, a junior clerk, is immersed in a law tome. The door opens; Essick and Figg enter heavily, carrying briefcases.

ESSICK: All right, Nostradamus, drop your domino. Were there any phone calls?

PROSSE: Not since the instrument was removed six months ago.

ESSICK (*harshly*): None of your chaff. I told you to sweep up, not sit there with your nose in a book.

PROSSE: At least I can get it into a book. That's more than you can do.

ESSICK: Why, you little roach—

FIGG: Ah, give over, it's too hot. What are you reading, Noel?

PROSSE: Blackstone on "Torts."

ESSICK: From the trollops I see him with, he'd be better off with Blackstone on "Tarts."

PROSSE (*with hatred*): You've a sharp tongue in your head, Mr. Essick. Look out it doesn't cut your throat.

ESSICK: I've had enough of your sauce, you young squirt. You're fired!

PROSSE (*taking his hat*): The usual severance pay, I presume?

ESSICK (*sweetly*): You know the code, Counselor. Go ahead and sue.

PROSSE: I'll see you in the small-claims court. Goodbye, you leech. (*He exits, a penholder flung by Essick quivering in the door after him.*)

FIGG: Gosh, Essick, that's no way. Only yesterday you fired Mandamus, our old colored retainer.

ESSICK: You use that word "retainer" once more and I'll put a slug in your back. (*Figg shrugs, buries himself in a law journal. Essick scrawls disconsolately on his blotter. A footstep sounds in the corridor.*)

FIGG (*jumping up*): A client!

ESSICK: Don't blow your top. Probably a sneak from the Bar Association.

(*A small man in a rumpled mohair suit and dry-cleaned panama enters, looks about anxiously.*)

MAN: I got to see a lawyer right away. My name is Minneapolis—Leo Minneapolis.

ESSICK: What are you—a Greek?

MAN: Well, I'm not a Greek's brother.

FIGG: You mean your brother's not a Greek?

MAN (*plaintively*): I don't know what I mean. I got a lot of trouble.

ESSICK: We all have. What is it?

MAN: I want to sue a massage parlor on Alta Yenta Drive. Yesterday I was a little acid, see? So I figure I'll go down to the Friendly Fevers and get a good baking out.

ESSICK (*wearily*) : Keep it short.

MAN : Today I couldn't hardly do my brain-breathing exercises. My bile don't function properly and my whole left side is numb.

ESSICK : Listen, brother, you haven't got a leg to stand on. (*His diagnosis is accurate; the petitioner's knees buckle sharply and he almost founders. Essick elbows him roughly out the door.*) Go on, you stew-bum, sleep it off in the park!

FIGG : What did you do that for? I heard some change jingling in his pants.

ESSICK : Nah, strictly a moocher. (*A knock at the door; a woman bustles in.*)

WOMAN (*importantly*) : I guess you heard about me. My name is Venezuela.

ESSICK : Aha! And your principal exports are coffee and bananas. Look here, lady—

WOMAN : Didn't you read in the paper where the streetcar came in my house?

ESSICK (*desperately*) : I don't read the papers. I have a radio in my head.

WOMAN : I can remember it just as plain. I was sitting in the kitchen with Morris the night of August fourth when I heard a noise like a streetcar in the living room.

ESSICK : Yes, yes, the wind—your imagination, no doubt.

WOMAN : I said to Morris, "Morris, there's a streetcar in the next room." He just laughed.

ESSICK (*hoarsely*) : Figg, reach me that paperweight.

WOMAN : The next thing, the curtains parted and there stood—

ESSICK : I know. There stood Morris, kicking the gong around. Now, Madam, I'll tell you something. You've got a doormat, haven't you?

WOMAN : Sure, but—

ESSICK : What does it say on it?

WOMAN : Why, "Welcome," I guess.

ESSICK : And you expect me to get up in court and convince a jury you didn't invite that streetcar in? I wouldn't touch—

278

(*She wheels, listening intently.*)

WOMAN: There's somebody in the hall!

ESSICK (*inspired*): Quick, hide in the closet! (*He opens a door, bundles her in, turns exultantly.*) We're in the chips, Figg! There's bound to be a reward!

FIGG: But on second thought I did read something—

ESSICK: Don't *you* start, for Pete's sake. (*Jiggling the hook of the telephone, which has reappeared mysteriously*) Where the hell's that operator? (*Another knock. A second woman enters, with a determined scowl.*)

SECOND WOMAN: How soon can I get a divorce?

ESSICK (*rubbing his hands*): Well, this is more like it. Under Mexican law, in about three weeks.

SECOND WOMAN: Fine. Now, my name is Brazil—

ESSICK (*faintly*): Oh, my God!

SECOND WOMAN: My husband's a motorman on the Gage Avenue shuttle line. Ever since last August fourth he keeps bending my ear about steering into some woman's living room.

ESSICK (*rocking back and forth, head in hands*): It's a judgment on me.

FIGG: You better come back tomorrow, Mrs. Brazil. My partner's not well. He ate a bad avocado—

SECOND WOMAN: I can't wait. That man's got me frantic!

ESSICK (*suddenly*): What's that—a footstep?

SECOND WOMAN: My husband! He must have followed me!

ESSICK: Here, duck in the closet! (*He whisks her in, slams the door.*) August fourth, eh? Remember what happened fifty years ago on August fourth, Figg?

FIGG: Why, no, I can't say I do.

ESSICK (*rummaging in his desk*): Fall River. Party by the name of Borden.

FIGG: *Hey!* What are you doing with that hatchet?

ESSICK: I'll get some business for this Goddam firm. (*Crossing to closet*) Call up the D.A. and tell him you've got a case!

CURTAIN

Let Old Acquaintance

Be Forgot

I CAN TAKE wistful humor or leave it alone, and I am not one of those who choke up at the memory of Harry Langdon, but about forty years ago there was a sequence in a film of his—called, I seem to remember, *His Wedding Day*—that still haunts my memory. In his usual hapless fashion, Langdon, through the machinations of a petulant, dish-faced girl and her scheming mother, was being tricked into matrimony. Just as the principals had assembled at the altar, Langdon's attention was drawn to a mysterious guest, in a black cape, studying him fixedly from a nearby pew. Who he was or why his baleful scrutiny should have unsettled the bridegroom-to-be was never elucidated, but it was clear the stranger possessed some horrid hypnotic power. Struggle as he would, Langdon could not detach his eyes from him, and when the other, satisfied that his will had triumphed, beckoned him to follow, Langdon complied with an obedient, fearful smile. As the wedding party looked on aghast—in movies of this genre, nobody ever made any effort to intervene—the two left the church, got into a ramshackle touring car, and drove off. The ensuing action was fairly violent automobile comedy of the period; hurtling along through traffic, the Svengali character removed the steering wheel and passed it to Langdon, who manipulated it dutifully for a good thirty seconds before the implications hit home. The moment they did, of course, his companion tossed the wheel out of the car altogether, and it became apparent to Langdon, as it had somewhat earlier to the audience, that he was in a most peculiar fix.

The same foreboding that dire consequences impended overcame me several afternoons ago when, rubbering into the window of a West Fourth Street bookshop, I was dealt a crippling slap on the back and spun around to find Osric Barber intently regarding me. My association with Barber, although meager, is longlived; we met originally at some Webster Hall saturnalia in the gladsome twenties, and across the years have ricocheted into each other in places as dissimilar as Cuernavaca, the Hudson Tubes, and the Deux Magots. That he was a *Künstler* of sorts, a painter or sculptor, I was dimly aware, but I had never seen his work. Every few years, a flamboyant announcement of a show of his would arrive, printed on buckram or asbestos, from a gallery that had gone bankrupt in the interim. The titles gave no clue to the nature of the art; some, such as "Sinfonietta No. 7," were musical, others ("Nerve Gas") medical, and I concluded that he must be mingling half a dozen media, none of which awoke my curiosity. His energy, I saw in the instant of recognition, had not lessened in the decade since our last encounter. The pointed beard jutting from his chin, of the kind one observes on Spanish grandees and stomach specialists, was as sable as ever. His coalblack eyes sparkled in their sockets, and I was sure that his flashing incisors, even if capped, were equal to any Brazil nut.

"How the hell are you?" he demanded, thumping my chest. "I thought you were in Siam or one of those godforsaken places." Had I been wearing a panung, I might have pretended I still was, but he was already busy with his own saga. "You can have that tropical bit," he said, with aversion. "I spent two years in Haiti, and, let me tell you, it's strictly for vultures. The Shell people wanted me to decorate their commissary in Dhahran last winter, but I just laughed in their face. *I* should eat figs and shrivel up with malaria so some old bag in Wisconsin draws her dividend? Not for me, Charlie. Anyway, I was tied up with the Oslo Museum at the time. That's how I got into industrial design, you know."

"Is that what— Is that your field now?" I asked, and edged toward the curb. "Must be absorbing."

"The greatest," he said, and blocked my path. "I've done a couple of revolutionary things—the sardine tin I worked out for one of the Norwegian canneries, for instance. Remember how the key always broke off when you forced it, and you tore your hand to pieces? Well, no more. I designed a foolproof can that uses magnetic tape. Even a baby could open it."

"A baby who eats sardines, that is," I amended.

"Just a figure of speech," he said impatiently. "I also did over another medieval contraption—the pants hanger with the two wooden clips and the spring. I told the client, 'A man gets tired of finding his trousers on the bottom of the closet every morning. Give me carte blanche.' I tackled the problem, and, by jingo, I licked it the same way."

"With magnetic tape?"

"What else?" Barber returned. "I tell you, there's nothing that plastic won't do—it practically *thinks*. Look," he said, abruptly commandeering my arm, "have you got five minutes? Come on over to my drop, on Morton Street. I want to show you something."

We rocked back and forth in a tug of war like two men testing overalls as I interposed every excuse I could contrive, but resistance was futile. Employing the whole arsenal of cajolery, reproach, and flattery, Barber maneuvered me westward into the heartland of the Village. In front of a tall, dingy building zigzagged by fire escapes and whose façade displayed innumerable bananalike protuberances buried under its stucco, Barber paused and turned to me. His eyes glittered with anticipation. "You'll flip when you get a load of this," he promised cryptically. "I guarantee you haven't seen anything like it in Siam—or anywhere else, for that matter. Follow me."

Robbed of my will, I trailed after him through a fake-marble entryway lined with broken mailboxes and up five precipitous flights. His apartment, a railroad flat painted the color professionally known as cockroach green, was stifling, if not exotic, enough to revive memories of Bangkok. Halfway down its central corridor, Barber flung open a door and pressed a switch.

"My vivarium," he said, with a flourish toward a large shadow box illuminated on one wall. The enclosure was roughly five feet square, banked with gravel, rocks, and herbage, and shielded by a thick pane of plate glass. Writhing tumidly in its depths were six or seven snakes of assorted caliber; a pair of lizards, startled out of their torpor by the sudden light, scurried into hiding under a plant. "What do you think of that for a collection?" demanded Barber pridefully. "I've got a couple of specimens in there that'll stand up alongside anything in the Bronx Zoo. But that's not the reason I brought you here. Like porpoises, these reptiles *talk*."

"You don't say," I said, humoring him. In dealing with mystics, I always feel, a placatory attitude is indicated. "You can hear 'em palaver, can you?"

"Plainer than I hear you," he averred. "Listen to this." He strode to the vivarium and fingered a panel beside it. A high-pitched, sustained hum became audible, punctuated at intervals by snorts and gurgles vaguely resembling Arabic labials. "Did you get that?" Barber crowed. "The blacksnake's teasing one of the lizards! Ho-ho— Listen to him! He's a sketch."

Viewed as entertainment, the foolery impressed me as inferior to Bert Lahr's, but I withheld comment. "How long has this been going on?" I asked uncomfortably. "I thought serpents were—er—noiseless."

"So does everyone," my host replied. "Before I applied the

principle of magnetic tape to 'em, nobody ever broke through the barrier. I still have a couple of bugs to iron out, but when I do, scientific circles will be agog.'' He shut off the sound and slid aside the glass front. "I may patent the idea—''

"Hey, what are you doing?'' I exclaimed, recoiling.

"Opening the door so you'll get a better look,'' he said agreeably. "Come over here.''

"No, no— I see them clear as can be,'' I protested. "Listen, Barber, that glass thingumajig— You don't seem to realize! They're liable to get out on the *floor*.''

"That wouldn't hurt 'em,'' he said, in the tolerant voice one adopts toward an overwrought child. "I often let 'em crawl out and play for an hour before bedtime.'' He was a trifle surprised, he continued, that a man who had crisscrossed Southeast Asia should betray such antipathy to reptiles and so little knowledge of their characteristics. "I bet you believe that old bromide about their skins being cold and clammy,'' he said, reaching into the cage. "Have you ever handled one?''

I have watched a Malay deckhand run amuck, and I once passed a night in a reputedly haunted temple, but never before had I been confronted by an *exalté* with six feet of rock python twisting in his grasp importuning me to stroke its flesh. The fact that its name was Teddy and that, as Barber pleaded, it was an affectionate, harmless pet struck me as totally irrelevant. Short of fainting, therefore, I did the only practical thing under the circumstances. I cowered back into the farthest corner of the room, knees pressed together and fingers intertwined in a gesture of supplication. The pantomime, and the squeals I added to implement it, convinced Barber of my inflexibility. With a grunt of disgust, he tossed the constrictor back among its fellows and shut the glass front.

"I thought you liked animals,'' he grumbled. "I wouldn't have asked you up otherwise. No, not that way!'' he called as I started for the street. "The living room's in here.''

"I can't stay," I said distractedly. "I left my cat to be blocked—I mean, my hat—and the store closes at five."

"Then I'll walk you to the corner," he offered. "I have to get some stuff to feed Teddy." I knew what stuff he meant—with long ears and a pink nose—but at least he had the grace not to particularize. As we pounded downstairs, Barber evidently decided to restore my *amour-propre,* if only for auld lang syne. "A lot of people have that same unreasoning fear of snakes," he confided chattily. "The two dames that lived under me moved out when they heard I had the vivarium. Some drunk in the building's always calling up the Board of Health to complain that there's a viper or an adder on his window sill, though they know damn well I haven't any."

"How do they know that?" I asked.

"Their instinct should tell 'em, if they weren't so full of prejudice," he retorted. "Just because it squirms, does that say it's poisonous?" He laughed tonelessly. "But the experience I had in the subway a couple of weeks ago—that was the living end. You've seen the reptile house at the Zoo?"

"Only in the distance."

"Well," said Barber, "I often drop up there from time to time to see what's new, like you probably do to the public library. So this day I speak of, I was ready to leave when I noticed two cops outside with a small boy, yacketing to the assistant curator. The kid was an amateur collector, a nice wide-awake youngster about thirteen, and he had a pillowcase full of snakes on the ground nearby. Seemed that one of 'em, a garter or something, had crept down a vent into the neighbors' bathroom, the way they will, and the cops, with their typical mentality, had confiscated the poor kid's property and brought him in for a lecture. Well, nobody was paying attention to the pillowcase, so I sashayed over and quietly teased open the top. What do you think I saw?"

"Something with scales," I ventured.

"*And* colors like the rainbow!" Barber said orgiastically.

"Four little beauties—a hognose, a sidewinder, and a pair of baby racers. Just what I needed to round out my aggregation! Naturally, I couldn't let a chance like that slip by. I figured the Zoo couldn't use them, since it already had duplicates galore. The only problem was where to hide them, because I wasn't wearing a coat—just a sports shirt. The devil with it, I thought. I reached in and grabbed two in each hand, jammed them into my hip pockets, and took off—so fast that no one even gave me a second glance. Luckily—"

"Watch out!" I broke in as a truck backed out of a garage we were abreast of and almost cut us down.

"Boy, you've certainly got jumpy over the years," he observed, raising his eyebrows. "But as I was saying, the breaks were with me. Going through the turnstile at the main gate, I spot a woman with a baby carriage. She loans me a few safety pins from her child's blanket, I fasten my pockets neat and sweet, and I head for the I.R.T. Now comes the payoff. It's a long ride downtown, and the train fills up pretty well after Seventy-second Street. I'm hanging on to a strap—I couldn't sit down for fear of bruising the little guys—and all of a sudden they start acting up, leaping and twisting like crazy. I guess they were stimulated by my body heat. Anyhow, it must have looked as if I was doing a cooch, because everyone around me went into hysterics. I don't blame them for laughing, but then, just like that, the roof fell in. As the doors opened at Columbus Circle, the woman next to me let out a screech that paralyzed the whole car. Simultaneously, I reached for my hip and felt this critter wriggle past the safety pin."

"Well, I'm glad you were on deck to reassure everybody," I said inanely, and stuck out my hand. "This is my corner, old man. Lots of luck with the vivarium."

"Wait a minute." He stopped me. "Where is this hat place of yours?"

"In—er—Flatbush," I replied quickly. "On Borsalino Avenue. It's kind of far out, but they specialize in puggrees—"

"I'll drive you there," Barber decided. "I've got my car parked in the next block. You'll flip over it, I guarantee. It's a classic—a 1920 Stevens-Duryea model."

I could feel the cold perspiration start from my forehead. "Just tell me one thing," I said. "Can you detach the steering wheel when the car's in motion?"

"Why, I never tried," he said, his eyes widening in surprise.

"You will, Osric, you will," I predicted, and left him to work it out. And I'm sure he's done so, with his magnetic tape.